Sifted Silver

Sifted Silver

a treasury of quotations for Christians

compiled by
JOHN BLANCHARD

 EVANGELICAL PRESS

EVANGELICAL PRESS
12 Wooler Street, Darlington, Co. Durham, DL1 1RQ, England

© Evangelical Press

First published 1995

ISBN 0 85234 334 5

British Library Cataloguing in Publication Data avalable for this title

Other Books by John Blanchard
Gathered Gold
How to enjoy your Bible
Invitation to live
Luke comes alive
More Gathered Gold
Pop goes the gospel
Read Mark learn
Training for triumph
Truth for life
Ultimate Questions
Whatever happened to Hell?
What in the world is a Christian?
Will the real Jesus please stand up?

Printed and bound in Great Britain by The Bath Press, Avon

Affectionately dedicated to

HENRY AND MARJORIE THOMAS

Prayer Partners Extraordinary

Introduction

The volume you are holding in your hands is not accidental — though for a long time it was unintentional. In 1984, Evangelical Press published a collection of 5,000 quotations which I had brought together under the title *Gathered Gold*. These had been accumulated over a period of many years of reading and listening and I hoped that presenting them in this way would be of great help, not only to preachers, teachers and other Christian communicators, but to all who read them.

Gathered Gold had such an enthusiastic reception that in 1986 a second volume of 5,000 quotations was published under the title *More Gathered Gold*.

That was meant to be the end of the story. The introduction to the second volume specifically said, 'A third is not intended' — but two things changed the plot. Firstly, both volumes continued to be widely used in many countries around the world; secondly, my trawling eye continued to harvest thousands of other quotations which it seemed selfish to hoard in my own filing system. My publisher agreed: *Sifted Silver* is the result.

It might be helpful if I underlined from the introductions to the first two volumes a few points that will be relevant to anyone using the present work.

Firstly, the inclusion of any quotation does not mean that I endorse the author's stance on any other issue of faith or practice. The person concerned may not even be a Christian; readers with raised eyebrows are referred to Acts 17:28 as a precedent!

Secondly, not all the quotations have the same depth or tone. Some are technical explanations; others make a serious devotional or practical point; in some cases the quotation is in the form of a witty or humorous comment.

Thirdly, I have deliberately excluded from the material at my disposal hundreds of quotations which are of a negative nature — statements reflecting unbiblical or anti-Christian attitudes about God, man, life, death, eternity and so on. These obviously have their place, but I wanted this collection to be wholly positive and more widely useful than as a technical reference book.

Fourthly, I have not taken up space with titles, ranks, positions and dates, preferring to let the quotations stand on their own merit. However, a subject index has been provided, including cross-references where it was thought these would be helpful.

Fifthly, a limited number of quotations from my own written and spoken ministry have been included (without claiming any particular merit for them) where it was felt that they might be useful. These always appear in italics at the beginning of a section.

As with previous volumes, this collection is sent forth with the prayer that the wit and wisdom gathered over the passing years might help to illuminate the unchanging truth of 'the living and enduring word of God' (1 Peter 1:23).

John Blanchard
Banstead
Surrey

July 1995

ABANDONMENT

(See also: Consecration; Submission; Zeal)

To be another than I am, I must abandon that I am.

Chrysostom

God doesn't want our success; he wants us. He doesn't demand our achievements; he demands our obedience.

Charles Colson

Self, service, substance is the divine order, and nothing counts until we give ourselves.

Vance Havner

(God) cannot bless us until he has us. When we try to keep within us an area that is our own, we try to keep an area of death. Therefore, in love, he claims all. There's no bargaining with him.

C. S. Lewis

It is not so much of our time and so much of our attention that God demands; it is not even all of our time and all our attention: it is our selves.

C. S. Lewis

ABORTION

Abortion must be looked upon as an eventuation that runs counter to the biological stream of life.

I. Galdston

To eliminate the scourge of illegitimate children more self-discipline to prevent their conception is required, not more freedom to destroy them in the womb.

Immanuel Jakobovits

Every induced abortion, whether legal or criminal, is an expression of failure — failed contraceptive technique, irresponsibility by one or both partners, ignorance, betrayal of trust or denial of human dignity.

John Stallworthy

It is only a short step from disposable babies to disposable people.

Margaret White

ACTIONS

(See also: Duty; Good Deeds; Service)

Do every act in thy life as if it were the last.

Marcus Antoninus

Think like a man of action and act like a man of thought.

Henri Bergson

1

Unless a man has to do more than he can do, he will not do all that he can do.

Gordon Cooper

An acre of performance is worth a whole world of promise.

James Howell

Great ideas need landing gears as well as wings.

C. D. Jackson

There are no non-religious activities; only religious and irreligious.

C. S. Lewis

Make no distinction in your conduct between small things and great.

William Taylor

The conduct of our lives is the only proof of the sincerity of our hearts.

Robert Wilson

Knowing is not enough; we must apply. Willing is not enough; we must do.

Johann Wolfgang

ACTIVISM
(See also: Service)

Activity and theology are no substitutes for God.

Activity can be a hiding-place from reality.

Idleness is the devil's workshop, but so is busyness if, while we are busy here and there we fail in our main responsibility.

Vance Havner

When we are too busy to sharpen the axe we are too busy.

Vance Havner

We are not always doing the most business for God when we are the busiest.

John Henry Jowett

What is the use of travelling at a fast speed when you are going in the wrong direction?

Bernhard Langer

As long as we continue to trust to our own abilities and activities we shall avail nothing.

D. Martyn Lloyd-Jones

The child is generally much more active than the adult person; so that if we estimate our growth merely in terms of activity we are setting up a characteristic of childhood and the childish state as the measure of growth.

D. Martyn Lloyd-Jones

Activity which lacks thought is blind.

John Murray

It is more important to know where you are going than to get there quickly. Do not mistake activity for achievement.

Mabel Newcomer

Satan is far more anxious to keep us off our knees than he is to keep us off our feet!

Ivor Powell

Our religious activities should be ordered in such a way as to have plenty of time for the cultivation of the fruits of solitude and silence.

A.W. Tozer

Apart from God every activity is merely a passing whiff of insignificance.

Alfred Whitehead

ADOPTION

We can only begin an upright course of life when God, of his good pleasure, adopts us into his family.

John Calvin

I am a pilgrim and a stranger on the earth, but I am not an orphan.

Vance Havner

ADVICE

Four eyes see more than two.

Anon.

Most of us would get along well if we used the advice we give to others.

Anon.

Two quick ways to disaster are to take nobody's advice and to take everybody's advice.

Anon.

It takes a great man to give sound advice tactfully, but a greater to accept it graciously.

J. C. MacAulay

Men give advice; God gives guidance.

Leonard Ravenhill

I not only use all the brains I have but all I can borrow.

Woodrow Wilson

AGNOSTICISM
(See also: Atheism; Unbelief)

When agnosticism has done its withering work in the mind of man, the mysteries remain as before; all that has been added to them is a settled despair.

Vincent McNabb

3

I could not bear to be an 'ignoramus' or an 'agnostic' about
God! I must have a God! I cannot do without him.

C. H. Spurgeon

We should all be incurably agnostic if God had not revealed
himself.

David Watson

ALCOHOL
(See also: Drunkenness)

Is it any merit to abstain from
wine if one is intoxicated with
anger?

Augustine

Alcohol does not drown care,
but waters it and makes it grow
faster.

Benjamin Franklin

I am more afraid of King Alcohol than of all the bullets of the
enemy.

Robert E. Lee

AMBITION

It's dangerous to try to be
number one, because it's next
to nothing.

Anon.

Honour ought to seek thee, not
thou seek it.

Augustine

Ambition deludes men so
much that by its sweetness it
not only intoxicates but drives
them mad.

John Calvin

Ambition is blind — man's
favour is blind — the world's
applause is blind.

John Calvin

There is nothing less tolerable
in the servants of Christ than
ambition and vanity.

John Calvin

Ambition is greed for power.

C. C. Colton

The fruit of the Spirit is not
push, drive, climb, grasp and
trample ... Life is more than a
climb to the top of the heap.

Richard J. Foster

Seek not greatness, but seek
truth, and you will find both.

Horace Mann

It is doubtless an easy enough
matter to drop certain forms of
outer worldliness ... but quite

another to lay carnal ambition in the dust.
James Philip

When we have yearnings and cravings that never seem to be satisfied, we should ask ourselves whether in fact there is something wrong with the desire itself.
James Philip

Ambition is the grand enemy of all peace.
John C. Powys

I charge thee, fling away ambition: by that sin fell the angels.
William Shakespeare

I know of nothing which I would choose to have as the subject of my ambition for life than to be kept faithful to my God till death.
C. H. Spurgeon

There is no greater unreasonableness in the world than in the designs of ambition.
Jeremy Taylor

If we are taken up with our own personal needs, or if we are looking for position and status in the church, we shall be of little use to God.
David Watson

Your ambition, not your worded prayer, is your real creed.
Ella Wheeler Wilcox

ANGELS
(See also: Demons)

Angels are the ministers of God's wrath, as well as of his grace.
John Calvin

They who think that each of us is defended by one angel only wickedly depreciate the kindness of God.
John Calvin

Under Christ, as the Head, angels are the guardians of the church.
John Calvin

We rob ourselves of much joy if we forget the loving and caring presence all round about us of the angels of God.
Maurice Roberts

Take away purity from an angel and he is no more an angel but a devil.
Thomas Watson

ANGER
(See also: Hatred; Passion)

When anger enters the mind wisdom departs.

Thomas à Kempis

Anger is often more hurtful than the injury that caused it.

Anon.

Don't fly into a rage unless you are prepared for a rough landing.

Anon.

Nothing can cook your goose quicker than boiling anger.

Anon.

Sharp words make more wounds than surgeons can heal.

Anon.

Two things a man should never be angry at: what he can help, and what he cannot help.

Anon.

A man that does not know how to be angry does not know how to be good. Now and then a man should be shaken to the core with indignation over things evil.

Henry Ward Beecher

Anger is usually inexhaustible.

John Calvin

Intemperate anger deprives men of their senses.

John Calvin

Anger and jealously can no more bear to lose sight of their objects than love.

George Eliot

Do not do to others what angers you if done to you by others.

Isocrates

Anger's the anaesthetic of the mind.

C. S. Lewis

No man can think clearly when his fists are clenched.

George J. Nathan

Unrestrained anger is often more hurtful to us than the injury that provoked it.

Seneca

When anger is present, look for the pain.

R. C. Sproul

Anger is temporary insanity.

C. H. Spurgeon

I have no more right as a Christian to allow a bad temper to dwell in me than I have to allow the devil himself to dwell there.

C. H. Spurgeon

To be angry against sin is a high and holy thing.

C. H. Spurgeon

Wrath in man is a tormenting fiend.

David Thomas

Ask permission from God before you dare do anything in an angry way.

John Trapp

That anger is without sin that is against sin.

Thomas Watson

ANNIHILATION
(See also: Death; Eternity; Judgement)

The Bible annihilates annihilationism.

God does not annihilate his work, however much he may change its form. The biblical idea of death has nothing in common with annihilation.

Louis Berkhof

In every culture, and apparently throughout history, it has been normal for man to assume that he has some continuance beyond the grave.

Arthur C. Custance

That man is a spiritual being, who survives the death of his physical body, is a basic human instinct which is denied only with the greatest effort.

Dave Hunt

No man, regardless of his theoretical system, is content to look at himself as a finally meaningless machine which can and will be discarded totally and for ever.

Francis Schaeffer

ANTICHRIST
(See also: Satan — Existence and Nature)

The name Antichrist does not designate a single individual, but a single kingdom, which extends throughout many generations.

John Calvin

When Scripture speaks of Antichrist it includes the whole duration of his reign.

John Calvin

ANTINOMIANISM

Nothing could be further from the truth than the suggestion that God's choice destroys moral effort on our part.

Sinclair Ferguson

The greatest curse that ever entered the church of God is dirty antinomianism.

Rowland Hill

If the 'grace' you have received does not help you to keep the law, you have not received grace.

D. Martyn Lloyd-Jones

In the denial of the permanent authority and sanctity of the moral law there is a direct thrust at the very centre of our holy faith, for it is a thrust at the veracity and authority of our Lord himself.

John Murray

ANXIETY
(See also: Fear; Worry)

Anxiety is the interest paid on trouble before it is due.

William R. Inge

APATHY
(See also: Complacency)

One does evil enough when one does nothing good.

Anon.

When apathy is the master, all men are slaves.

Anon.

Nothing is so fatal to religion as indifference.

Edmund Burke

No man need stay the way he is.

Harry Emerson Fosdick

Many Christians have enough religion to make them decent, but not enough to make them dynamic.

Kenneth Grider

He who passively accepts evil is as much involved in it as he who helps to perpetrate it.

Martin Luther King

At the final bar of judgement the gravest charge that will be made against us Christians will be that we were so unconcerned.

D. Martyn Lloyd-Jones

Apathy is the acceptance of the unacceptable.

John R. W. Stott

APOSTASY

The evil consequences of apostasy from God are not confined to the original apostates.

Charles Hodge

Scripture does not need to be denied for apostasy to begin: all that is needed is that Scripture takes second place in our calculations.

Iain H. Murray

How can they be true who have departed from the truth?

James Philip

ART

Art is the gift of God and must be used for his glory. That in art is highest which aims at this.

Michelangelo

Genuine art was never created for its own sake, it was always a means of worship, an affirmation of belief, an aspiration pointing beyond itself. The beauty of art is reflected beauty.

Thomas Molnar

We shall have no art until we remember that it is a reward, given us only when we reach beyond ourselves to the Author of beauty.

George Roche

ASSURANCE

Let us not seek any other ground of assurance than God's own testimony.

John Calvin

The inward testimony of conscience, the sealing of the Spirit ... far exceeds all the evidence of the senses.

John Calvin

There is no better assurance of salvation to be found anywhere than can be gained from the decree of God.

John Calvin

Assurance does not lie in what we are, be we great or small. It lies in what God has done in his plan of salvation to secure us to himself.

Sinclair Ferguson

Our assurance must be founded, built up and established on the mercy of God alone.

Will Metzger

Feelings of confidence about our salvation need to be tested before they are trusted.

J. I. Packer

The assurance that we are called of God, chosen in Christ before the foundation of the world, affords a safe and secure anchorage from which no tempest can ever dislodge us.

James Philip

Your Rock is Christ, and it is not the Rock which ebbs and flows, but your sea.

Samuel Rutherford

Christians should never rest until the soul evidences that it is the Lord's ... While our interest in his favour is doubtful, what happiness can we enjoy?

Charles Simeon

Our assurance is only as strong as our faith.

R. C. Sproul

Assurance is a jewel for worth but not for rarity.

C. H. Spurgeon

Full assurance is not essential to salvation, but it is essential to satisfaction.

C. H. Spurgeon

We count it no presumption to say that we are saved, for the Word of God has told us so in those places where salvation is promised to faith in Christ. The presumption would lie in doubting the Word of God.

C. H. Spurgeon

ATHEISM
(See also: Agnosticism; Unbelief)

One of the bleakest things about atheism is that it provides no basis for virtue.

An atheist is someone who believes that what you see is all you get.

Anon.

Atheism is rather in the lip than in the heart of man.

Francis Bacon

There are more atheists than believe themselves to be such.

Albert Barnes

It is hard to see how a great man can be an atheist. Doubters do not achieve. Sceptics do not contribute. Cynics do not create.

Calvin Coolidge

If there is no God, everything is permitted.

Fydor Dostoyevski

Atheism stabs the soul to death at one stroke.

John Flavel

Atheists are worse than devils, for they believe, and tremble; these banish God out of their thoughts.

John Flavel

Men may deny God with their voices, but cannot escape his presence or judgement with fanciful theories and exculpatory formulas.

P. G. Fothergill

I was ... living, like so many atheists or antitheists, in a whirl of contradictions. I maintained that God did not exist. I was also very angry with God for not existing. I was equally angry with him for creating a world.

C. S. Lewis

Every effort to prove there is no God is in itself an effort to reach for God.

Charles Edward Locke

When people tell me they are atheists, they are not just telling me about the way they think.

They also tell me something about the way they live.

Will Metzger

God's world is never friendly to those who forget its Maker.

J. I. Packer

There is no greater blasphemy than to will God out of existence.

J. I. Packer

It is non-believers who are most vociferous in demanding some explanation from God.

Frank Retief

No one is so much alone in the universe as a denier of God.

Johann P. F. Richter

The adoption of atheism is a sin without necessity. It is the voluntary action of man.

W. G. T. Shedd

If ever man appears as a consummate ass, it's when he denies the existence of God.

Billy Sunday

Was every man on earth to become an atheist, it could not affect God in any way.

A. W. Tozer

All atheists are wilful atheists.

John Urquhart

Atheism springs not from a clear head but from a disordered heart.

W. L. Watkinson

Those who hope for no other life are dead even for this.

Johann Wolfgang

ATONEMENT
(See also: Cross; Forgiveness by God; Jesus Christ — Death; Redemption)

The death of Jesus was not a proposition for sinners but the purchase of salvation.

The atonement is the real reason for the Incarnation.

James Montgomery Boice

Blest cross! Blest sepulchre!
  Blest rather be
The man that there was put to
  shame for me.

John Bunyan

Grace first inscribed my name
In God's eternal book;
'Twas grace that gave me to the
  Lamb,
Who all my sorrows took.

Philip Doddridge

The work of atonement took place in the presence of the God of heaven. Indeed, it involved a transaction within the fellowship of the eternal Trinity in their love for us: the Son was willing, with the aid of the Spirit, to experience the hiding of the face of the Father.

Sinclair Ferguson

Sin's debt, that fearful burden,
Let not your soul distress;
Your guilt the Lord will
  pardon,
And cover by his grace.
He comes for men procuring
The peace of sins forgiven;
For all God's sons securing
Their heritage in heaven.

Paul Gerhardt

It was to save sinners that Christ Jesus came into the world. He did not come to help them save themselves, nor to induce them to save themselves, nor even to enable them to save themselves. He came to save them!

William Hendriksen

If our Saviour had committed all the sins of the world ... his agony that he suffered should have been no greater nor grievouser than it was.

Hugh Latimer

It was not for societies or states that Christ died, but for me.

C. S. Lewis

There is not a ray of hope for man outside of substitution.
D. L. Moody

The atonement is the crucial doctrine of the faith. Unless we are right here, it matters not, it seems to me, what we are like elsewhere.
Leon Morris

Atonement by the blood of Jesus is not an arm of Christian truth; it is the heart of it.
C. H. Spurgeon

Atonement is the brain and spinal cord of Christianity.
C. H. Spurgeon

If our Lord's bearing our sin for us is not the gospel, I have no gospel to preach.
C. H. Spurgeon

One thing I know — substitution. And one thing I do — preach it.
C. H. Spurgeon

What God was satisfying on the cross was his very own self. It was not the law conceived as something above him, but the law of his own infinite being.
John R. W. Stott

AUTHORITY

A leading authority is anyone who has guessed right more than once.
Anon.

There is nothing holier, or better, or safer, than to content ourselves with the authority of Christ alone.
John Calvin

The authority of the saints rests upon the authority of the Scriptures, the Saviour and the Spirit.
Vance Havner

AWE
(See also: Fear of God; Worship)

Christ never permitted anybody to be commonly familiar with him, and if you knew him you would never be familiar with him — you would be reverent.
Rolfe Barnard

Reverence excludes speculation about things that God has not mentioned in his Word.
J. I. Packer

The true scientist never loses the faculty of amazement. It is the essence of his being.
Hans Seyle

13

The larger the island of knowledge, the longer the shoreline of wonder.

Ralph W. Sockman

BACKSLIDING

Whoever strives to withdraw from obedience withdraws from grace.

Thomas à Kempis

However deep you fall, you are never out of God's reach.

Anon.

Life's greatest tragedy is to lose God and not miss him.

Anon.

It is better to help our friends to recover lost grace than lost money.

Augustine

The unhappiest person in this world is a rebellious Christian.

Roy Clements

There's no slipping uphill again, and no standing still when once you've begun to slip down.

George Eliot

The man who has lost contact with God lives on the same dead-end street as the man who denies him.

Milton Marcy

It is dangerous to backslide in any degree, for we know not to what it may lead.

C. H. Spurgeon

BEAUTY

Beauty is God's handwriting.

Ralph Waldo Emerson

The beautiful can have but only one source — God.

Arthur Schopenhauer

BIBLE — and Christ

A man who can read the New Testament and not see that Christ claims to be more than mere man can look all over the sky at high noon on a cloudless day and not see the sun.

W. E. Biederwolf

We do not find Christ in the Old Testament by spotting accidental references or similarities here and there; he is the centre, the structure of the whole history of the Old Testament.

Edmund P. Clowney

We cannot have a reliable Saviour without a reliable Scripture.

Brian H. Edwards

It is Christ himself, not the Bible, that is the true Word of God. The Bible, read in the right spirit and with the guidance of good teachers, will bring us to him.

C. S. Lewis

If you want to interpret well and confidently, set Christ before you, for he is the man to whom it all applies, every bit of it.

Martin Luther

The Jesus of the New Testament has at least one advantage over the Jesus of modern reconstruction — he is real.

J. Gresham Machen

BIBLE — Divine Authorship
(See also: Revelation)

When you drink from the stream, remember the spring.

Anon.

God cannot endure the contempt of his Word.

John Calvin

God is not to be separated from his Word.

John Calvin

The first thing that is essential when anyone begins to read the Bible is to know what it claims for itself.

Brian H. Edwards

Throughout its pages the Bible never expresses one sentence or word of doubt about either its divine origin or its absolute trustworthiness; on the contrary, it constantly asserts both.

Brian H. Edwards

A belief in strictly verbal inspiration will indeed make all Scripture a book by a single Author.

C. S. Lewis

We have a speaking God ... the clear speech of a God who reveals himself in words which we can grasp, that are meaningful.

Peter Lewis

One proof of the inspiration of the Bible is that it has withstood so much poor preaching.

A. T. Robertson

Because we believe the Scriptures to be God's Word and we

believe God does not lie, we begin by accepting all its statements, including those which are historical, as true, rather than suspending judgement about them until they are proved to be true.

David Samuel

The Scriptures do not breathe out God. God breathes out Scripture.

Bob Sheehan

There is a living God. He has spoken in the Bible. He means what he says and will do all he has promised.

J. Hudson Taylor

BIBLE — Fulness

Old truths are always new to us if they come with the smell of heaven upon them.

John Bunyan

There is no justification for any new interpretation of the faith.

R. C. Lucas

The great argument of Scripture is the glory of God's own name.

Charles Simeon

BIBLE — and the Holy Spirit

God does not bestow the Spirit on his people in order to set aside the use of his Word, but rather to render it fruitful.

John Calvin

Unless God imparts the spiritual ability to hear his voice, one hears nothing but meaningless words.

Ronald Dunn

(The Holy Spirit) has not promised to reveal new truths, but to enable us to understand what we read in the Bible; and if we venture beyond the pale of Scripture we are upon enchanted ground and exposed to all the illusions of imagination and enthusiasm.

John Newton

We are directed to expect the teaching and assistance of the Holy Spirit only within the limitations and by the medium of the written word.

John Newton

The Holy Spirit is always in, with and by the Word.

Philipp Spener

The Bible is a supernatural book and can be understood only by supernatural aid.

A. W. Tozer

BIBLE — Inerrancy

Here is rock; all else is sand.

J. C. Ryle

If the Bible is trustworthy then we must take seriously the claim that it is more than trustworthy.

R. C. Sproul

I am prepared to believe whatever it says, and to take it believing it to be the Word of God. For if it is not all true, it is not worth one solitary penny to me.

C. H. Spurgeon

If I did not believe in the infallibility of this book I would rather be without it. If I am to judge the book, it is no judge of me.

C. H. Spurgeon

BIBLE — Influence and Power

God brings about reformation when his people return to the Word of God as their sole source of doctrine and practice.

John H. Armstrong

It is not the man who brings the Word that saves the soul, but the Word which the man brings.

Thomas Arthur

The Word of the Lord is a light to guide you, a counsellor to counsel you, a comforter to comfort you, a staff to support you, a sword to defend you, and a physician to cure you. The Word is a mine to enrich you, a robe to clothe you, and a crown to crown you.

Thomas Brooks

I know the Bible is inspired because it finds me at a greater depth of my being than any other book.

Samuel Taylor Coleridge

Nothing has affected the rise and fall of civilization, the character of cultures, the structure of governments, and the lives of the inhabitants of this planet as profoundly as the words of the Bible.

Charles Colson

Philosophy and religion may reform, but only the Bible can transform.

Brian H. Edwards

It is not the Word hidden in the head but in the heart that keeps us from sin.

Vance Havner

The Bible redirects my will, cleanses my emotions, enlightens my mind, and quickens my total being.

E. Stanley Jones

A single line in the Bible has consoled me more than all the books I have ever read.

Immanuel Kant

The first thing the Bible does is to make man take a serious view of life.

D. Martyn Lloyd-Jones

God's chosen instrument in conversion is his Word, not our reasoning ability.

Will Metzger

All of God's work is done by God's Word.

Stuart Olyott

The Word is both a glass to show us the spots of our soul and a laver to wash them away.

Thomas Watson

BIBLE — Preservation

The Christian can take the whole Bible in his hand and say

without fear or hesitation that he holds in it the true Word of God, handed down without essential loss from generation to generation.

Frederick Kenyon

The Jews would die 10,000 times rather than to permit one single word to be altered of their Scriptures.

Philo

A thousand times over the death-knell of the Bible has been sounded, the funeral procession formed, the inscription cut on the tombstone, and committal read. But somehow the corpse never stays put.

Bernard Ramm

BIBLE — Purpose

The Bible is not an entertainment. It was never designed to amuse.

J. I. Packer

If you wish to know God you must know his Word.

C. H. Spurgeon

When we go to the doctor and are given a prescription, his purpose is that we should eat the medicine, not the prescription!

John R. W. Stott

BIBLE — Relevance

There is nothing on which the Bible has nothing to say.

The Bible is meant to be bread for our daily use, not just cake for special occasions.
Anon.

Where Scripture leads we may safely follow.
Loraine Boettner

All Scripture is profitable for us, even passages that seem so difficult to understand.
Jerry Bridges

The entire Bible is a book on godliness.
Jerry Bridges

There can be no courage in men unless God supports them by his Word.
John Calvin

There is no faith without God's Word.
John Calvin

It is not commentaries, councils or creeds that should mould our Christian beliefs, however valuable some of them may be, but the Word of God.
Brian H. Edwards

All that needs to be spoken or written about prayer is in the Bible.
E. F. Hallock

Any spiritual experience that is not Bible-based is not of God but of the devil. It may be spiritual, but it is the wrong spirit.
Vance Havner

He who hath heard the Word of God can bear his silences.
Ignatius of Loyola

All things desirable to men are contained in the Bible.
Abraham Lincoln

He who has the Holy Spirit in his heart and the Scriptures in his hands has all he needs.
Alexander MacLaren

There's far more truth in the book of Genesis than in the quantum theory.
Malcolm Muggeridge

The fundamental mode whereby our rational Creator guides his rational creatures is by rational understanding and application of his written Word.
J. I. Packer

Scripture is relevant to a disenchanted era, for it holds the

only hope of its deliverance.
Clark H. Pinnock

God's Word interprets nature, providence and grace.
William S. Plumer

If we want to know where our pathway is to lead and where our feet are to walk, the best place to look is into that Book which God has called the Light and the Lamp.
Robert G. Rayburn

The Lord has more truth yet to break forth out of his holy Word.
John Robinson

Take away the cross of Christ from the Bible and it is a dark book.
J. C. Ryle

I hold one single sentence out of God's Word to be of more certainty and of more power than all the discoveries of all the learned men of all the ages.
C. H. Spurgeon

It is impossible to rightly govern the world without God and the Bible.
George Washington

We need every word that God speaks.
David Watson

BIBLE — Submission to

If you believe what you like in the Bible, and reject what you like, it is not the Bible you believe but yourself.
Augustine

All who forsake the Word fall into idolatry.
John Calvin

I do not venture to make any assertion where Scripture is silent.
John Calvin

Let us so adhere to the Word of God that no novelty may captivate us and lead us astray.
John Calvin

Men are fools till they submit to the Word of God.
John Calvin

We should yield this honour to the Word, to believe what is otherwise incredible.
John Calvin

We have hungered to be masters of the Word much more than we have hungered to be mastered by it.
Don Carson

Men do not reject the Bible because it contradicts itself,

but because it contradicts them.

E. Paul Hovey

The law of God is the royal law of liberty and liberty consists in being captive to the word and law of God. All other liberty is not liberty but the thraldom of servitude to sin.

John Murray

When we reach the outer limits of what Scripture says it is time to stop arguing and start worshipping.

J. I. Packer

Be walking Bibles.

C. H. Spurgeon

Never be afraid of your Bibles. If there is a text of Scripture you dare not meet, humble yourself till you can.

C. H. Spurgeon

The place for God's Word is not an outside place, but an inside place.

C. H. Spurgeon

BIBLE — Supremacy

A glory gilds the sacred page,
Majestic like the sun;
It gives a light to every age,
It gives, but borrows none.

William Cowper

The Bible never claims to be one holy book among many, but the holy book above all.

Brian H. Edwards

BIBLE — Unity

Any part of the human body can only be properly explained in reference to the whole body. And any part of the Bible can only be properly explained in reference to the whole Bible.

F. F. Bruce

The new covenant does not destroy the old in substance, but only in form.

John Calvin

The Bible has a story-line. It traces an unfolding drama.

Edmund P. Clowney

I take it as a first principle that we must not interpret any one part of Scripture so that it contradicts other parts.

C. S. Lewis

It is impossible that Scripture should contradict itself; it only appears so to senseless and obstinate hypocrites.

Martin Luther

Truly, the inner unity of the Bible is miraculous; a sign and

21

wonder, challenging the unbelief of our sceptical age.
J. I. Packer

BIBLE STUDY

As we search the Scriptures, we must allow them to search us, to sit in judgement upon our character and conduct.
Jerry Bridges

It is impossible to practise godliness without a constant, consistent and balanced intake of the Word of God in our lives.
Jerry Bridges

Memorization is the first step to meditation.
Jerry Bridges

A well-understood Bible is the only basis of a sound theology, an enlightened piety, practical godliness, solid comfort and extensive usefulness.
John Brown

Continual meditation on the Word is not ineffectual ... God, by one and another promise, establishes our faith.
John Calvin

Those only are worthy students of the law who come to it with a cheerful mind, and are so delighted with its instruction as to account nothing more desirable or delicious than to make progress therein.
John Calvin

The longer I'm a Christian, the more I'm in fear of misinterpreting the Bible. It's an awesome responsibility.
Charles Colson

Never leave a passage of Scripture until it has said something to you.
Robert Cook

If I had to choose between reading the Bible and prayer, I would choose to read the Bible. It is more important for me to hear what God is saying than for God to hear what I am saying.
E. F. Hallock

A man can't always be defending the truth; there must be a time to feed on it.
C. S. Lewis

Every time we consider or study the Bible we are, of necessity, worshipping.
D. Martyn Lloyd-Jones

It is a good thing to be a student

of the Word, but only in order to be a practiser and experiencer of the Word.

D. Martyn Lloyd-Jones

I study my Bible as I gather apples. First, I shake the whole tree that the ripest may fall. Then I shake each limb, and when I have shaken each limb I shake each branch and every twig. Then I look under every leaf.

Martin Luther

Our natural eyesight is so defective that to read the Bible aright we must put on the spectacles of faith.

Graham Miller

The reading of Scripture is intended to awaken our minds, not to send them to sleep.

J. I. Packer

A thorough knowledge of the Bible is worth more than a college education.

Theodore D. Roosevelt

Make it the first morning business of your life to understand some part of the Bible clearly, and make it your daily business to obey it in all that you do understand.

John Ruskin

The main reason why we should study the Bible is because it is our duty. God is our Sovereign, it is his Word, and he commands that we study it.

R. C. Sproul

Bible study is the metal that makes a Christian.

C. H. Spurgeon

I have always found that the meaning of a text can be better learned by prayer than in any other way.

C. H. Spurgeon

The deeper you dig into Scripture, the more you find that it is a great abyss of truth.

C. H. Spurgeon

The sight of the promises themselves is good for the eye of faith; the more we study the words of grace, the more grace shall we derive from the words.

C. H. Spurgeon

One of the highest and noblest functions of a man's mind is to listen to God's Word, and so to read his mind and think his thoughts after him.

John R. W. Stott

The Bible only comforts those who think.

Geoff Thomas

BIGOTRY

No physician can cure the blind in mind.

Anon.

It is with narrow-minded as with narrow-necked bottles; the less they have in them, the more noise they make in pouring it out.

Alexander Pope

BOASTING

(See also: Conceit; Egotism; Pride; Vanity)

He who sings his own praise is usually off key.

Anon.

People who sing their own praises usually do so without accompaniment.

Anon.

Self-praise is no recommendation.

Anon.

Men arrogate too much to themselves when they think that they excel in anything.

John Calvin

Nobody's so apt to be a soloist as the fellow who blows his own horn.

Franklin P. Jones

Anyone who thinks he can live the Christian life himself is just proclaiming that he is not a Christian.

D. Martyn Lloyd-Jones

Do you wish people to think well of you? Don't speak well of yourself.

Blaise Pascal

Boasting is an evidence that we are pleased with self; belittling, that we are disappointed in it. Either way, we reveal that we have a high opinion of ourselves.

A. W. Tozer

There is not a more dangerous precipice than self-righteousness.

Thomas Watson

CHARACTER

There is no such thing as salvation by character; what men need is salvation from character.

A man shows his character by what he laughs at.

Anon.

Being a character and having character are poles apart.

Anon.

Character is always lost when a high ideal is sacrificed on the altar of conformity and compromise.

Anon.

It's what you do when you have nothing to do that reveals what you are.

Anon.

The true worth of a man is to be measured by the objects he pursues.

Marcus Antoninus

One of the surest marks of good character is a man's ability to accept personal criticism without malice to the one who gives it.

O. A. Battista

God-like character is both the fruit of the Spirit as he works within us and the result of our personal efforts. We are both totally dependent upon his working within us and totally responsible for our own character development.

Jerry Bridges

Though the power for godly character comes from Christ, the responsibility for developing and displaying that character is ours.

Jerry Bridges

If we would judge rightly of any man we must see how he bears good and bad fortune.

John Calvin

Lighter is the loss of money than of character.

John Calvin

Character is that which can do without success.

Ralph Waldo Emerson

Character is not made in a crisis — it is only exhibited.

Robert Freeman

You cannot dream yourself into a character; you must hammer and forge yourself one.

James Froude

Character tends to congeal, to solidify as time goes on.

Vance Havner

Character and reputation are not synonymous.

George Johnstone Jeffrey

Nearly all men can stand adversity, but if you want to test a man's character, give him power.

Abraham Lincoln

Our behaviour in times of need and crisis proclaims what we really are.

D. Martyn Lloyd-Jones

Reputation is what folks think you are. Personality is what you seem to be. Character is what you really are.
Alfred Montapert

There is no stronger test of a man's character than power and authority.
Plutarch

God is more concerned about character than our comfort.
Paul W. Powell

All men are good company in fair weather; but the storms of life prove spiritual character.
Maurice Roberts

It is in little things not in great that weakness of character is to be found.
Charles Simeon

I am quite certain that the safest way to defend your character is never to say a word about it.
C. H. Spurgeon

Character is a plant that grows more sturdily for some cutting back.
Verna Wright

CHARITY
(See also: Generosity; Giving; Kindness)

Piety is the root of charity.
John Calvin

Charity to the soul is the soul of charity.
Elizabeth Fry

Charity is money put to interest in another world.
Robert Southey

The lamp of faith must be filled with the oil of charity.
Thomas Watson

CHASTENING
(See also: Trials)

Our sovereign God never lets so much as a shadow fall across our lives without intending it to be for his glory and our good.

Not till the loom is silent,
And the shuttles cease to fly,
Shall God unfold the pattern
And explain the reason why
The dark threads were as needful
(In the Master's skilful hand)

As the threads of gold and silver
In the pattern which he planned.

Anon.

God punishes his enemies but chastises his children.

Alistair Begg

Adversity does not fall out to us by chance, but is the method by which God arouses us to repentance.

John Calvin

The Lord blesses us more by punishing us than he would have done by sparing us.

John Calvin

The scourges by which God chastises his children are testimonies of his love.

John Calvin

God teaches us, by affliction, to prize and long for heaven.

Thomas Case

God often makes his people pass through the furnace, not that they may perish, but that they may be purified, and thus reach a better salvation.

Thomas V. Moore

It is God's way commonly to deepen his people by placing them under periodic providential strains and pressures.

Maurice Roberts

Whatever is good for God's children, they shall have it, for all is theirs to further them to heaven. If crosses be good, they shall have them, if disgrace be good, they shall have it, for all is ours, to serve our main good.

Richard Sibbes

The anvil, the fire and the hammer are the making of us; we do not get fashioned much by anything else. That heavy hammer falling on us helps to shape us; therefore, let affliction and trouble and trial come.

C. H. Spurgeon

God will wean us from the earth some way — the easy way if possible, the hard way if necessary.

A. W. Tozer

CHRISTIAN
(See also: Christianity)

Holiness is to be the driving ambition of the Christian.

It doesn't take much of a man to be a Christian, but it takes all of him.

Anon.

Every believer is God's miracle.

Philip Bailey

There is no higher compliment that can be paid to a Christian than to call him godly.

Jerry Bridges

Holiness is the everyday business of every Christian.

Charles Colson

If we really understand what being a Christian means — that this Christ, the living God, actually comes in to rule one's life — then everything must change: values, goals, priorities, desires and habits.

Charles Colson

Knowing God is your single greatest privilege as a Christian.

Sinclair Ferguson

The Scriptures give four names to Christians — saints, for their holiness; believers, for their faith; brethren, for their love; disciples, for their knowledge.

Andrew Fuller

Christians are not just nice people. They are new creatures. If you are what you have always been you are not a Christian.

Vance Havner

Faith makes a Christian; life proves a Christian; trials confirm a Christian; and death crowns a Christian.

Johann G. C. Hopfner

Holiness is the distinguishing mark of the Christian.

Michael Howell

A man finally proclaims whether he is a Christian or not by the view he takes of this world.

D. Martyn Lloyd-Jones

By definition a Christian should be a problem and an enigma to every person who is not a Christian.

D. Martyn Lloyd-Jones

The Christian is a man who expects nothing from this world. He does not pin his hopes on it, because he knows that it is doomed.

D. Martyn Lloyd-Jones

The Christian is not a good man. He is a vile wretch who

has been saved by the grace of God.

D. Martyn Lloyd-Jones

The Christian is sorrowful, but not morose; serious, but not solemn; sober-minded, but not solemn; grave, but never cold or prohibitive; his joy is a holy joy; his happiness a serious happiness.

D. Martyn Lloyd-Jones

The more Christian a person is, the simpler will that person's life be.

D. Martyn Lloyd-Jones

The ordinary Christian knows more about life than the greatest philosopher who is not a Christian.

D. Martyn Lloyd-Jones

A Christian is never in a state of completion but always in a process of becoming.

Martin Luther

The true reason for becoming a Christian is not that we may have a wonderful life but that we may be in a right relationship to God.

Will Metzger

What is a Christian? The question can be answered in many ways, but the richest answer I know is that a Christian is one who has God for his Father.

J. I. Packer

The Christian who has the smile of Christ needs no status symbols.

Leonard Ravenhill

There will be no possibility of standing before Christ but by standing in Christ.

William Secker

Christians are in the world to be witnesses, and they must concentrate on their calling.

Paul B. Smith

For the Christian, all of life is sacred.

Paul B. Smith

The distinguishing mark of a Christian is his confidence in the love of Christ, and the yielding of his affections to Christ in return.

C. H. Spurgeon

Nobody can call himself a Christian who does not worship Jesus.

John R. W. Stott

The Christian should resemble a fruit tree, not a Christmas tree! For the gaudy decorations of a Christmas tree are only tied on, whereas fruit grows on a fruit tree.

John R. W. Stott

A genuine Christian should be a walking mystery because he is surely a walking miracle. Through the leading and the power of the Holy Spirit, the Christian is involved in a daily life and habit that cannot be explained.

A. W. Tozer

The Christian is strong or weak depending upon how closely he has cultivated the knowledge of God.

A. W. Tozer

All Christ's subjects are kings.

Thomas Watson

The Christian is a God-explorer.

Tom Wells

CHRISTIANITY — Characteristics

Real Christianity is an invitation to the most costly and dangerous adventure the world can offer.

Roy Clements

A Christianity that does not lead to a transformation of the whole person is not Christianity.

Edward N. Gross

Salt seasons, purifies, preserves. But somebody ought to remind us that salt also irritates. Real living Christianity rubs this world the wrong way.

Vance Havner

The fresh air of normal New Testament Christianity would be a shock to the average professing Christian.

Vance Havner

Christianity promises to make men free; it never promises to make them independent.

William R. Inge

The Holy Spirit is the only authenticator of Christianity.

Arthur P. Johnson

If you want a religion to make you really feel comfortable, I certainly don't recommend Christianity.

C. S. Lewis

One of the reasons why it needs no special education to be a Christian is that Christianity is an education in itself.

C. S. Lewis

The mind which asks for a non-miraculous Christianity is a mind in process of relapsing from Christianity into mere 'religion'.

C. S. Lewis

Nothing in the Scripture indicates the church should lure people to Christ by presenting Christianity as an attractive option.

John MacArthur

Doctrinal Christianity is not a pastime for intellectuals. It is a matter of life and death.

Iain H. Murray

Real doctrinal Christianity has an obstinacy about it which no amount of modern opinion or religious excitement can change.

Iain H. Murray

Christianity is a battle — not a dream.

Wendell Phillips

Christianity is nothing without its history.

Clark H. Pinnock

Christianity is a demanding and serious religion. When it is delivered as easy and amusing, it is another kind of religion altogether.

Neil Postman

Christianity did not originate in a lie, and we can and ought to demonstrate this, as well as to believe it.

William Ramsay

The pessimist is not a representative of Christianity.

A. T. Robertson

Christianity is no more a bondage to men than wings are to birds.

O. Palmer Robertson

Christianity without dogma is a powerless thing.

J. C. Ryle

It is quite possible that some day there might evolve a world religion, but the Christianity of the Bible will never be a part of it.

Paul B. Smith

There is no authentic biblical Christianity without the cross at its centre.

John R. W. Stott

If Christianity has never disturbed us, we have not yet learned what it is.

William Temple

Christianity can do without the favour of the world.

David Thomas

Christianity promises us no escape from the opposition of wicked men; indeed it teaches us to expect it.

David Thomas

CHRISTIANITY — Definition

Christianity is either relevant all the time or useless anytime. It is not just a phase of life; it is life itself.

Richard Halverson

In science we have been reading only the notes to a poem; in Christianity we find the poem itself.

C. S. Lewis

Some tend to think that Christianity is a matter of being nice. But niceness is purely biological. One dog is nicer than another dog!

D. Martyn Lloyd-Jones

Christianity is primarily about truth and the doctrine of salvation.

Iain H. Murray

Christianity is more than a storm cellar; it is a way of life.

Gilbert Peters

Christianity is neither a creed

nor a ceremonial, but life vitally connected with a loving Christ.

Josiah Strong

Christianity is all about relationships with God and with others.

David Watson

CHRISTIANITY— Uniqueness

Christianity can no more be compared with other religions than Jesus Christ can be compared with other people.

Do not attempt to water Christianity down. There must be no pretence that you can have it with the supernatural left out. So far as I can see Christianity is precisely the one religion from which the miraculous cannot be separated.

C. S. Lewis

There is no Christianity apart from revelation.

D. Martyn Lloyd-Jones

The difficulties of Christianity no doubt are great; but depend on it, they are nothing compared to the difficulties of infidelity.

J. C. Ryle

No religion except Christianity has an atonement.

R. C. Sproul

CHRISTLIKENESS
(See also: Godliness; Holiness)

To become like Christ is the only thing in the world worth caring for, the thing before which every ambition of man is folly and all lower achievement vain.

John Drummond

The gospel does not make us like Adam in his innocence — it makes us like Christ, in all the perfection of his reflection of God.

Sinclair Ferguson

The duty as well as the destiny of believers is to be conformed to the image of God's Son.

William Hendriksen

From morning to night keep Jesus in your heart, long for nothing, desire nothing, hope for nothing, but to have all that is within you changed into the spirit and temper of the holy Jesus.

William Law

'Putting on Christ' is not one among many jobs a Christian has to do; and it is not a sort of special exercise for the top class. It is the whole of Christianity. Christianity offers nothing else at all.

C. S. Lewis

If you try to imitate Christ, the world will praise you; if you become like Christ, the world will hate you!

D. Martyn Lloyd-Jones

The goal of sanctification is to be conformed to Christ's image, not to be self-satisfied.

John MacArthur

CHURCH — Attendance and Membership

Any man in a church should be one whose character qualifies him for any office the church offers.

E. F. Hallock

Don't ever come to church without coming as though it were the first time, as though it could be the best time and as though it might be the last time.

Vance Havner

The New Testament does not envisage solitary religion.

C. S. Lewis

33

To stay away from church is to spit in God's face and to despise his gift of the kingdom.

R. C. Sproul

CHURCH — Blemishes

Whenever doctrine is devalued the church's worship is diminished, and no amount of enthusiasm, excitement or energy can replace what is lost.

Our whole problem is that we meet, and go through the motions, and the Lord is not there.

Rolfe Barnard

The levity in our services shows the blindness of our hearts.

Rolfe Barnard

Before the church can make an impact on the culture it must break with the idolatries and misconceptions that dominate the culture.

Donald Bloesch

People are driven from the church not so much by stern truth that makes them uneasy as by weak nothings that make them contemptuous.

George Buttrick

God's sacred barn-floor will not be perfectly cleansed before the last day.

John Calvin

The church cannot be rightly reformed except it be trained to obedience by the frequent scourges of God.

John Calvin

Those who wish to build the church by rejecting the doctrine of the Word build a hog's sty, and not the church of God.

John Calvin

A church with a little creed is a church with a little life.

B. H. Carroll

We do not want, as the newspapers say, a church that will move with the world. We want a church that will move the world.

G. K. Chesterton

A church without authority is like a crocodile without teeth; it can open its mouth as wide and as often as it likes, but who cares?

Brian H. Edwards

It is one of Satan's deep devices to call off the attention of the church from her own state to the condition of the world without and around her.

H. C. Fish

It is a stark tragedy to love the church and its work and not to love Jesus.

E. F. Hallock

Nothing will destroy a church and its power in a community and the world any quicker than to lose its first love.

E. F. Hallock

If even half of our church membership ever took Jesus Christ seriously we would start a major revolution!

Vance Havner

Many church people do not give Satan enough trouble to arouse his opposition.

Vance Havner

One serious malady of the church is infantile paralysis — too many babies who never grow.

Vance Havner

The besetting sin of our Christianity today, in private and public, is insipidity.

Vance Havner

The church has no greater need today than to fall in love with Jesus all over again.

Vance Havner

The devil's main business today is getting people to join a church without being saved.

Vance Havner

We are long on membership but short on discipleship. We are more anxious to gather statistics than to grow saints.

Vance Havner

Worldliness is rampant in the church. The devil is not fighting churches, he is joining them! He isn't persecuting Christianity, he is professing it.

Vance Havner

The chief trouble with the church is that you and I are in it.

Charles H. Heimsath

It is not only a mistake but a sin to trust attractions for the ear and the eyes, and to draw people to the church by the same methods by which they are drawn to a place of entertainment.

William G. Hughes

A self-satisfied church is either dead or dying.

R. B. Kuiper

By and large people do not go to church to learn about God from his infallible Word, but rather to be tranquillized.

R. B. Kuiper

I have no hesitation again in asserting that the failure of the church to have a greater impact upon the life of men and women in the world today is due entirely to the fact that her own life is not in order.

D. Martyn Lloyd-Jones

It is the lack of solid biblical conviction in the pulpit which has begotten the almost total absence of decisiveness in the pews.

Conrad Mbewe

We are producing Christian activities faster than we are producing Christian experience and Christian faith.

J. R. Mott

The church is most evangelistic when she is least concerned about impressing the world or with adding to her numbers.

Iain H. Murray

The real need of the church is not for new methods of evangelism or increased activity, but for a deep moral cleansing and a readjustment of heart and life that will clear away barriers to fruitful communication of the gospel.

James Philip

Going through any physical motions apart from the lifting of one's spirit to God or the humbling of one's spirit before God is without significance.

Robert G. Rayburn

I believe that in public worship we should do well to be bound by no human rules, and constrained by no stereotyped order.

C. H. Spurgeon

I believe that one reason why the church of God at this present moment has so little influence over the world is because the world has so much influence over the church.

C. H. Spurgeon

Some may say, 'If the minister preached better, we should be better hearers'; but the minister might say, 'If I had better hearers, I should preach better.'

William Tiptaft

I can safely say, on the authority of all that is revealed in the Word of God, that any man or woman on this earth who is bored and turned off by worship is not ready for heaven.

A. W. Tozer

I do not believe it is necessarily true that we are worshipping God when we are making a lot of racket.

A. W. Tozer

In the average church we hear the same prayers repeated each Sunday year in and year out with, one would suspect, not the remotest expectation that they will be answered.

A. W. Tozer

God preserve our churches from becoming mere bless-me-clubs!

George Verwer

The Christian church today suffers because so many of its members feel that *they* have made a decision for Christ, or that *they* have chosen to join a church. Such man-centred notions spell spiritual weakness and imbalance.

David Watson

When social action is mistaken for evangelism, the church has ceased to manufacture its own blood cells and is dying of leukaemia.

Sherwood Wirt

CHURCH — and Christ

What the world needs is neither a Christless churchianity nor a churchless Christianity, but Christ the Head living afresh in his body, the church.

Vance Havner

Christ is the essence of worship, and our understanding of the church's worship must take its starting-point from him.

Robert G. Rayburn

If the church goes wrong on Christ it goes wrong on everything.

John R. W. Stott

CHURCH — Divisions

You can't build a church with stumbling blocks.

Fred Beck

Divisions between Christians are a sin and a scandal, and Christians ought at all times to be making contributions towards reunion, if it is only by their prayers.

C. S. Lewis

Let's have no barriers against saints, only sins.

R. C. Lucas

The existence of over 9,000 Christian denominations throughout the world is an insult to Christ and a hindrance to the spread of the kingdom of God.

David Watson

CHURCH — Duties

The highest honour in the church is not government but service.

John Calvin

Wherever we find the Word of God surely preached and heard, and the sacraments administered according to the institution of Christ, there, it is not to be doubted, is a church of God.

John Calvin

The Scriptures know no clericalism. To all the people of God belongs the work of the ministry.

R. C. Lucas

The church is a workshop, not a dormitory.

Alexander MacLaren

Anything which makes it easier for us to worship spiritually should be encouraged while anything that draws attention to itself rather than to God should be eliminated from our corporate worship services.

Robert G. Rayburn

The church is under orders. Evangelistic inactivity is disobedience.

John R. W. Stott

Congregations never honour God more than when they reverently listen to his Word, intending not just to hear but to obey in response to what he has done, is doing and will do for them.

Geoff Thomas

I believe a local church exists to do corporately what each Christian believer should be doing individually — and that is to worship God. It is to show forth the excellencies of him who has called us out of darkness into his marvellous light. It is to reflect the glories of Christ ever shining upon us through the ministries of the Holy Spirit.

A. W. Tozer

CHURCH — Fellowship
(See also: Fellowship)

Christians may not see eye to eye, but they should walk arm in arm.

Anon.

It is best to be with those in time we hope to be with in eternity.

Thomas Fuller

We were neither made nor redeemed for self-sufficient aloneness.

J. I. Packer

Be united with other Christians. A wall with loose bricks is not good. The bricks must be cemented together.

Corrie ten Boom

CHURCH — Glory

The church has many critics but no rivals.

Anon.

Although God is concerned about the sin of the nation, he is more concerned about the spirituality of the church.

John Benton

Purity of doctrine is the soul of the church.

John Calvin

The source and origin of the church is the free love of God.

John Calvin

The most wonderful things that are now done on earth are wrought in the public ordinances.

David Clarkson

Is not the church the very cork on which the world remains afloat?

William Hendriksen

The glory of the gospel is that when the church is absolutely different from the world she invariably attracts it.

D. Martyn Lloyd-Jones

Sound doctrine always has been, is today, and ever will be the foremost mark of the true church.

Geoff Thomas

CHURCH — Security in God's purposes

The preservation of the church depends on the mere favour of God.

John Calvin

The salvation of the church is so precious in the sight of God that he regards the wrong done to the faithful as done to himself.

John Calvin

The welfare of the church is inseparably connected with the righteousness of God.

John Calvin

While the world stands God will have a church in it.

Matthew Henry

The church will outlive the universe; in it the individual person will outlive the universe. Everything that is joined to the immortal Head will share his immortality.

C. S. Lewis

I believe in the final perseverance of every saint as an individual. Furthermore, I believe in the final perseverance of the saints as a body: the church of God shall live, and continue her work till she has accomplished it. But far diviner is the thought to me of the final perseverance of the Christ of God.

C. H. Spurgeon

CHURCH UNITY

Peace is not to be purchased by the sacrifice of truth.

Anon.

Unity must not be sought at the expense of the gospel.

Walter J. Chantry

If all the churches in the world became amalgamated, it would not make the slightest difference to the man in the street. He is not outside the churches because the churches are disunited, he is outside because he likes his sin, because he is a sinner, because he is ignorant of spiritual realities. He is no more interested in unity than the man in the moon!

D. Martyn Lloyd-Jones

Cursed be that unity for which the Word of God is put at stake.

Martin Luther

That union which is not based on the truth of God is rather a conspiracy than a communion.

C. H. Spurgeon

CIRCUMSTANCES

Worship God in the difficult circumstances and, when he chooses, he will alter them in two seconds.

Oswald Chambers

The answer to decision-making is not putting the Lord to the test by ascribing arbitrary significance to events in his providence ... God has not authorized us to make oracles of events.

Edmund P. Clowney

Events of all sorts creep and fly exactly as God pleases.

William Cowper

Things do not happen in this world — they are brought about.

Will Hays

My whole outlook upon everything that happens to me should be governed by these three things: my realization of who I am, my consciousness of where I am going, and my knowledge of what awaits me when I get there.

D. Martyn Lloyd-Jones

All things harden the wicked for hell and ripen the godly for heaven.

Daniel Rowland

COMMUNION WITH CHRIST

(See also: Communion with God; Love for Christ; Meditation; Prayer)

Union with Christ is the foundation of all our spiritual experience and all spiritual blessings.

Sinclair Ferguson

Jesus showed to his disciples his hands and his side; he cannot send us into the world unless we are identified with him in his crucifixion.

Vance Havner

Have your heart right with Christ, and he will visit you often, and so turn weekdays into Sundays, meals into sacraments, homes into temples, and earth into heaven.

C. H. Spurgeon

There is no cure for lukewarmness like a good supper with Christ.

C. H. Spurgeon

True communion with Christ is not a mere spasm, not just an excitement of ecstasy.

C. H. Spurgeon

Our task is to live our personal communion with Christ with such intensity as to make it contagious.

Paul Tournier

To accept Christ is to know the meaning of the words 'as he is, so are we in this world'. We accept his friends as our friends, his enemies as our enemies, his ways as our ways, his rejection as our rejection, his cross as our cross, his life as

41

our life, and his future as our future.

A. W. Tozer

COMMUNION WITH GOD

(See also: Communion with Christ; Fellowship; Love for God; Prayer)

Everybody who belongs to Jesus belongs to everybody who belongs to Jesus.

Anon.

God is closest to those whose hearts are broken.

Anon.

Our sense of sin is in proportion to our nearness to God.

Thomas D. Bernard

Man never achieves a clear knowledge of himself until he has first looked upon God's face, and then descends from contemplating him to scrutinize himself.

John Calvin

God does not give us power to imitate him; he gives us his very self.

Oswald Chambers

True grace delights in secret converse with God.

Jonathan Edwards

Seeking the face of God turns us in a definite direction which cannot be confused with entertainment or superficiality.

Jim Elliff

Only to sit and think of God,
Oh what a joy it is!
To think the thought, to breathe
      the name
Earth has no higher bliss.

Frederick W. Faber

It is misguided to think that God will revive a people who find no time to commune with him from the heart.

Jim Faucett

We need to sit before God long enough for the sacredness and holiness of his person to overshadow the spirit and mind.

E. F. Hallock

God has no favourites, but he does have intimates.

Vance Havner

If our lives and ministry are to count for anything today we must solemnly resolve to make time for God.

Vance Havner

Man is at his greatest and highest when, upon his knees, he comes face to face with God.

D. Martyn Lloyd-Jones

Most Christians learned at an early age how to talk to God, but they did not learn to listen as well.

Gordon MacDonald

How can we expect to live with God in heaven if we love not to live with him on earth?

John Mason

Perhaps there are no truths about the Spirit that Christian people more urgently need to learn today than those which relate to the inner life of fellowship with God.

J. I. Packer

A man in touch with God has access to unimagined divine energies and is able to bend them to earth in blessing to men.

James Philip

In the light of God, human vision clears.

James Philip

It is scarcely ever that we can intercede with fervour unless we enjoy habitual nearness to God.

Charles Simeon

There is a pattern to human responses to the presence of God. The more righteous the person, the more he trembles when he enters the immediate presence of God.

R. C. Sproul

I know that people do not want to be alone with God, but if your longing heart ever finds the living water, it will be alone.

A. W. Tozer

COMPLACENCY
(See also: Apathy)

Show me a thoroughly satisfied man and I will show you a failure.

Anon.

The quickest and shortest way to crush whatever laurels you have won is for you to rest on them.

Donald P. Jones

A man who is always satisfied with himself is seldom satisfied with others.

François Rochefoucauld

COMPROMISE

We must never settle for harmony at the expense of holiness, nor for peace at the expense of principle.

Please all and you will please none.

Aesop

Those who follow the crowd are quickly lost in it.

Anon.

It is madness for sheep to talk peace with a wolf.

Thomas Fuller

A dog that follows everybody is of no good to anybody.

Vance Havner

If you try to be everything to everybody, you will end up being nothing to anybody.

Vance Havner

It is better to die for a conviction than to live with a compromise.

Vance Havner

The middle of the road is a poor place to walk. It is a poor place to drive. It is a poor place to live.

Vance Havner

We are not here to commune with darkness but to conquer it.

Vance Havner

Compromise makes a good umbrella but a poor roof; it is a temporary expedient.

James Russell Lowell

You cannot play with sin and overcome it at the same time.

J. C. MacAulay

To do what others do when, deep down, one knows it is wrong is moral cowardice, which does not lessen guilt but increases it.

J. I. Packer

He who offers to God a second place offers him no place.

John Ruskin

CONCEIT
(See also: Boasting; Egotism; Pride; Vanity)

Conceit makes a little squirt think that he is a fountain of knowledge.

Anon.

Confidence is keeping your chin up; overconfidence is sticking your neck out.

Anon.

If you will but totally disregard a conceited man, he will, after a while, be out of breath in blowing his own trumpet.

Anon.

Most self-made men worship their creator.

Anon.

Don't think yourself so big that other people look small.

Confucius

CONFESSION

(See also: Contrition; Conviction of Sin; Penitence; Repentance)

When man uncovers his sin, God covers it. When man cloaks, God strips bare. When man confesses, God pardons.

Augustine

How easily sin gets into the heart; how hardly it gets out of the mouth.

Joseph Hall

For him who confesses, shams are over and realities have begun.

William James

Never suffer sin to remain upon you; let it not grow old in you; wipe it off while it is fresh, else it will stain; let it not eat its way in and rust in you.

John Henry Newman

The time-lag between the moment of sinning and the moment of forsaking and confessing is a sure indication of the true nature of a man's walk with God.

Alan Redpath

We confess small faults in order to insure that we have no great ones.

François Rochefoucauld

Do not give fair names to foul sins. Call them what you will, they will smell no sweeter.

C. H. Spurgeon

It does not spoil your happiness to confess your sin. The unhappiness is in not making the confession.

C. H. Spurgeon

CONSCIENCE — and God

I have been a man of great sins, but he has been a God of great mercies, and now, through his mercies, I have a conscience as sound and quiet as if I had never sinned.

Donald Cargill

Conscience, which is the voice of God, is higher than all the voices of men.

J. H. Merle d'Aubigné

Every conscience is primed by God. He embosses upon our human nature an awareness of his standards.

Peter Masters

45

Whether trained in moral or religious values or not, all people have God's moral code written within them, and no technique on earth can totally delete or change it.

Peter Masters

We never do anything so secretly but that it is in the presence of two witnesses: God and our own conscience.

Benjamin Whichcote

CONSCIENCE — Importance

When a man says he has a clear conscience it often means he has a bad memory.

Anon.

A happy life depends on a good conscience.

John Calvin

All men stand condemned, not by alien codes of ethics, but by their own, and all men therefore are conscious of guilt.

C. S. Lewis

Disobedience to conscience makes conscience blind ... The moral blindness consequent on being a bad man must therefore fall on everyone who is not a good man.

C. S. Lewis

Conscience is the rudder of the ship of faith.

James Philip

Faith is strong only when the conscience is clear and the heart is pure.

James Philip

Before our conscience punishes us as a judge, it warns us as a friend.

Stanislus

A scar on the conscience is the same as a wound.

Publilius Syrus

A good conscience and a good name is like a gold ring set with a rich diamond.

Thomas Watson

A good conscience can sleep in the mouth of a cannon.

Thomas Watson

A conscience void of offence before God and man is an inheritance for eternity.

Daniel Webster

CONSCIENCE — Power

A good conscience is to the soul what health is to the body; it preserves a constant ease and serenity within us.

Joseph Addison

46

A guilty conscience needs no accuser.

Anon.

The only tyrant I accept in this world is the still voice within.

Mahatma Gandhi

Conscience is the still small voice that makes you feel still smaller.

James A. Sanaker

I would bear any affliction rather than be burdened with a guilty conscience.

C. H. Spurgeon

An uneasy conscience is a hair on the mouth.

Mark Twain

CONSCIENCE — and Sin

There is no greater torment than an evil conscience.

John Calvin

An evil conscience is the devil's anvil, on which he fabricates all those swords and spears on which the guilty sinner pierces and wounds himself.

John Flavel

Our consciences take no account of the Fall.

Donald MacLeod

This side of hell, what can be worse than the tortures of an awakened conscience?

C. H. Spurgeon

CONSECRATION
(See also: Abandonment; Submission; Zeal)

To my God, a heart of flame; to my fellow men, a heart of love; to myself, a heart of steel.

Augustine

The child of God has only one dread — to offend his Father; only one desire — to please and delight in him.

Charles Bridges

It does not take great men to do great things; it only takes consecrated men.

Phillips Brooks

God wants self before substance and service.

Vance Havner

Consecration is handing God a blank sheet to fill in with your name signed at the bottom.

M. H. Miller

Whatever the cost in rearrangement, including bravely coming to terms with loved ones, friends, not to say pursuits, pleasures and indulgences, you

47

must turn to the Lord and give yourself afresh to him.
William Still

CONTENTMENT

Contentment is an inexhaustible treasure.
Anon.

Contentment with what we have is absolutely vital to our spiritual health.
Jerry Bridges

If we have not quiet in our minds, outward comfort will do no more for us than a golden slipper on a gouty foot.
John Bunyan

The contented man is never poor, the discontented never rich.
George Eliot

I am always content with what happens, for what God chooses is better than what I choose.
Epictetus

A mind at leisure from itself beats all rest cures.
Vance Havner

He who desires nothing will always be free.
Edouard Laboulaye

Be content with what you have, but never with what you are.
W. B. Millard

The only person in this world who enjoys complete contentment is the person who knows that the only worthwhile and satisfying life is to be a means, however humble, to God's chief end — his own glory and praise.
J. I. Packer

Contentment is an embracing of the providence of God.
George Seevers

If you are not content with what you have, you would not be satisfied if it were doubled.
C. H. Spurgeon

The more we count the blessings we have, the less we crave the luxuries we haven't.
William A. Ward

The fewer desires, the more peace.
Joseph Wilson

CONTRITION
(See also: Confession; Conviction of Sin; Penitence; Repentance)

Remorse is the pain of sin.
Theodore Parker

Sorrow for sin should be the keenest sorrow; joy in the Lord should be the loftiest joy.

C. H. Spurgeon

The best rubrics of worship are those which are written on broken hearts.

C. H. Spurgeon

We can stand before the cross only with a bowed head and a broken spirit.

John R. W. Stott

CONTROVERSY

Some arguments are sound — and nothing more.

Richard Armour

Never encourage any degrees of heat without light.

David Brainerd

Hot heads and cold hearts never solved anything.

Billy Graham

Our divisions should never be discussed except in the presence of those who have already come to believe that there is one God and that Jesus Christ is his only Son.

C. S. Lewis

Controversy is a serious thing. All those who enter upon it are in great need of more grace.

Iain H. Murray

Truth often suffers more by the heat of its defenders than by the arguments of its opposers.

William Penn

Five minutes before I die it will not matter one whit to me who won the last argument. I will have other things of far greater importance on my mind.

Frank Retief

One of the marks of a mature person is the ability to dissent without creating dissension.

Don Robinson

That religion is suspicious which is full of faction and discord.

Thomas Watson

The gospel seldom thrives where the apple of strife grows.

Thomas Watson

CONVERSION
(See also: Faith — Saving; Regeneration; Repentance)

It is a sign of true conversion when a man's heart is melted to

49

love God's eternal law and when his will is bent to obey it.
Richard Alderson

God does not convert men without design; and his designs are not new, but are eternal.
Albert Barnes

Conversion cannot be separated from prayer.
John Calvin

In the conversion of man, the properties of our original nature remain entire.
John Calvin

Men by their own free will cannot turn to God until he first change their stony hearts into hearts of flesh.
John Calvin

True conversion is proved by the constant tenor of the life.
John Calvin

If Christ's lordship does not disrupt our own lordship, then the reality of our conversion must be questioned.
Charles Colson

Conversion is an empty-handed turning from sin to the Saviour.
Vance Havner

It takes a radical break to turn from earth's trash to heaven's treasure.
Vance Havner

Conversion requires an alteration of the will, and an alteration which, in the last resort, does not occur without the intervention of the supernatural.
C. S. Lewis

Every conversion is the story of a blessed defeat.
C. S. Lewis

Unless God changes a person's heart, nothing lasting will be achieved.
Will Metzger

Whenever a profession of conversion is not accompanied by holiness of life it must be understood that the person concerned is not yet a Christian.
Iain H. Murray

Conversion is the standing miracle of the church.
C. H. Spurgeon

When Christ came into my life I came about like a well-handled ship.
Robert Louis Stevenson

The change of a sinner's heart is as great a miracle as any Jesus Christ wrought on earth.

Joseph Wilson

CONVICTION OF SIN

(See also: Confession; Contrition; Penitence; Repentance)

Conviction is not repentance. It is one thing to be awakened at five o'clock in the morning, but it is another thing to get up.

Anon.

Nobody has ever been convicted of his sinfulness until he has been confronted with the living Lord in his holiness.

Rolfe Barnard

The flesh cannot endure the doctrine of the gospel; none can endure to have their vices reproved.

John Calvin

Measure your growth in grace by your sensitiveness to sin.

Oswald Chambers

Our salvation begins when we condemn ourselves.

Didymus

The conviction that causes men to think it worth the while to seek salvation is hardly ever a conviction of the worth of the reward, but of the dreadfulness of the punishment.

Jonathan Edwards

Grace often grows strongest where conviction of sin has pierced deepest.

Sinclair Ferguson

The deepest levels of conviction may be experienced after rather than before conversion.

Sinclair Ferguson

Those who are most conscious of forgiveness are invariably those who have been most acutely convicted of their sin.

Sinclair Ferguson

Who was the guilty? Who
   brought this upon thee?
Alas, my treason, Lord Jesus,
   hath undone thee.
'Twas I, Lord Jesus, I it was
   denied thee;
I crucified thee!

Johann Heermann

If faith without works is dead, then conviction without action is worthless.

Jay Hudson

The sorest injury we can do to any man is to lighten his conception of the enormity of sin.

John Henry Jowett

51

A man only comes to Christ when he is desperate.
D. Martyn Lloyd-Jones

The first sign of spiritual life is to feel that you are dead!
D. Martyn Lloyd-Jones

A man must completely despair of himself in order to become fit to obtain the grace of Christ.
Martin Luther

A sense of defilement before God is not morbid, neurotic or unhealthy in any way. It is natural, realistic, healthy, and a true perception of our condition.
J. I. Packer

A right knowledge of sin lies at the root of all saving Christianity.
J. C. Ryle

The beginning of the way to heaven is to feel that we are on the way to hell.
J. C. Ryle

If you can look on sin without sorrow then you have never looked on Christ.
C. H. Spurgeon

Only let a man once feel sin for half an hour, really feel its tortures, and I warrant you he would prefer to dwell in a pit of snakes than to live with his sins.
C. H. Spurgeon

Whenever you think about your own conversion, regard it as a miracle.
C. H. Spurgeon

The only way to arrive at faith in the Holy Spirit is along the road of self-despair.
John R. W. Stott

To mourn only for fear of hell is like a thief that weeps for the penalty rather than the offence.
Thomas Watson

A sense of spiritual poverty is a blessing when it leads the humble soul to God.
Edwin T. Winkler

CONVICTIONS

A belief is what you hold; a conviction is what holds you.
Anon.

A conviction is not truly a conviction unless it includes a commitment to live by what we claim to believe.
Jerry Bridges

You can have such an open mind that it is too porous to hold a conviction.

George Crane

Beware lest we mistake our prejudices for our convictions.

Harry A. Ironside

A dogmatic belief in objective value is necessary to the very idea of a rule which is not tyranny or an obedience which is not slavery.

C. S. Lewis

You never know how much you really believe anything until its truth or falsehood becomes a matter of life and death to you.

C. S. Lewis

Great saints have always been dogmatic. We need a return to a gentle dogmatism that smiles while it stands stubborn and firm on the Word of God.

A. W. Tozer

Convictions are the root on which the tree of vital Christianity grows.

Benjamin B. Warfield

COURAGE

The scars you acquire by exer-

cising courage will never make you feel inferior.

O. A. Battista

There can be no courage in men unless God supports them by his Word.

John Calvin

A man without courage is a knife without an edge.

Benjamin Franklin

Only he who can say, 'The Lord is the strength of my life' can say, 'Of whom shall I be afraid?'

Alexander MacLaren

Take courage. We walk in the wilderness today and in the Promised Land tomorrow.

D. L. Moody

Perfect courage consists in doing without a witness all that we should be capable of doing before the whole world.

François Rochefoucauld

Courage is the mastery of fear, not the absence of fear.

Mark Twain

COURTESY

Politeness is like an air cushion; there may be nothing in it,

53

but it eases our jolts wonderfully.

Samuel Johnson

If you will be cherished when you are old, be courteous while you are young.

John Lyly

Nothing is ever lost by courtesy. It is the cheapest of the pleasures; costs nothing and conveys much.

Erastus Wiman

COVETOUSNESS
(See also: Gluttony; Greed)

He who coverts is poor, notwithstanding all he may have acquired.

Ambrose

Gold is the heaviest of all metals, but it is made more heavy by covetousness.

Anon.

Covetousness makes us the slaves of the devil.

John Calvin

Covetousness is not only in getting riches unjustly, but in loving them inordinately, which is a key that opens the door to all sin.

Thomas Watson

The sin of covetousness is the most hard to root out.

Thomas Watson

COWARDICE

Cowards run the greatest danger of any men in a battle.

Anon.

A man without courage cannot long remain virtuous, for he is unable to resist vice.

Chrysostom

To sin by silence when they should protest makes cowards out of men.

Abraham Lincoln

CREATION
(See also: Evolution; Nature)

The glory of creation is its infinite diversity.

Anon.

The work of God was completed, not in one moment but in six days, that it might not be tedious to us to occupy the whole of life in the consideration of it.

John Calvin

God is the true origin of species.

Don Garlington

The universe seems to have been designed by a pure mathematician.

James Jeans

No philosophical theory which I have yet come across is a radical improvement on the words of Genesis, that 'in the beginning God made heaven and earth'.

C. S. Lewis

The serious scientist's comment on Genesis 1 is 'I have nothing to say. I was not there.'

Graham Miller

If the universe reveals its order to us through rational science, it is because the universe is so ordered by the Author of reason.

George Roche

The idea of creation confounds me and surpasses my conception, though I believe as much of it as I am able to conceive. But I know that God has formed the universe and all that exists in the most consummate order.

Jean Jacques Rousseau

Man is the captain of creation, and thus his job is to work with the world, organizing it and transforming it for God's glory.

R. C. Sproul

Our ecological responsibility rests in our prior responsibility to obey our Creator.

R. C. Sproul

Without God the world would be a maze without a clue.

Woodrow Wilson

CRITICISM BY OTHERS
(See also: Criticism of Others)

Many can bear adversity, but few contempt.

Anon.

To reply to a nasty remark with another nasty remark is like trying to remove dirt with mud.

Anon.

We would rather be ruined by praise than saved by criticism.

Anon.

I have seldom ever heard a criticism about myself that didn't indeed contain a kernel of useful truth.

Gordon MacDonald

Many people believe that admitting a fault means they no longer have to correct it.

Marie von Ebner-Eschenbach

CRITICISM OF OTHERS
(See also: Criticism by Others)

Finding fault is not difficult to those who are determined to find it.

Do not condemn the judgement of another because it differs from yours. You may both be wrong.

Anon.

Do not remove a fly from your friend's forehead with a hatchet.

Anon.

Rare is the person who can weigh the faults of others without putting his thumb on the scales.

Anon.

When looking for faults, use a mirror, not a telescope.

Anon.

The accuser should be better than the accused.

Aristotle

Any fool can criticize, condemn and complain — and usually does.

Dale Carnegie

No one so thoroughly appreciates the value of constructive criticism as the one who is giving it.

Hal Chadwick

It is the peculiar quality of a fool to perceive the faults of others and forget his own.

Cicero

Criticism, like rain, should be gentle enough to nourish a man's growth without destroying his roots.

Frank A. Clark

It is not necessary to blow out your neighbour's light to let your own shine.

M. R. de Haan

We have a bat's eye for our own faults, and an eagle's for the faults of others.

James L. Gordon

Giving away pieces of our mind is poor business. We can't afford it, for one thing, because we do not have that much mind to spare!

Vance Havner

He has the right to criticize who has the heart to help.

Abraham Lincoln

Forebear to judge, for we are sinners all.

William Shakespeare

A smile in giving honest criticism can make the difference between resentment and reform.

Philip Steinmetz

CROSS
(See also: Atonement; Jesus Christ — Death)

The cross of Christ destroyed the equation religion equals happiness.

Dietrich Bonhoeffer

Our salvation consists in the doctrine of the cross.

John Calvin

The cross means nothing apart from the law.

Walter J. Chantry

You do not understand Christ until you understand his cross.

P. T. Forsyth

A crossless Christ would mean no more than a Christless cross.

Vance Havner

What brought Jesus to the cross was ultimately not the authorities of the Jews and the Romans but God's love and purpose.

Alex Luc

Take away the cross of Christ from the Bible and it is a dark book.

J. C. Ryle

It is the cross ... that reveals the most violent and mysterious outpouring of the wrath of God that we find anywhere in Scripture.

R. C. Sproul

I wish that our ministry — and mine especially — might be tied and tethered to the cross.

C. H. Spurgeon

Nothing provokes the devil like the cross.

C. H. Spurgeon

The world's one and only remedy is the cross.

C. H. Spurgeon

CYNICISM

Never, never, never be a cynic, even a gentle one. Never help out a sneer, even at the devil.

Vachel Lindsay

Sour godliness is the devil's religion.

John Wesley

What is a cynic? A man who knows the price of everything and the value of nothing.

Oscar Wilde

DEATH — Anticipation

Nothing has contributed more powerfully to wean me from all that held me down to earth than the thought, constantly dwelt upon, of death and of the last judgement.

Augustine

But this is the privilege of saints, that they shall not die until the best time, not until when, if they were but rightly informed, they would desire to die.

Samuel Bolton

My dying shows me to be mortal, but I shall be immortal after that.

Donald Cargill

To me there is nothing more fatuous about mankind than the statement that to think about death is morbid. The man who refuses to face facts is a fool.

D. Martyn Lloyd-Jones

Who would live always in such a world as this?

John Newton

It is the very joy of this earthly life to think that it will come to an end.

C. H. Spurgeon

DEATH — Blessings
(See also: Death — and Heaven)

Death cancels everything but truth.

Anon.

Those who live in the Lord never see each other for the last time.

Anon.

Christ has made of death a narrow starlit strip between the companionships of yesterday and the reunions of tomorrow.

William Jennings Bryan

Death is God's delightful way of giving us life.

Oswald Chambers

Death is not death if it rids us of doubt and fear, of chance and change, of space and time, and all which space and time bring forth and then destroy.

Charles Kingsley

What message from heaven speaks louder to us than the daily dying and departure of our fellow creature?

William Law

Has this world been so kind to you that you would leave it with regret? There are better things ahead than any we leave behind.

C. S. Lewis

If we really believe that home is elsewhere and that this life is a 'wandering to find home', why should we not look forward to the arrival?

C. S. Lewis

I have heard of people being afraid of the pains of death. There are no pains of death: the pain is in life. Death is the end of pain. It is all over. Put the saddle on the right horse. Do not blame death for what he does not do. It is life that brings pain.

C. H. Spurgeon

The best moment of a Christian's life is his last one, because it is the one that is nearest heaven.

C. H. Spurgeon

If you have one grain of grace, you must die to know how rich you are.

William Tiptaft

Death is only putting out the lamp at the rise of a new dawn.

David Watson

Faith builds a bridge across the gulf of death.

Edward Young

DEATH — Certainty

The time of every man's death has been fixed by God ... We are safe from all risk until God is pleased to call us away.

John Calvin

Death is oftentimes as near to the young man's back as it is to the old man's face.

Bernard of Clairvaux

Death keeps no calendar.

Thomas Fuller

Dying my death is the one thing no one else can do for me.

Martin Heidegger

We are but tenants, and ... shortly the great Landlord will give us notice that our lease has expired.

Joseph Jefferson

It is heard to have patience with people who say 'There is no death' or 'Death doesn't matter.' There is death. And whatever is matters. And whatever happens has consequences, and it and they are irrevocable and irreversible. You might as

59

well say that birth doesn't matter.

C. S. Lewis

The longest life is a lingering death.

John Mason

The death rate is still one per person.

Robert A. Morey

Death is not a spectator sport.
Samuel E. Waldron

DEATH — and Heaven
(See also: Death — Blessings)

I have talked to doctors and nurses who have held the hands of dying people, and they say that there is as much difference between the death of a Christian and a non-Christian as there is between heaven and hell.

Billy Graham

Death to a Christian is a putting off of rags for robes.

John Mason

First infancy dies, then childhood, then youth, then manhood, then old age; and then we make an end of dying.

John Mason

DEATH — Indiscriminate

There's no dying by proxy.
Anon.

DEATH — and Judgement

Let us make a friend of death and our Judge; and then we shall die out of choice as well as necessity.

John Mason

The bed of death brings every human being to his pure individuality, to the intense contemplation of that deepest and most solemn of all relations — the relation between the creature and his Creator.

Daniel Webster

DEATH — Meaning

The human body is formed for immortality ... By sinking into death it does not utterly perish.
John Calvin

Death is an incident, not an end.

Billy Graham

We have a date with Deity, an appointment with the Almighty.

Vance Havner

The intellectual critic is soon answered. We have but to ask him to explain the meaning of life and death.

D. Martyn Lloyd-Jones

DEATH — Preparation for

Do every act in thy life as if it were the last.

Marcus Antoninus

Happy is that Christian who falls asleep with his Lord's work in his hand.

Francis Burkitt

The mind of a Christian ought not to be filled with thoughts of earthly things, or find satisfaction in them, for we ought to be living as if we might have to leave this world at any moment.

John Calvin

You cannot pass a day devoutly unless you think of it as your last.

John Climacus

It is difficult for me to understand how an intelligent person can spend all of his time building for this world and have no time for the future world.

Billy Graham

There is nothing morbid about getting ready to die. For a Christian, it is preparation for life's greatest adventure.

Vance Havner

There are, aren't there, only three things we can do about death: to desire it, to fear it, or to ignore it.

C. S. Lewis

We should think of death, not as though we were thinking, but as though we were dying.

John Mason

He who lives to live forever never fears dying.

William Penn

Is it not dangerous living one hour at a time in a state that we would not die in?

Richard Sibbes

No man would find it difficult to die who died every day. He would have practised it so often, that he would only have to die but once more; like the singer who has been through his rehearsals, and is perfect in his part, and has but to pour forth the notes once for all, and have done.

C. H. Spurgeon

If rich men only knew when they died, how their relatives would scramble for their money, the worms for their bodies, and the devil for their souls, they would not be so anxious to save money.

William Tiptaft

No one can live well until they can die well.

David Watson

DEATH — Triumph over

The fear of death is worse than death.

Robert Burton

No man ever repented of being a Christian on his deathbed.

Hannah More

The only real answer to death is life.

Derek Prime

What greater encouragement can a man have to fight against his enemy than when he is sure of the victory before he fights — of final victory?

Richard Sibbes

DEMOCRACY

Democracy assumes that there are extraordinary possibilities in ordinary people.

Harry Emerson Fosdick

A society which becomes democratic in ethos as well as in constitution is doomed. And not much loss either.

C. S. Lewis

Democracy is all very well as a political device. It must not be allowed to intrude into the spiritual, or even the aesthetic, world.

C. S. Lewis

DEMONS
(See also: Angels)

There are two equal and opposite errors into which our race can fall about the devils. One is to disbelieve in their existence. The other is to believe, and to feel an excessive and unhealthy interest in them.

C. S. Lewis

It is no more difficult to believe in demons than to believe in God, Christ, the Holy Spirit, angels or the devil.

J. W. Roberts

DEPRAVITY
(See also: Guilt; Man — a Sinner; Sin; Sinful Nature)

Man sins not because he is deprived, but because he is depraved.

Fallen human nature has neither grace nor truth in it, but the human nature of Christ was full of grace and truth.
W. E. Best

Original sin is more than negative absence of original righteousness; it is positive corruption.
W. E. Best

According to the constitution of our nature, oil might be extracted from a stone sooner than we could perform a good work.
John Calvin

Every sin should convince us of the general truth of the corruption of our nature.
John Calvin

Original sin is sufficient for the condemnation of all men.
John Calvin

The general character of men's lives is nothing else but a continual departure from the law of God.
John Calvin

The Holy Spirit teaches us in Scripture that our mind is smitten with so much blindness, that the affections of our heart are so depraved and perverted, that our whole nature is vitiated, that we can do nothing but sin until he forms a new will within us.
John Calvin

There is not a man who knows the hundredth part of his own sin.
John Calvin

We ... are born lions, tigers, wolves and bears, until the Spirit of Christ tames us, and from wild and savage beasts forms us to be mild sheep.
John Calvin

The magnitude of man's sin is also the measure of his need of salvation.
Sinclair Ferguson

The ultimate tragedy of man's self-understanding is that he believes himself to be free, has all the feelings of a free agent, but does not realize that he is a slave to sin and serves the will of Satan.
Sinclair Ferguson

Whoever has a proper knowledge of himself will be convinced that naturally there is nothing good in him.

Robert Haldane

Temptation has its source not in the outer lure but in the inner lust.

D. Edmund Hiebert

Crime is inherent in human nature; the germ is in every man.

H. B. Irving

In the last analysis, we sin not because we have to but because we want to.

Henry Jacobsen

The wickedness of the ordinary man can be explained only by recognizing a radical defect that runs from top to bottom in his moral nature.

C. E. M. Joad

The Fall is simply and solely disobedience — doing what you have been told not to do; and it results from pride — from being too big for your boots, forgetting your place, thinking that you are God.

C. S. Lewis

We are all fallen creatures and all very hard to live with.

C. S. Lewis

We have come to realize that a man can be educated and cultured and still be a beast!

D. Martyn Lloyd-Jones

When a man truly sees himself, he knows that nobody can say anything about him that is too bad.

D. Martyn Lloyd-Jones

As no man can give himself faith, neither can he take away his unbelief.

Martin Luther

The history of man is his attempt to escape his own corruption.

Daniel Mullis

The sinner is free to do as he pleases ... but his pleasure is to sin.

A. W. Pink

Wrong views about holiness are generally traceable to wrong views about human corruption.

J. C. Ryle

Man's will is free to follow his inclinations, but fallen man's inclinations are always and invariably away from God.

R. C. Sproul

As the salt flavours every drop in the Atlantic, so does sin affect every atom of our nature.
C. H. Spurgeon

I would never have been saved if I could have helped it.
C. H. Spurgeon

Sin not only makes us unlike God but contrary to God.
Thomas Watson

The answer to the wickedness of human nature is not found in human eloquence or attractiveness. It is not even found in the miraculous. The answer is found in God!
Tom Wells

'Know thyself'? If I knew myself I would run away.
Johann Wolfgang

DESPAIR

The logical outcome of genuine despair would seem to be suicide. If a man is not prepared for that, he does not really despair, but only fancies so.
Anon.

In a really dark night of the soul it is always three in the morning, day after day.
F. Scott Fitzgerald

We do not usually learn that Christ is all we need until we reach that point where he is all we have!
Vance Havner

Despair is a greater sin than any of the sins which provoke it.
C. S. Lewis

The pessimist is not a representative of Christianity.
A. T. Robertson

The Christian's chief occupational hazards are depression and discouragement.
John R. W. Stott

DETERMINATION

Great souls have wills, feeble ones have only wishes.
Anon.

I can plod.
William Carey

All excellence involves discipline and tenacity of purpose.
John W. Gardner

DIFFICULTIES

No crisis is greater than Christ.

An obstacle is often an unrecognized opportunity.

Anon.

Difficulties either make us better or bitter.

Anon.

In the presence of trouble some people grow wings; others buy crutches.

Anon.

Shall light troubles make you forget weighty mercies?

John Flavel

The reason some people know the solution is because they created the problem.

Kelly Fordyce

You must live with people to see their problems, and live with God in order to solve them.

P. T. Forsyth

Problems are opportunities in work clothes.

Henry J. Kaiser

If a man in his heart is right with God, God will deal with the problem.

Alan Redpath

If God be God, then no insoluble problems exist. And if God be *my* God, then no problem of mine is without its appropriate solution.

Maurice Roberts

Many men owe the grandeur of their lives to their tremendous difficulties.

C. H. Spurgeon

Let God's promises shine on your problems.

Corrie ten Boom

Our greatest problem in suffering is unbelief.

Geoff Thomas

DIGNITY

If your dignity cannot take care of itself, but requires nursing, it is worth but little.

Anon.

Dignity does not consist in possessing honours, but in deserving them.

Aristotle

Where is there dignity unless there is honesty?

Cicero

DISCIPLESHIP

Jesus didn't commit the gospel to an advertising agency; he commissioned disciples.

Joseph Bayly

No man is qualified to be a disciple of Christ until he has been divested of self.

John Calvin

Our Lord had only one desire, and that was to do the will of his Father, and to have this desire is characteristic of a disciple.

Oswald Chambers

The walk of a disciple is gloriously different, but gloriously certain.

Oswald Chambers

Salvation is free, but discipleship costs everything we have.

Billy Graham

Our Lord made discipleship hard and lost many prospective followers because he called them to a pilgrimage, not to a parade — to a fight, not to a frolic.

Vance Havner

Does it not fill our hearts with a thrilling excitement to think that the costly disciplines and lonely agonies that make up

our earthly discipleship may at any moment, and without any warning, be transformed into everlasting splendours the like of which we can scarcely conceive, let alone understand?

James Philip

DISCIPLINE

Discipline is proof of sonship.

Discipline is a privilege because it is an evidence of our sonship.

Alistair Begg

Guarding our hearts begins with guarding our eyes and ears.

Jerry Bridges

You cannot sharpen an axe on a cake of butter.

Vance Havner

Discipline, while the word is unfallen, exists for the sake of what seems its very opposite — for freedom, almost for extravagance.

C. S. Lewis

The great need in the Christian life is for self-discipline. This is not something that happens to you in a meeting; you have got to do it!

D. Martyn Lloyd-Jones

Discipline is the basic set of tools we require to solve life's problems.

M. Scott Peck

Better be pruned to grow than cut up to burn.

John Trapp

Discipline without direction is drudgery.

Donald S. Whitney

DISCONTENT

The poorest man in the world is the one who is always wanting more than he has.

Anon.

Discontent is one of the most satanic of all sins, and to indulge in it is to rebel against God just as Satan did.

Jerry Bridges

The contented man is never poor, the discontented never rich.

George Eliot

Discontent follows ambition like a shadow.

Henry H. Haskins

A man's discontent is his worst evil.

George Herbert

DISHONESTY
(See also: Lying)

There are people so addicted to exaggeration that they cannot tell the truth without lying.

John Billings

Truth exists, only falsehood has to be invented.

Georges Braque

A lie stands on one leg, truth on two.

Benjamin Franklin

You can fool some of the people all of the time, and all of the people some of the time, but you cannot fool all of the people all of the time.

Abraham Lincoln

A lie is the refuge of weakness. The man of courage is not afraid of the truth.

J. C. MacAulay

He who tells a lie is forced to invent twenty more to sustain it.

Alexander Pope

DIVORCE

Divorce is always a bombshell. However much it has been anticipated and even thought through, it almost invariably turns out to be much harder for both partners than either ever imagined.

Andrew Cornes

So many people who think divorce a panacea for every ill find out when they try it that the remedy is worse than the disease.

Dorothy Dix

It is not marriage that fails, it is people that fail.

Harry Emerson Fosdick

I have such hatred of divorce that I prefer bigamy to divorce.

Martin Luther

DOCTRINE
(See also: Theology)

Every Christian should have an insatiable appetite for sound doctrine.

The life of Christian doctrine is its practical application.

Anon.

Purity of doctrine is the soul of the church.

John Calvin

The design of Christian doctrine is that believers should

exercise themselves in good works.

John Calvin

Zeal without doctrine is like a sword in the hand of a lunatic.

John Calvin

A church with a little creed is a church with a little life.

B. H. Carroll

The modern cry 'Less creed and more liberty' is a degeneration from the vertebrate to the jellyfish.

B. H. Carroll

Some who demonstrate a passion for accurate doctrine place a question mark over their love for God by evidencing no active love for lost sinners.

Walter J. Chantry

Invariably when a great doctrine is misused there is a tendency for it to be devalued.

Sinclair Ferguson

The New Testament always ties up prophetic doctrine with practical duty.

Vance Havner

True doctrine is a master key to all the world's problems. With it the world can be taken apart and put together.

Eric Hoffer

The church is where the truth is. Sound doctrine always has been, is today, and ever will be the foremost mark of the true church.

R. B. Kuiper

Doctrines are not God: they are only a kind of map. But that map is based on the experience of hundreds of people who were really in touch with God.

C. S. Lewis

I always find that those who are driven with every wind of doctrine are those who are too lazy to study doctrine.

D. Martyn Lloyd-Jones

If your knowledge of doctrine does not make you a great man of prayer, you had better examine yourself again.

D. Martyn Lloyd-Jones

The man whose doctrine is shaky will be shaky in his whole life.

D. Martyn Lloyd-Jones

There is nothing so fatuous as the view that Christian doctrine is removed from life. There is nothing which is more practical.

D. Martyn Lloyd-Jones

Doctrine and life have been married by God.

Will Metzger

A creed is the road or street. It is very good as far as it goes, but if it doesn't take us to Christ it is worthless.

D. L. Moody

Doctrinal Christianity is not a pastime for intellectuals. It involves life and death.

Iain H. Murray

Real doctrine Christianity has an obstinacy about it which no amount of modern opinion or religious excitement can change.

Iain H. Murray

Doctrine is never meant merely to make us knowledgeable, but to make us godly.

James Philip

True holiness flows from the soundness of a man's doctrine.

Robert A. Richey

The Christian faith is the most exciting drama that ever staggered the imagination — and the dogma is the drama.

Dorothy L. Sayers

It is a positive and very hurtful sin to magnify liberty at the expense of doctrine.

Walter Shurden

To separate doctrine from life or life from doctrine is to sue for a groundless divorce. God has joined them together, and what he has joined together we must never put asunder.

R. C. Sproul

Certain doctrines would not make a mouse stir its ears; the grand old doctrines of grace stir our blood, quicken our pulse, and fill our whole being with enthusiasm.

C. H. Spurgeon

A doctrine has practical value only as far as it is prominent in our thoughts and makes a difference in our lives.

A. W. Tozer

Doctrine won't make you happy unless it is translated into life.

Henry Van Dyke

DOUBT

Doubt is not always a sign that a man is wrong; it may be a sign that he is thinking.

Oswald Chambers

The truth, however dreadful it is, is not so dreadful as uncertainty.

Anton Chekov

He is a fool who leaves a certainty to pursue an uncertainty.

Hesiod

Clouds of doubt are created when the warm, moist air of our expectations meets the cold air of God's silence. The problem is not as much in God's silence as it is in your ability to hear.

Max Lucado

Chronic doubt is a sin that is not to be tolerated.

C. H. Spurgeon

The teachers of doubt are doubtful teachers.

C. H. Spurgeon

DRUNKENNESS
(See also: Alcohol)

The drunken man is a living corpse.

Chrysostom

A drinker has a hole under his nose that all his money runs into.

Thomas Fuller

Drinking is the refuge of the weak; it is crutches for lame ducks.

E. Stanley Jones

Drunkenness is temporary suicide.

Bertrand Russell

DUTY
(See also: Actions; Good Deeds; Responsibility; Service)

Do what you know to be your present duty and God will acquaint you with your future duty as it comes to be present.

Samuel Annesley

In doing what we ought we deserve no praise.

Augustine

Do not let not being able to do it any better keep you from doing what you can.

Vance Havner

The consciousness of a duty performed gives us music at midnight.

George Herbert

I ought, therefore I can.

Immanuel Kant

Every duty is a religious duty, and our obligation to perform every duty is therefore absolute.

C. S. Lewis

The world might stop in ten minutes; meanwhile, we are to go on doing our duty. The great thing is to be found at one's post as a child of God, living each day as though it were our last, but planning as though the world might last a hundred years.

C. S. Lewis

There are no great principles for great duties and little ones for little duties.

Alexander MacLaren

The best motive to present duty is to be drawn from future destiny.

Thomas V. Moore

Faithfulness knows no difference between small and great duties.

John Ruskin

If God should call me into judgement before him, according to the strictness of his perfect law, for the best duty I have ever performed, and for nothing else, I must be condemned as a transgressor; for when weighed in these exact balances, it would be found wanting.

Thomas Scott

Duties come from doctrines.
Richard Seume

Consequences and usefulness are nothing to us. Duty and right — these are to be our guides.

C. H. Spurgeon

EDUCATION
(See also: Knowledge; Mind; Reason)

Anyone who stops learning is old, whether at twenty or eighty.

Anon.

Education is never as expensive as ignorance.

Anon.

Education is what is left over when you subtract what you have forgotten from what you have learned.

Anon.

Education is a progressive discovery of our own ignorance.
Will Durant

Many learned men, with all the rich furniture of their brain,

live and die slaves to the spirit of this world.

William Law

One of the reasons why it needs no special education to be a Christian is that Christianity is an education in itself.

C. S. Lewis

The great aim of education is not knowledge but action.
Herbert Spencer

It is better to learn late than never.

Publilius Syrus

Education is useless without the Bible.
Noah Webster

EGOTISM
(See also: Boasting; Conceit; Pride; Vanity)

An egotist is a man whose self-importance makes his mind shrink while his head swells.
Anon.

Egotism is an odd disease. It makes everybody sick but the one who has it.

Anon.

The egotist is an 'I' specialist.
Anon.

Most of the trouble in the world is caused by people wanting to be important.

T. S. Eliot

An egotist is a man who talks about himself so much that you don't have a chance to talk about yourself.

Vance Havner

ELECTION — and Calling

God never chooses on merit.

God prepares his elect for hearing, and gives them ears for that purpose.

John Calvin

At the heart of the election doctrine throbs God's freedom.

Carl F. H. Henry

ELECTION —
and Conversion
(See also: Predestination)

A Christian has been selected to live; to live essentially in Christ, to live effectively for Christ and to live eternally with Christ.

Grace and election are the essence and mystery of history.

Augustine

Election is ... the parent of faith.

John Calvin

None believe but those whom God, of free grace, enlightens for his own good pleasure.

John Calvin

When God elects us, it is not because we are handsome.

John Calvin

Until we have come to the place where we can sing about election with a full heart we have not grasped the spirit of the New Testament teaching.

Sinclair Ferguson

God's choices are without human precedent.

R. C. Lucas

Election is ascribed to God the Father, sanctification to the Spirit, and reconciliation to Jesus Christ ... The Son cannot die for them whom the Father never elected, and the Spirit will never sanctify them whom the Father hath not elected nor the Son redeemed.

Thomas Manton

This doctrine affords comfort: thy unworthiness may dismay thee, but remember that thy election depends not upon thy worthiness but upon the will of God.

Elnathan Parr

To either deny sovereign election or to store it away in some theological closet on shelves labelled 'good for nothing' or 'harmful' is to rob the people of God of the fullest view of God's glory and to limit the church's worship to the realms of human logic.

Robert B. Selph

From the Word of God I gather that damnation is all of man, from top to bottom, and salvation is all of grace, from first to last. He that perishes chooses to perish; but he that is saved is saved because God has chosen to save him.

C. H. Spurgeon

It is one of the axioms of theology that if a man be lost God must not be blamed for it; and it is also an axiom of theology that if a man be saved God must have the glory for it.

C. H. Spurgeon

At the heart of election is a particular and passionate love that was the cause of God sending his Son to be the Saviour of his people.

G. Steveson

Election keeps no one out of heaven who would otherwise have been there, but it keeps a whole multitude of sinners out of hell who would otherwise have been there.

Mark Webb

ELECTION — and Eternal Security
(See also: Eternal Security)

The doctrine of election is not meant to confuse the Christian but to comfort him.

God watches over the scattered dust of his own children, gathers it again, and will suffer nothing of them to perish.

John Calvin

There is no better assurance of salvation to be found anywhere than can be gained from the decree of God.

John Calvin

Should any man be fully persuaded that God had decreed his eternal happiness, however groundless that persuasion might be, he would find his aversion to the doctrine of election exceedingly abated by it.

Thomas Scott

Candles which are lit by God the devil can never blow out.

C. H. Spurgeon

They are well kept whom the Lord keeps.

William Tiptaft

ELECTION — and Faith

It is God who causes faith in the believer by prompting his will and enlightening his intellect.

Thomas Aquinas

Election depends on the promise of God.

John Calvin

No man believes with a true and saving faith unless God inclines his heart; and no man when God does incline his heart can refrain from believing.

Blaise Pascal

God alone can make a man a believer. Our part is to accept or reject his initiative.

John Powell

ELECTION — and Holiness

The end of our election is that we might show forth the glory of God in every way.

John Calvin

Nothing could be further from the truth than the suggestion that God's choice destroys moral effort on our part.

Sinclair Ferguson

The only certain proof of my election is that today I am following the Lord.

R. C. Lucas

God has not chosen us because we were holy, or because he foresaw we should become holy, but in order that we might be holy.

Charles Simeon

As chastity distinguishes a virtuous woman from a harlot, so sanctification distinguishes God's people from others.

Thomas Watson

Purity is the end of our election.

Thomas Watson

ELECTION — Mystery of

Grace and election are the essence and mystery of history.

Augustine

The difference which exists between the elect and the rest of the world is the mere good pleasure of God.

John Calvin

The election of God is anterior to Adam's fall.

John Calvin

When we come to election, we see nothing but mercy on every side.

John Calvin

You must first deny the authenticity and full inspiration of the Holy Scripture before you can legitimately and truly deny election.

C. H. Spurgeon

EMOTIONS

If you are limping around on the crutches of feelings, throw them away and walk on the legs of faith.

Ronald Dunn

Don't bother much about your feelings. When they are humble, loving, brave, give thanks for them; when they are conceited, selfish, cowardly, ask to have them altered.

C. S. Lewis

Feelings come and go, and when they come a good use can be made of them; they cannot be our regular spiritual diet.

C. S. Lewis

Confidence that one's impressions are God-given is no guarantee that this is really so, even when they persist and grow stronger through long seasons of prayer. Bible-based wisdom must judge them.

J. I. Packer

There is no great Christianity where there is no great feeling.

Maurice Roberts

ENCOURAGEMENT

A good word costs no more than a bad one.

Anon.

More people fail for lack of encouragement than for any other reason.

Anon.

A compliment is verbal sunshine.

Robert Orben

We cannot hold a torch to another's path without brightening our own.

Ben Sweetland

Correction does much, but encouragement does more. Encouragement after censure is as the sun after a shower.

Johann Wolfgang

77

ENTHUSIASM
(See also: Zeal)

Wherever you are, be all there. Live to the hilt every situation you believe to be the will of God.

Jim Elliot

We have stage fire and strange fire and satanic fire, but not much Spirit fire.

Vance Havner

A man can succeed at almost anything for which he has unlimited enthusiasm.

Charles M. Schwab

Enthusiasm and persistence can make an average person superior; indifference and lethargy can make a superior person average.

William A. Ward

ENVY
(See also: Jealousy)

As rust corrupts iron, so envy corrupts man.

Antisthenes

If there is any sin more deadly than envy, it is being pleased at being envied.

Richard Armour

Love looks through a telescope, envy through a microscope.

John Billings

The envious man is an enemy to himself, for his mind is always spontaneously occupied with his own unhappy thoughts.

Menander

Envy always implies inferiority, wherever it resides.

Pliny

ETERNAL SECURITY
(See also: Election — and Eternal Security; Heaven — the Christian's Eternal Home)

We have not the slightest cause to fear that our integrity will make us a prey to the ungodly when God promises us safety under his hand.

John Calvin

Whoever falls from God's right hand is caught into his left.

Edwin Markham

If God maintains sun and planets in bright and ordered beauty he can keep us.

F. B. Meyer

The earth shall soon dissolve
  like snow,
The sun forbear to shine;
But God, who called me here
  below,
Will be for ever mine.
> *John Newton*

Perseverance is the rope that
ties the soul to the doorpost of
heaven.
> *Frances J. Roberts*

He that formed me in the
  womb,
He shall guide me to the tomb;
All my times shall ever be
Ordered by his wise decree.
> *John Ryland*

Child of God, you cost Christ
too much for him to forget you.
> *C. H. Spurgeon*

God promises to keep his people, and he will keep his promises.
> *C. H. Spurgeon*

He that takes care of our times
will take care of our eternity.
> *C. H. Spurgeon*

It is a glorious truth that God
will keep his people, but it is an
abominable falsehood that sin
will do them no harm.
> *C. H. Spurgeon*

The doctrine of final perseverance of believers seems to me
to be written as with a beam of
sunlight throughout the whole
of Scripture.
> *C. H. Spurgeon*

When Christ can die, then can
the believer perish.
> *C. H. Spurgeon*

We can call out even to the
demons in hell, 'Which of you
is going to condemn me?' And
there will be no answer.
> *John R. W. Stott*

When God calls a man, he does
not repent of it ... This is the
blessedness of a saint; his condition admits of no alteration.
> *Thomas Watson*

ETERNITY
(See also: Heaven; Hell; Judgement)

The created world is but a small
parenthesis in eternity.
> *Thomas Browne*

I've read the last page of the
Bible. It's going to turn out all
right.
> *Billy Graham*

Do not so contemplate eternity
that you waste today.
> *Vance Havner*

The thirst for infinity proves infinity.
Victor Hugo

Life is only lived wisely to the extent that it is spent in preparation for the eternity which follows.
Dave Hunt

Live near to God, and all things will appear little to you in comparison with eternal realities.
Robert Murray M'Cheyne

Learn to hold loosely all that is not eternal.
Agnes Maude Royden

Eternity is a jewel of the saints' crown.
Thomas Watson

Eternity is duration without beginning and without end.
Thomas Wilson

The solution of the riddle of life in space and time lies *outside* space and time.
Ludwig Wittgenstein

ETHICS
(See also: Goodness; Morality; Virtue)

Without transcendent norms, laws are either established by social elites or are merely bargains struck by competing forces in society.
Charles Colson

All men stand condemned, not by alien codes of ethics, but by their own, and all men therefore are conscious of guilt.
C. S. Lewis

Let us very clearly understand that, in a certain sense, it is no more possible to invent a new ethic than to place a new sun in the sky.
C. S. Lewis

Every human being has some ethical sense within him, a light of nature by which he can distinguish right from wrong.
R. C. Sproul

The essence of Christian ethics is gratitude.
R. C. Sproul

True ethical absolutes can only be grounded in the fear of a living God.
R. C. Sproul

EVANGELISM — Divine Initiative

God is a communicating being.
Jonathan Edwards

God had only one Son and he made him an evangelist.

R. C. Lucas

EVANGELISM — and Doctrine

The fashionable doctrine, 'God loved you, Christ died for you, believe that and be happy', is but daubing immortal souls with 'untempered mortar'.

John Kennedy

All true theology has an evangelistic thrust, and all true evangelism is theology in action.

J. I. Packer

EVANGELISM — Message

If we think wrongly about our definition of evangelism, we are likely to act wrongly in our methods of evangelism.

Will Metzger

We are not to try to entice people by methods appealing to their desires.

Will Metzger

Cling to the great truth of electing love and divine sovereignty, but let not these bind you in fetters when, in the power of the Holy Ghost, you become fishers of men.

C. H. Spurgeon

The medicine of the gospel has been prescribed by the Good Physician; we may neither dilute it nor add ingredients to make it more palatable; we must serve it neat.

John R. W. Stott

EVANGELISM — Principles

Many of us cannot reach the mission fields on our feet, but we can reach them on our knees.

T. J. Bach

I just want to lobby for God.

Billy Graham

We cannot evangelize unless we understand the Word; and we cannot evangelize unless we understand the world.

Donald MacLeod

It is our privilege to have world evangelism as a passion, not our responsibility to have as a burden.

Mary Nordstrom

Most people are brought to faith in Christ, not by argument for it, but by exposure to it.

Samuel Shoemaker

EVANGELISM — Responsibility for

(See also: Soul-Winning; Witnessing)

Every Christian who is not called to preach is called to send other Christians to do so.

Missions are a must, not a maybe.

Anon.

The special person called to do missionary work is every person who is a member of the church of Christ. The call does not come to a chosen few, it is to every one of us.

Oswald Chambers

Too many are missionaries by proxy but not in person.

Vance Havner

Every Christian is either a missionary or an imposter.

C. H. Spurgeon

If sinners will be damned, at least let them leap to hell over our bodies.

C. H. Spurgeon

It will not matter whether I live or die if you all become ministers.

C. H. Spurgeon

EVANGELISM — Scope

In the offer of the gospel we must make no limitation whatever, because 'God commandeth *all men everywhere* to repent.'

Thomas Chalmers

The world will never be Christianized, but it should be evangelized.

Vance Havner

EVOLUTION

(See also: Creation; Nature)

The theory of evolution is a stab in the dark that has acquired the status of a dogma.

There is no more reason to believe that man descended from an inferior animal than there is to believe that a stately mansion has descended from a small cottage.

William Jennings Bryan

What shall we say of the intelligence ... of those who distinguish between fishes and

reptiles and birds, but put a man with an immortal soul in the same circle with the wolf, the hyena and the skunk?
William Jennings Bryan

Evolution is a good example of that modern intelligence which, if it destroys anything, destroys itself.
G. K. Chesterton

We are not a chance collision of atoms in an indifferent universe or islands amid cold currents of modern culture.
Charles Colson

If evolution works, how come mothers still have only two hands?
Ed Dussault

So far, evolution has been nothing but staggering from one error to the other.
Henrik Ibsen

It seems at times as if many of our modern writers on evolution have had their views by some sort of revelation.
G. A. Kerkut

Blithely to accept that evolution succeeded against all odds is to believe in a long series of miracles.
George Roche

How do we celebrate our emergence from a chaos of chance without undermining the validity of human thought?
George Roche

The odds against random life would swallow the history of the universe as the oceans swallow a raindrop.
George Roche

There is no 'fact' of evolution. Insisting on the 'fact' is simply the anti-hero's way of saying he believes in evolution, regardless of the evidence.
George Roche

A number of materialist thinkers have ascribed to blind evolution more miracles, more improbable coincidences and wonders, than all those who believe in God's purpose and design could ever devise.
Isaac Bashevis Singer

Modern evolutionary secularism provides no foundation for valuing human life.
R. C. Sproul

EXAMPLE
(See also: Influence)

Conduct is an unspoken sermon.
Henri Amiel

A good example is the best sermon.

Anon.

Precepts may lead, but examples draw.

Anon.

A person who lives right, and is right, has more power in his silence than another has by words.

Phillips Brooks

One example is worth a thousand arguments.

Thomas Carlyle

Well done is better than well said.

Benjamin Franklin

No man is so insignificant as to be sure his example can do no harm.

Edward Hyde

The world takes its notions of God from the people who say they belong to God's family.

Alexander MacLaren

More depends on my walk than talk.

D. L. Moody

Live to explain thy doctrine by thy life.

Matthew Prior

Let him that would move the world first move himself.

Socrates

Truth in propositions is powerful; truth in example is more powerful.

David Thomas

Good example is a language and an argument which everybody understands.

Thomas Wilson

EXCUSES

An excuse is only the skin of a reason, stuffed with a lie.

Vance Havner

He who wants to know people should study their excuses.

Friedrich Hebbel

He who excuses himself accuses himself.

Gabriel Meurier

An excuse is a lie guarded.

Alexander Pope

It is easy to make excuses when we ought to be making opportunities.

Warren Wiersbe

EXPERIENCE

Experience is not always the kindest of teachers, but it is the best.

Anon.

Experience is the best of schoolmasters, only the school fees are heavy.

Thomas Carlyle

Do not confuse great experiences with great grace.

Sinclair Ferguson

Experience is a costly school, yet some learn no other way.

Benjamin Franklin

Today is yesterday's pupil.

Thomas Fuller

Nothing shuts the mouth, seals the lips, ties the tongue, like the poverty of our own spiritual experience. We do not bear witness for the simple reason that we have no witness to bear.

John R. W. Stott

Practice is the best of all instructors.

Publilius Syrus

Every experience God gives us, every person he puts in our lives, is the perfect preparation for the future that only he can see.

Corrie ten Boom

Experience is the one thing you can't get for nothing.

Oscar Wilde

FAILURE

Half the failures of life arise from pulling in one's horse as he is leaping.

J. C. Hare

No amount of falls will really undo us if we keep picking ourselves up each time.

C. S. Lewis

It is very difficult to be humble if you are always successful, so God chastises us with failure at times in order to humble us, to keep us in a state of humility.

D. Martyn Lloyd-Jones

Failure is an invitation to have recourse to God.

Antonin Sertillanges

The greatest failure is the failure to try.

William A. Ward

FAITH — and Deeds

(See also: Faith — Saving; Good Deeds; Holiness — and Justification)

Only he who believes is obedient; only he who is obedient believes.
Dietrich Bonhoeffer

Faith and love must be inseparable companions. There is a necessary connection between them. Faith without love is no living grace, and love without faith is no saving faith.
Francis Burkitt

Practice is the incarnation of faith.
John Donne

Man fell by a desire to be independent of God, and now man wishes to be equally independent of God in returning to him.
T. C. Hammond

Works without faith are like a suit of clothes without a body, empty. Faith without works is a body without clothes; no warmth.
John P. K. Henshaw

Wherever there is genuine faith it must blossom into works.
Joseph B. Mayor

A life of faith involves hard work, courage and discipline.
Philip Nunn

To live by faith is to live a reasonable life based on God's Word, a life which reflects God's values and priorities.
Philip Nunn

To assume that a holy God winks at sin and grants eternal life on the basis of our performance is the greatest deception plaguing mankind.
R. C. Sproul

There is never a doubt in our heart about the experience of faith while it is in action.
C. H. Spurgeon

You may as well separate weight from lead or heat from fire as works from faith.
Thomas Watson

No more, my God, I boast no
    more
Of all the duties I have done:
I quit the hopes I held before,
To trust the merits of thy Son.
Isaac Watts

Works? Works? A man get to heaven by works? I would as soon think of climbing to the moon on a rope of sand.
George Whitefield

FAITH — Definition

(See also: Faith — Saving)

Faith is to the soul what a mainspring is to a watch.

Anon.

What is faith, unless it is to believe what you do not see?
Augustine

Faith is the resurrection of the soul.

John Calvin

Faith is more than assent, but it is never *less* than assent.

Sinclair Ferguson

Faith is the capacity to trust God while not being able to make sense out of everything.

James Kok

Faith is a humble, self-effacing grace; it makes the Christian nothing in himself and all in God.

Robert Leighton

Faith is the open hand of the soul to receive all the bounteous supplies of God.

Thomas Manton

Faith, to put it simply, is the conviction that God does not tell lies.

Frank Retief

Faith is our acceptance of God's acceptance of us.

Adrian Rogers

Faith is not shelter against difficulties, but belief in the face of all contradictions.

Paul Tournier

FAITH — Essence

Faith has no merit with God when it is not the testimony of divine authority that leads us to it, but the evidence of human reason.

Peter Abelard

Faith is not an achievement. It is a gift.

Roland Bainton

Faith brings a man empty to God, that he may be filled with the blessings of God.

John Calvin

True faith is ever connected with hope.

John Calvin

The best hold that faith can have of God is to take him by his word.

David Dickson

Biblical faith is more than simply transferring our natural faith to spiritual objects.
Ronald Dunn

Faith is not idle; it works while it waits.
Ronald Dunn

Faith will give you a positive attitude; but a positive attitude is not necessarily faith.
Ronald Dunn

God wants to bring us to the place where we trust in him and him alone, without the aid of emotional crutches.
Ronald Dunn

We make faith more difficult than God ever made it.
Vance Havner

Faith is not a question of majorities.
Auguste Lecerf

Faith is always an obedience.
D. Martyn Lloyd-Jones

Faith abandons hope in man's own accomplishments, leaves all works behind, and comes to Christ alone and empty-handed, to cast itself on his mercy.
J. I. Packer

Faith and obedience are bound up in the same bundle. He that obeys God, trusts God; and he that trusts God, obeys God.
C. H. Spurgeon

Faith in faith is faith astray.
A. W. Tozer

Faith means believing in advance what will only make sense in reverse.
Philip Yancey

FAITH — Ground

Faith cannot stand unless it be founded on the promises of God.
John Calvin

Faith does not depend on miracles, or on any extraordinary sign, but is the peculiar gift of the Spirit, and is produced by means of the Word.
John Calvin

Faith does not proceed from ourselves, but is the fruit of spiritual regeneration.
John Calvin

Faith should fix its whole attention on the power of God alone.
John Calvin

There is no faith without God's Word.

> *John Calvin*

No faith is genuine faith which believes that something extra needs to be added to the death of Jesus to make me acceptable to God.

> *John C. Chapman*

Faith is not on this side of knowledge but beyond it.

> *John Donne*

The character of God is the foundation of faith.

> *Ronald Dunn*

True faith takes its character and quality from its object and not from itself.

> *Sinclair Ferguson*

Real true faith is man's weakness leaning on God's strength.

> *D. L. Moody*

My faith has no bed to sleep on but omnipotency.

> *Samuel Rutherford*

Faith brings with it to Christ nothing but a sinful man's soul.

> *J. C. Ryle*

At the root of the Christian life lies belief in the invisible. The object of the Christian's faith is unseen reality.

> *A. W. Tozer*

FAITH — Importance

Trust the past to the mercy of God, the present to his love and the future to his providence.

> *Augustine*

If we love Christ much, surely we shall trust him much.

> *Thomas Brooks*

Faith is the identifying mark of the Christian.

> *Ronald Dunn*

To believe is our chief duty and the fountain from which all other duties flow.

> *Ronald Dunn*

The man who prays without faith has a radical defect in his character.

> *H. W. Fulford*

Nothing is more disastrous than to study faith, analyse faith, make noble resolves of faith, but never actually to make the leap of faith.

> *Vance Havner*

There can be no hope without faith in Christ, for hope is rooted in him alone. Faith without hope would, by itself, be empty and futile.

Ernst Hoffmann

The time of fear is the time to trust.

John MacBeath

Be careful for nothing, prayerful for everything, thankful for anything.

D. L. Moody

We shall never believe with a vigorous and unquestioning faith unless God touches our hearts; and we shall believe as soon as he does so.

Blaise Pascal

Panic is possible only when God is obscured from our thoughts by visible circumstances.

Maurice Roberts

Whatever our trust is most in, that is our God.

Richard Sibbes

If you are not seeking the Lord, judgement is at your heels.

C. H. Spurgeon

When you have nothing but God, see all in God.

C. H. Spurgeon

Every man lives by faith, the non-believer as well as the saint; the one by faith in natural laws and the other by faith in God.

A. W. Tozer

Our limitless trust in God seems to satisfy him as nothing else can do, because it corresponds with his eternal faithfulness, it honours his veracity, and is a constant, silent worship of all his perfections.

G. D. Watson

FAITH — Increase

If we desire an increase of faith we must consent to its testings.

Anon.

Our faith is never perfect ... we are partly unbelievers.

John Calvin

Unless our faith be now and then raised up, it will lie prostrate; unless it is warmed, it will be frozen; unless it be roused, it will grow torpid.

John Calvin

We learn to trust by trusting.

Ronald Dunn

Faith grows as it feeds on facts, not on feelings nor on fancies.

Geoffrey Grogan

90

Faith rises or falls according to the measure in which we remember the things which are unseen.

Maurice Roberts

The larger the God we know, the larger will be our faith. The secret of power in our lives is to know God and expect great things from him.

A. B. Simpson

FAITH — and Knowledge

(See also: Reason)

I do not seek to understand that I may believe, but I believe that I may understand: for this I also believe, that unless I believe I will not understand.

Anselm

Understanding is the reward of faith. Therefore seek not to understand that you may believe, but believe that you may understand.

Augustine

Faith does not mean believing without evidence. It means believing in realities that go beyond sense and sight — for which a totally different sort of evidence is required.

John Baillie

Faith requires no surrender of the intellect.

Charles Colson

Faith is not anti-intellectual. It is an act of man that reaches beyond the limits of our five senses.

Billy Graham

A Christian with faith has nothing to fear from the facts.

Paul Johnson

Faith is greater than learning.

Martin Luther

Faith is a ... form of knowledge which transforms the intellect.

Malcolm Muggeridge

It is poor philosophy to say we will believe nothing unless we can understand everything!

J. C. Ryle

The natural man must know in order to believe; the spiritual man must believe in order to know.

A. W. Tozer

To those who believe, no explanation is necessary. To those who do not believe, no explanation is possible.

Franz Werfel

We are as much obliged to believe God with reluctance to our understanding as to obey him with reluctance to our will.
Thomas Wilson

Faith often outreaches reason, but it does not outrage it.
Verna Wright

FAITH — Power

He who feeds his faith will starve his doubts to death.
Anon.

Faith is the master key of the Christian life.
Ronald Dunn

If only a soul can believe in God, to the extent to which it believes it can obtain anything that is in the heart of God to bestow.
Ronald Dunn

We persevere through faith and never apart from it.
Sinclair Ferguson

Faith is blind — except upward. It is blind to impossibilities and deaf to doubt. It listens only to God.
S. D. Gordon

Faith will not always get for us what we want, but it will get what God wants us to have.
Vance Havner

As we must not trust to an arm of flesh when it is engaged for us, so we must not be afraid of an arm of flesh when it is stretched out against us.
Matthew Henry

Faith draws the poison from every grief, takes the sting from every loss, and quenches the fire of every pain; and only faith can do it.
Josiah Holland

Faith will lead you where you cannot walk. Reason has never been a mountain climber.
E. W. Kenyon

Faith instructs us in the depths of God.
Jacques Maritain

Faith is the soul's mouth, whereby the hunger of the heart is removed.
C. H. Spurgeon

Faith is the surest of all sin-killers.
C. H. Spurgeon

Faith sees the invisible, believes the unbelievable, and receives the impossible.
Corrie ten Boom

Faith fetches Christ's strength into the soul.
Thomas Watson

Faith gives a true map of the world.
Thomas Watson

Faith paves a causeway to heaven.
Thomas Watson

Faith reconciles providences and promises.
Thomas Watson

Faith, mighty faith, the promise sees,
And looks to that alone;
Laughs at impossibilities,
And cries it shall be done.
Charles Wesley

Faith builds a bridge across the gulf of death.
Edward Young

FAITH — and Prayer
(See also: Prayer — and Faith)

The true proof of faith is the assurance when we pray that God will really perform what he has promised us.
John Calvin

Let's keep our chins up and our knees down — we're on the victory side!
Alan Redpath

Mature faith does not live by answers to prayer, but by prayer.
R. E. O. White

FAITH — Rewards

God is most glorified in the faith of his servants.
William Gouge

The Christian faith is not a way to explain, enjoy or endure this world, but to overcome it.
Vance Havner

Those that are acquainted with God and Christ are already in the suburbs of life eternal.
Matthew Henry

The function of faith is to turn God's promises into facts.
J. Oswald Sanders

Faith unlocks the divine storehouse, but unbelief bars its doors.
Curtis Vaughan

93

FAITH — Saving

(See also: Conversion; Faith — Definition; Regeneration; Repentance)

Faith is the evidence of divine adoption.

John Calvin

The gospel can be understood by faith alone — not by reason, nor by the perspicacity of the human understanding.

John Calvin

The seat of faith is not in the brain but in the heart.

John Calvin

Repentance and faith are Siamese twins.

Walter J. Chantry

Faith and repentance must be seen as marriage partners and never separated.

Sinclair Ferguson

That faith can save a man, and that nothing else can, is written throughout the Scriptures as with a pencil of light.

Robert Johnstone

True faith is never found alone; it is accompanied by expectation.

C. S. Lewis

Faith is not of some good work which God must reward with salvation. Faith is not the cause of salvation, but the means through which we receive it.

Philip Nunn

Most people are brought to faith in Christ, not by argument for it, but by exposure to it.

Samuel Shoemaker

It is not a brave thing to trust God: for true believers it is a simple matter of sweet necessity.

C. H. Spurgeon

It will not save me to know that Christ is a Saviour; but it will save me to trust him to be my Saviour.

C. H. Spurgeon

Little faith will bring your soul to heaven; great faith will bring heaven to your soul.

C. H. Spurgeon

Never make a Christ out of your faith, nor think of it as if it were the independent source of your salvation.

C. H. Spurgeon

There is no sin that shall damn the man who believes, and nothing shall save the man who will not believe.

C. H. Spurgeon

Spurious faith has no saving power.

> *R. V. G. Tasker*

God is never found accidentally.

> *A. W. Tozer*

True faith commits us to obedience.

> *A. W. Tozer*

FAITH — Supremacy

To believe is our chief duty and the fountain from which all other duties flow.

> *Ronald Dunn*

Faith is a mother grace, a breeding grace.

> *William Gouge*

Get the queen bee of faith and all the other virtues will attend her.

> *C. H. Spurgeon*

It is very well to rest on God when you have other props, but it is best of all to rest on him when every prop is knocked away.

> *C. H. Spurgeon*

FAITH — Testing

An untried faith is a worthless faith.

> *Ronald Dunn*

You don't know what faith you have until it is tested.

> *Rees Howells*

Better a baffled faith than no faith at all.

> *Albert Knudson*

Faith is such a vital matter to the children of God that it must needs be put to the test, first in order to prove that it is genuine, and second to purge and strengthen it.

> *Philip Mauro*

We never test the resources of God until we attempt the impossible.

> *F. B. Meyer*

Pray for a faith that will not shrink when washed in the waters of affliction.

> *Ernest Wadsworth*

FAITH — Weak

The faith that will shut the mouth of lions must be more than a pious hope that they will not bite.

> *Anon.*

To believe only possibilities is not faith but philosophy.
Thomas Browne

Distrust is cured by meditating upon the promises of God.
John Calvin

A fellow shouldn't abandon his faith when it weakens, any more than he would throw away a suit because it needs pressing.
Frank A. Clark

If we are spiritually impoverished, it is not because the hand of grace is tight-fisted; it is because the hand of faith is too weak.
Ronald Dunn

Even those of us who have weak faith have the same strong Christ as others!
Sinclair Ferguson

True faith may be weak faith, and weak faith true faith.
Richard Glover

Better to be slow of head to understand than slow of heart to believe!
Vance Havner

The Lord Jesus does not cast off his believing people because of failures and imperfections.
J. C. Ryle

FAITHFULNESS

God has no larger field for the man who is not faithfully doing his work where he is.
Anon.

Christians do not have to live; they have only to be faithful to Jesus Christ, not only *until* death but *unto* death if necessary.
Vance Havner

There is no guarantee that men faithful to God will be recognizable by their numbers, their talents or their success.
Iain H. Murray

Faithfulness is our business; fruitfulness is an issue that we must be content to leave with God.
J. I. Packer

Faithfulness knows no difference between small and great duties.
John Ruskin

I know of nothing which I would choose to have as the

subject of my ambition for life than to be kept faithful to my God till death.

C. H. Spurgeon

It is impossible to be faithful to Jesus Christ and not incur the opposition of the world.

William Still

FAME
(See also: Popularity)

He is genuinely great who considers himself small and cares nothing about high honours.

Thomas à Kempis

The honours of this world: what are they but puff, and emptiness, and peril of falling?

Augustine

Fame is a fickle food
Upon a shifting plate.

Emily E. Dickinson

Men think highly of those who rise rapidly in the world; whereas nothing rises quicker than dust, straw and feathers.

August W. Hare

Seeking to perpetuate one's name on earth is like writing on the sand by the seashore.

D. L. Moody

It is better to be faithful than famous.

Theodore D. Roosevelt

For a man to spend his life in pursuit of a title that serves only when he dies to furnish out an epitaph is below a wise man's business.

Seneca

FAMILY LIFE —
Importance

Woman takes her being from man, man takes his well-being from woman.

Thomas Adams

The greatest benefits conferred on human life, fatherhood, motherhood, childhood, home, become the greatest curse if Jesus Christ is not the Head.

Oswald Chambers

No other structure can replace the family.

Charles Colson

The Christian is supposed to love his neighbour, and since his wife is his nearest neighbour, she should be his deepest love.

Martin Luther

I believe the family was established long before the church, and my duty is to my family first.

D. L. Moody

FAMILY LIFE — Influence on Children

The religion of a child depends on what its father and mother are, and not on what they say.

Henri Amiel

Every word and deed of a parent is a fibre woven into the character of a child that ultimately determines how that child fits into the fabric of society.

Anon.

The mother who spoils her child fattens a serpent.

Anon.

The surest way to make it hard for your children is to make it soft for them.

Anon.

Whatever parent gives his children good instruction, and sets them at the same time a bad example, may be considered as bringing them food in one hand and poison in the other.

John Balguy

A child, like your stomach, doesn't need all you can afford to give it.

Frank A. Clark

What we desire our children to be, we must endeavour to be before them.

Andrew Combe

Ideal parenting is modelled after the relationship between God and man.

James C. Dobson

No job can compete with the responsibility of shaping and moulding a new human being.

James C. Dobson

Do not handicap your children by making their lives easy.

Robert Heinlein

Fathering is a marathon, not a sprint.

Paul L. Lewis

Let us not fool ourselves — without Christianity, without Christian education, without the principles of Christ inculcated into young life, we are simply rearing pagans.

Peter Marshall

Better a little chiding than a great deal of heartache.

William Shakespeare

Every child has a right to be both well fed and well led.

Ruth Smelter

One of the best legacies a father can leave his children is to love their mother.

C. Neil Strait

FAMILY LIFE — a Test of Character

He that has not rest at home is in the world's hell.

Anon.

A home is no home unless it contains food and fire for the mind as well as for the body.

Margaret Fuller

If the Saviour cannot manifest himself at your breakfast table he will not shine through you at any other table.

Vance Havner

It is a poor light that is made to shine brighter in the distance than close at hand.

Vance Havner

Praise will transform the humblest dwelling to a hallowed heaven.

Frances J. Roberts

When home is ruled according to God's Word, angels might be asked to stay with us, and they would not find themselves out of their element.

C. H. Spurgeon

FEAR

(See also: Anxiety; Worry)

Fear is generated by unbelief, and unbelief strengthened by fear. Nothing can cure us of fear till God cures us of unbelief.

Francis Burkitt

The right fear is the fear of losing God.

Meister Eckhart

Who lives in fear will never be a free man.

Horace

Fear is the sand in the machinery of life.

E. Stanley Jones

The time of fear is the time to trust.

John MacBeath

Only he who can say, 'The Lord is the strength of my life' can say, 'Of whom shall I be afraid?'

Alexander MacLaren

Panic is the sinful failure to apply our knowledge of God to particular problems.

Maurice Roberts

Half our fears are the result of ignorance.

C. H. Spurgeon

There is nothing in the world more ridiculous than unbelieving fears.

C. H. Spurgeon

Fear enfeebles.

Thomas Watson

Fear is the root of apostasy.

Thomas Watson

FEAR OF GOD

(See also: Awe; Worship)

The fear of God is the greatest antidote against the fear of man.

Anon.

Godly fear shrinks from sin, worldly fear from punishment; the one influences our thoughts, the other only our actions.

Ayguan

If Jesus in his humanity delighted in the fear of God, surely we need to give serious thought to cultivating this attitude in our lives.

Jerry Bridges

He that fears God fears nothing else.

Edmund Burke

Nothing is more powerful to overcome temptation than the fear of God.

John Calvin

Righteousness flows from only one principle — the fear of God.

John Calvin

The fear of God is the root and origin of all righteousness.

John Calvin

There is no wisdom but that which is founded on the fear of God.

John Calvin

The remarkable thing about fearing God is that when you fear God you fear nothing else.

Oswald Chambers

The fear of the Lord is not just the end of wisdom but its beginning.

Edmund P. Clowney

Let us familiarize our minds with the fear due to Christ the Judge, and a new power will enter into our service, making it at once more urgent and more wholesome than it could otherwise be.

James Denney

The essential ingredients of the fear of God are correct concepts of the character of God, a pervasive sense of the presence of God and a constant awareness of our obligation to God.

Al Martin

No man acts with true wisdom till he fears God and hopes in his mercy.

William S. Plumer

The fear of men weakens, but the fear of the Lord strengthens.

Remigius

True ethical absolutes can only be grounded in the fear of a living God.

R. C. Sproul

It is a blessed fear which drives us to trust.

C. H. Spurgeon

Unregenerate fear drives from God, gracious fear drives to him.

C. H. Spurgeon

The fear of God promotes spiritual joy; it is the morning star that ushers in the sunlight of comfort.

Thomas Watson

FELLOWSHIP
(See also: Church — Fellowship; Friendship)

Genuine fellowship comes when Christians stop relating to one another as righteous saints and accept one another as unrighteous sinners.

David Watson

As the communion of saints is in our creed, so it should be in our company.

Thomas Watson

FLATTERY

Flattery is the art of telling a person exactly what he thinks of himself.

Anon.

Like a bee, the flatterer has honey in his mouth and a sting in his tail.

Anon.

Praise undeserved is poison in disguise.

Anon.

101

How can we conquer the world when it rages, if we cannot vanquish it when it flatters?

Augustine

It is better to be persecuted for having said the truth than to be favoured for having flattered.

Augustine

Flattery pleases those who wish to appear more virtuous than they are.

Cicero

Flattery is a device for getting somebody to pay attention to what you're saying.

Franklin P. Jones

There is nothing so shabby and mean and nauseating as the spirit of flattery because its motives are always of the lowest.

James Philip

Did we not flatter ourselves, the flattery of others would not hurt us.

François Rochefoucauld

Flattery is a sort of bad money, to which our vanity gives currency.

François Rochefoucauld

The voice of the flatterer stays long in the ear.

Seneca

What really flatters a man is that you think him worth flattering.

George Bernard Shaw

Flattery and friendship never go together.

C. H. Spurgeon

None but the silliest of geese would go to the fox's sermon.

C. H. Spurgeon

FORGIVENESS BY GOD
(See also: Atonement; Cross; Jesus Christ — Death)

Forgiveness from others is charity; from God, grace; from oneself, wisdom.

Anon.

If God were not willing to forgive sin heaven would be empty.

Anon.

If anybody imagines that God could simply forgive us in the same way that we forgive one another, he has not yet considered the seriousness of sin.

Anselm

God does not wish us to remember what he is willing to forget.

George A. Buttrick

When God designs to forgive us he changes our hearts and turns us to obedience by his Spirit.

John Calvin

Those who are most conscious of forgiveness are invariably those who have been most acutely convicted of their sin.

Sinclair Ferguson

Do you think that you deserve forgiveness? If you do, you are not a Christian.

D. Martyn Lloyd-Jones

To divorce forgiveness of sins from the actual living of the Christian life is nothing but rank heresy!

D. Martyn Lloyd-Jones

True forgiveness breaks a man, and he must forgive.

D. Martyn Lloyd-Jones

The pleasures of being forgiven are as superior to the pleasures of an unforgiven man as heaven is higher than hell.

Robert Murray M'Cheyne

Should we leave this world unforgiven, it will be a dire event.

J. I. Packer

The basic fact of biblical religion is that God pardons and accepts believing sinners.

J. I. Packer

We cannot experience God's forgiveness until our sins have been dealt with.

Frank Retief

When God pardons, he consigns the offence to everlasting forgetfulness.

Merv Rosell

You can have forgiven all your sin in half the tick of the clock, and pass from death to life more swiftly than I can utter the words.

C. H. Spurgeon

No man is rich enough to buy back his past.

Oscar Wilde

Our God has a big eraser.

Billy Zeoli

FORGIVENESS OF OTHERS

The Christian can always afford to forgive — and can never afford not to!

If you are suffering from a bad man's injustice, forgive him lest there be two bad men.

Augustine

The noblest revenge is to forgive.

Thomas Fuller

Forgiveness is not an occasional act, it is a permanent attitude.

Martin Luther King

If God forgives us, we must forgive others. Otherwise it is almost like setting up ourselves as a higher tribunal than him.

C. S. Lewis

I say to the glory of God and in utter humility that whenever I see myself before God and realize even something of what my blessed Lord has done for me, I am ready to forgive anybody anything.

D. Martyn Lloyd-Jones

Forgiveness is a funny thing — it warms the heart and cools the sting.

William A. Ward

Friendship flourishes at the fountain of forgiveness.

William A. Ward

FORMALISM
(See also: Hypocrisy)

God requires an inward purity as well as an outward performance.

Orthodoxy of words is atheism unless backed up by excellent character.

Anon.

Sunday-morning Christianity is the greatest hindrance to true revival.

Vance Havner

God is not deceived by externals.

C. S. Lewis

Many of us who profess to be Christians are so busy with the mechanics of our religion that we have no time left for the spiritual part of it.

William B. Martin

Religion that is merely ritual and ceremonial can never satisfy. Neither can we be satisfied by a religion that is merely humanitarian or serviceable to mankind. Man's craving is for the spiritual.

Samuel Shoemaker

A dead creed is of no use; we must have our creed baptized with the Holy Ghost.

C. H. Spurgeon

One can grasp orthodox religion while having no grasp of the Saviour.

Geoff Thomas

You can be as straight as a gunbarrel theologically — and as empty as one spiritually.

A. W. Tozer

No matter how spiritual the song you are singing, no matter how poetic the prayer you are praying, if it isn't sincere then it isn't worship, it's hypocrisy.

Donald S. Whitney

FREE WILL
(See also: Will)

The sinner, apart from grace, is unable to be willing and unwilling to be able.

W. E. Best

Because we are conscious of volition, we suppose our volition is free. What we discover by experience is that our freedom of will is unidirectional. We are truly free only when we sin, for we are then acting according to our nature, a fact which accounts for the pleasures of sin.

Arthur C. Custance

The phrase 'free will' is only used by the Bible in the context of stewardship. It is never used in the context of coming to Christ in faith.

Sinclair Ferguson

Sinners are free in working their own destruction, notwithstanding the divine work on them; just as the saints are free in working out their own salvation, while God works in them to will and to do of his good pleasure.

Basil Manly

Man's will is free to follow his inclinations, but fallen man's inclinations are always and invariably away from God.

R. C. Sproul

Free will I have often heard of, but I have never seen it. I have met with will, and plenty of it, but it has either been led captive by sin or held in blessed bonds of grace.

C. H. Spurgeon

FRIENDSHIP
(See also: Fellowship)

A real friend warms you by his presence, trusts you with his secrets, and remembers you in his prayers.

Anon.

Friendship doubles our joy and divides our grief.

Anon.

There are not many things in life so beautiful as true friendship, and there are not many things more uncommon.

Anon.

There is no better proof of friendship than to help our friends with their burdens.

Augustine

A friend is someone with whom you dare to be yourself.

C. Raymond Beran

Friendship is like money, easier to make than to keep.

Samuel Butler

A friend is a person with whom I may be sincere. Before him I may think aloud.

Ralph Waldo Emerson

It is best to be with those in time we hope to be with in eternity.

Thomas Fuller

A friend is never known until a man has need.

John Heywood

One should keep his friendships in constant repair.

Samuel Johnson

Friendship is the greatest of worldly goods. Certainly to me it is the chief happiness of life.

C. S. Lewis

Better it is to go with a few to heaven, than with a multitude to hell, and be damned for the sake of company.

Elnathan Parr

A man is known by the company he shuns as well as by the company he keeps.

C. H. Spurgeon

Show me a man's books and show me a man's companions and I will tell you what sort of man he is.

William Tiptaft

Friendship flourishes at the fountain of forgiveness.

William A. Ward

Association begets assimilation.

Thomas Watson

Tell me with whom thou art found and I will tell thee who thou art.

Johann Wolfgang

FRUITFULNESS

If I were fruitless, it mattered not who commended me; but if

I were fruitful, I cared not who did condemn.

John Bunyan

The fruit of the Spirit is not push, drive, climb, grasp and trample ... Life is more than a climb to the top of the heap.

Richard J. Foster

Judge a tree by its fruit, not its leaves.

Phaedrus

FULNESS OF LIFE

Fulness of the Spirit is not a press-button panacea; it is the growing experience of those who hunger and thirst after righteousness.

There is one thing we cannot imitate; we cannot imitate being full of the Holy Ghost.

Oswald Chambers

The Spirit-filled life is no mystery revealed to a select few, no goal difficult of attainment. To trust and to obey is the substance of the whole matter.

Victor Edman

I've never known a person whom I thought was truly filled with the Holy Spirit who went out and bragged about it or

sought to draw attention to himself.

Billy Graham

God commands us to be filled with the Spirit, and if we are not filled it is because we are living beneath our privileges.

D. L. Moody

The Spirit-filled life is not a special, deluxe edition of Christianity. It is part and parcel of the total plan of God for his people.

A. W. Tozer

FUTURE
(See also: Hope)

We should all be concerned about the future because we will have to spend the rest of our lives there.

Charles Kettering

Never be afraid to trust an unknown future to a known God.

Corrie ten Boom

GENEROSITY
(See also: Charity; Giving; Kindness)

Stretch your purse to the utmost, and do all the good you can.

Richard Baxter

Without the rich heart, wealth is an ugly beggar.

Ralph Waldo Emerson

It is much better to have your gold in the hand than in the heart.

Thomas Fuller

Not possession, but use, is the only riches.

Thomas Fuller

As the purse is emptied the heart is filled.

Victor Hugo

GENTLENESS

There is nothing stronger than gentleness.

Anon.

Only the truly strong and great can be truly tender. Tenderness is a mark of nobility, not of weakness.

James Philip

GIVING

(See also: Charity; Generosity; Kindness)

If men do not give according to their means, they must answer for it to God.

Albert Barnes

Not how much we give, but how much we do not give, is the test of our Christianity.

Oswald Chambers

God has given us two hands — one to receive with and the other to give with. We are not cisterns made for hoarding; we are channels made for sharing.

Billy Graham

The manner of giving shows the character of the giver, more than the gift itself.

J. C. Lavater

The limit of giving is to be the limit of our ability to give.

C. S. Lewis

The only safe rule is to give more than we can spare. Our charities should pinch and hamper us. If we live at the same level of affluence as other people who have our level of income, we are probably giving away too little.

C. S. Lewis

The only valid and virtuous motive in our giving is to give God pleasure.

Arthur Neil

We expect our young people to lay down their lives for God,

but most of us are not willing to lay down our bank accounts.
Paul B. Smith

Many people will always be poor because they never give to the cause of God.
C. H. Spurgeon

The way to lay up is to lay out.
Thomas Watson

GLUTTONY
(See also: Covetousness; Greed)

The minutes spent at the dinner table won't make you fat — but the seconds will.
Anon.

Gluttony is an emotional escape, a sign that something is eating us.
Peter Devries

GOD — Eternity

Time is nothing to God.
Oswald Chambers

All but God is changing day by day.
Charles Kingsley

God is not hurried along in the time-stream of this universe any more than an author is hurried along in the imaginary time of his own novel.
C. S. Lewis

God is not subject to time.
Dorothy L. Sayers

Our life is scarcely the twinkle of a star in God's eternal day.
Bayard Taylor

In God there is no was or will be, but a continuous and unbroken is. In him history and prophecy are one and the same.
A. W. Tozer

GOD — Existence

God is more truly imagined than expressed, and he exists more truly than is imagined.
Augustine

The truth of God is immortal.
John Calvin

We trust not because 'a god' exists, but because *this* God exists.
C. S. Lewis

You have to go outside the sequence of engines, into the world of men, to find the real originator of the rocket. Is it not equally reasonable to look outside nature for the real Originator of the natural order?

C. S. Lewis

Belief in God is an instinct as natural to man as walking on two legs.

G. C. Lichtenberg

God is the great reality.

J. B. Phillips

Men and women who refuse to acknowledge God's existence do so, in the final analysis, because it is contrary to their manner of living. They do not want to bow to the moral claims of a holy God on their lives.

R. C. Sproul

Who ... has ever seen an idea? ...Who has ever seen love? ... Who has ever seen faith? ... The real things in the world are the invisible spiritual realities. Is it so difficult, then, to believe in God?

Charles Templeton

GOD — Faithfulness

Divine faithfulness is a wonderful comfort for those who are loyal. It is a very earnest warning for those who might be inclined to become disloyal.

William Hendriksen

Believing prayer takes its stand upon the faithfulness of God.

D. Edmond Hiebert

The quality of faithfulness is essential to God's being.

Frank Retief

GOD — Glory

We should give God the same place in our hearts that he holds in the universe.

Anon.

The reverent, godly Christian sees God first in his transcendent glory, majesty and holiness before he sees him in his love, mercy and grace.

Jerry Bridges

Outside of God there is nothing but nothing.

Meister Eckhart

In commanding us to glorify him, God is inviting us to enjoy him.

C. S. Lewis

God's overriding goal is to glorify himself.

J. I. Packer

The only thing that God is bound to do is the very thing that he requires of us — to glorify himself.

J. I. Packer

The glory of God refers to who God is, not what he does.

R. C. Sproul

God is the source of all truth, and every discovery is a means of glorifying him.

Gene Veith

The glory of God is more worth than the salvation of all men's souls.

Thomas Watson

As the light of the moon is swallowed up by the brightness of the sun, so the shining achievements of men and women are swallowed up by the glory of God.

Janice Wise

GOD — Goodness

The Lord's goodness surrounds us at every moment. I walk through it almost with difficulty, as through thick grass and flowers.

R. W. Barbour

God's goodness is equal to his greatness.

Richard Baxter

God's gifts put man's best dreams to shame.

Elizabeth Barrett Browning

God's judgements are always founded on his goodness.

John Calvin

For those who have everything, as well as for those who have nothing, there is only one single good — God himself.

J. H. Merle d'Aubigné

Good when he gives,
  supremely good,
Nor less when he denies,
E'en crosses from his
  sovereign hand
Are blessings in disguise.

James Hervey

When we declare that God is good we are saying that he is in every way all that he as God should be, something that marks him out as altogether different from us.

Derek Prime

Putting our trust in God and depending on his intrinsic goodness frees us from the need to find explanations for everything.

Frank Retief

There are no days when God's fountain does not flow.

Richard Owen Roberts

The treasury of the church is the liberality of God.

C. H. Spurgeon

We cannot always trace God's hand but we can always trust God's heart.

C. H. Spurgeon

God is ever giving to his children, yet has not less.

Thomas Watson

God is patron of all the graces.

Thomas Watson

GOD — Holiness

Holiness is the glory of every perfection in the Godhead.

Stephen Charnock

If every attribute of the Deity were a distinct member, purity would be the form, the soul, the spirit to animate them. Without holiness, his patience would be an indulgence to sin, his mercy a fondness, his wrath a madness, his power a tyranny, his wisdom an unworthy subtlety. Holiness gives decorum to them all.

Stephen Charnock

A true love to God must begin with a delight in his holiness, and not with a delight in any other attribute.

Jonathan Edwards

If we stress the love of God without the holiness of God, it turns out to be only compromise.

Francis Schaeffer

Holiness is a dimension of God that consumes his very essence.

R. C. Sproul

Holiness is not just an attribute, it is God's very essence.

R. C. Sproul

When we see even a small glimpse of God's holiness, we will bow in worship.

R. C. Sproul

God permits sin but does not promote it.

Thomas Watson

GOD — Independence

God without man is still God; man without God is nothing.

God has no need of his creatures, but everything created has need of him.

Meister Eckhart

The greatest and best man in the world must say, 'By the grace of God I am what I am'; but God says absolutely — and that is more than any creature, man or angel, can say — 'I am that I am.'

Matthew Henry

God has no needs.

C. S. Lewis

God cannot be limited by anything outside of himself, because he created all that exists outside of himself.

R. C. Sproul

Dear me, the Lord got on very well before I was born, and I'm sure he will when I am dead.

C. H. Spurgeon

When we think of anything that has origin, we are not thinking of God. God is self-existent, while all created things necessarily originated somewhere at some time. Aside from God, nothing is self-caused.

A. W. Tozer

GOD — Inscrutability

The Almighty does nothing without reason, though the frail mind of man cannot explain the reason.

Augustine

Though we can know that God is, we cannot know what God is.

Augustine

God is at work in the world in ways far beyond our power to comprehend.

Nancy B. Barcus

You may know God, but not comprehend him.

Richard Baxter

We demand proof of God, forgetting that if we could prove God we would be within the compass of our rationalities, and then our logical mind would be our own grotesque God.

George A. Buttrick

The wisdom of the flesh is always exclaiming against the mysteries of God.

John Calvin

God ... cannot be fitted into a diagram.

Empedocles

With God there are mysteries, but no mistakes.

Michael Griffiths

Our safest eloquence concerning God is silence, when we confess without confession that his glory is inexplicable, his greatness above our capacity and reach.

Richard Hooker

All that which we call the attributes of God are only so many human ways of our conceiving that abyssal All which can neither be spoken nor conceived by us.

William Law

The very being of God is so transcendent and eternal that all our efforts to arrive at an understanding are doomed at the very outset to failure.

D. Martyn Lloyd-Jones

God's actual divine essence and his will, administration and works are absolutely beyond all human thought, human understanding or wisdom; in short, they are and ever will be incomprehensible, inscrutable, and altogether hidden to human reason.

Martin Luther

We know God but as men born blind know the fire. They know that there is such a thing as fire, for they feel it warm them, but what it is they know not. So, that there is a God we know, but what he is we know little, and indeed we can never search him out to perfection; a finite creature can never fully comprehend that which is infinite.

Thomas Manton

Incomprehensible? But because you cannot understand a thing, it does not cease to exist.

Blaise Pascal

God is not discoverable or demonstrable by purely scientific means, unfortunately for the scientifically-minded. But that really proves nothing. It simply means that the wrong instruments are being used for the job.

J. B. Phillips

What we can know about God is so great and glorious that we can confidently trust what we do not know about him. Our God is a good God.

Frank Retief

The infinity of God is not mysterious, it is only unfathomable — not concealed but incomprehensible. It is a clear infinity — the darkness of the pure, unsearchable sea.

John Ruskin

The more I learn about God, the more aware I become of what I don't know about him.

R. C. Sproul

We will never understand God exhaustively, but what we do understand about him is real, not myth.

R. C. Sproul

Do not try to imagine God, or you will have an imaginary God.

A. W. Tozer

God is spirit and to him magnitude and distance have no meaning.

A. W. Tozer

If God can be understood and comprehended by any of our human means, then I cannot worship him.

A. W. Tozer

Our concepts of measurement embrace mountains and men, atoms and stars, gravity, energy, numbers, speed, but never God. We cannot speak of measure or amount or size or weight and at the same time be speaking of God, for these tell of degrees and there are no degrees in God. All that he is he is without growth or addition or development.

A. W. Tozer

In vain our haughty reason swells,
For nothing's found in thee
But boundless inconceivables
And vast eternity.

Isaac Watts

God would not be God if he could be fully known to us, and

God would not be God if he could not be known at all.

H. G. Wood

GOD — Jealousy

The jealousy of God is one of the Christian's greatest challenges — and comforts.

The jealousy of God is nothing else but the vehemence and ardour of his paternal love.

John Calvin

GOD — Justice

God is not always a God of immediate justice, but he is a God of ultimate justice.

Whenever you hear the glory of God mentioned, think of his justice.

John Calvin

Belief in a just God is not optional.

John Rowland

As long as there is eternity, God has time enough to reckon with his enemies.

Thomas Watson

God of all mercy is a God unjust.

Edward Young

115

GOD — Love

God's hand is sometimes turned against his people, but never his heart.

There is nothing the Christian can do to make God love him more, or love him less. God's love for his people is infinite and unconditional.

It is but right that our hearts should be on God, when the heart of God is so much on us.
Richard Baxter

There is no parental abuse in the character of God's fatherhood.
Alistair Begg

God was love long before he had made any creatures to be the objects of his love, even from all eternity.
George Bethune

We must see our circumstances through God's love instead of, as we are prone to do, seeing God's love through our circumstances.
Jerry Bridges

To believers a persuasion of God's fatherly love is more delightful than all earthly enjoyments.
John Calvin

The springs of love are in God, not in us.
Oswald Chambers

God is holy love.
P. T. Forsyth

God loves us; not because we are loveable but because he is love; not because he needs to receive but because he delights to give.
C. S. Lewis

God, who needs nothing, loves into existence wholly superfluous creatures in order that he may love and perfect them.
C. S. Lewis

Though our feelings for (God) come and go, his love for us does not. It is not wearied by our sins, or our indifference; and, therefore, it is quite relentless in its determination that we shall be cured of those sins, at whatever cost to us, at whatever cost to him.
C. S. Lewis

To ask that God's love should be content with us as we are is to ask that God should cease to be God.
C. S. Lewis

The love of God is anchored to his character. He can only love in ways that are suitable to the sort of person he is.

J. A. Motyer

Even though there is no final answer to the mystery of evil prospering in the world, the overriding consideration that more than offsets everything else is God's unchanging love and care.

James Philip

God has a holy love and a holy wrath, but not a loving wrath or a wrathful love.

R. C. Sproul

Nothing binds me to my Lord like a strong belief in his changeless love.

C. H. Spurgeon

At the heart of election is a particular and passionate love that was the cause of God sending his Son to be the Saviour of his people.

G. Steveson

Divine love can admit no rival.

Johann Tauler

God loves his children as well in adversity as in prosperity.

Thomas Watson

GOD — Name

To know God's name is to know something of his nature.

The greatest argument of Scripture is the glory of God's own name.

Charles Simeon

GOD — Omnipotence

Marvel not that God does great things. Marvel that he stoops to do such little things.

Anon.

There are some things which God cannot do, and that because of the very reason of his omnipotence.

Augustine

There is power in God to lay prostrate the whole world, and to tread it under his feet, whenever it may please him.

John Calvin

When a man makes alliance with the Almighty, giants look like grasshoppers.

Vance Havner

A man with God on his side is always in the majority.

John Knox

117

There is an Arm that never
   tires,
When human strength gives
   way.
                George Matheson

If God be God, then no insoluble problems exist. And if God be *my* God, then no problem of mine is without its appropriate solution.
                Maurice Roberts

When we have nothing left but God, then we become aware that God is enough.
                Agnes M. Royden

The power of God is identified with his will; what he cannot do is what he will not do.
                Tertullian

GOD — Omnipresence

We cannot get away from God, though we can ignore him.
                James Cabot

God is as present as the air.
                Michael Hollings

We may ignore, but we can nowhere evade, the presence of God. The world is crowded with him.
                C. S. Lewis

Begin where we will, God is there first.
                A. W. Tozer

Within thy circling power I
   stand;
On every side I find thy hand;
Awake, asleep, at home,
   abroad,
I am surrounded still with God.
                Isaac Watts

GOD — Omniscience

Though the Lord is out of sight, we are not out of his.
                Matthew Henry

Do not let us deceive ourselves. No possible complexity which we can give to our picture of the universe can hide us from God: there is no copse, no forest, no jungle thick enough to provide cover.
                C. S. Lewis

If there is ever any one thought, full, distinct, vivid, thoroughly comprehended by yourself, then, just what that is to you, *all* knowledge is to God.
                Basil Manly

God does not learn things; he knows them from the beginning.
                R. C. Sproul

There is not a moment of privacy from God.

Geoff Thomas

We can never sin but there will be two witnesses present to observe and register it: our own selves and God.

Ralph Venning

We never do anything so secretly but that it is in the presence of two witnesses: God and our own conscience.

Benjamin Whichcote

GOD — Patience

There is no divine attribute more wonderful than the patience of God.

John Benton

The Almighty is working on a great scale and will not be hustled by our peevish impetuosity.

W. Graham Scroggie

The deep and due consideration of the infinite patience of God towards us will greatly promote the patience of *our* spirits, and transform us into the same image.

John Trapp

GOD — Perfection

God is self-centred — and rightly so.

God is equal to each of his attributes, whereas he 'possesses' each attribute in an infinite degree.

William Hendriksen

God is unsusceptible to evil; evil never has any appeal to him.

D. Edmond Hiebert

The fact that God is untemptable of evil is the foundation for the Christian belief in a moral universe.

D. Edmond Hiebert

God stands in such a relationship to evil that it is not outside of his rule yet he cannot be held responsible for it.

Frank Retief

If God is not just, he is not righteous; if he is not righteous, he is not holy; if he is not holy, he is not good.

John Rowland

Those who lose faith in God's perfection increasingly believe in the perfection of all kinds of false messiahs and their promises.

Isaac Bashevis Singer

Scripture says that the one thing God cannot do, and cannot because he will not, is to contradict himself.

John R. W. Stott

Our love of God will always be according to our knowledge of him and his perfections.

Thomas Wilson

GOD — Purposes

God knows what he is going to make of us.

James Montgomery Boice

God is not running an antique shop! He is making all things new!

Vance Havner

Though God has many things in his purposes, he has nothing in his prophecies but what are in his purposes.

Matthew Henry

In spite of all appearances to the contrary, God has a plan for this bankrupt world.

Helmut Thielicke

GOD — Sovereignty

God's cause is never in any danger.

Nothing that happens to the Christian is accidental or incidental.

God is never in a hurry, but he is always on time.

Anon.

Man drives, but it is God who holds the reins.

Anon.

God is so powerful that he can direct any evil to a good end.

Thomas Aquinas

God's sovereignty does not negate our responsibility to pray, but rather makes it possible for us to pray with confidence.

Jerry Bridges

God has in himself all power to defend you, all wisdom to direct you, all mercy to pardon you, all grace to enrich you, all righteousness to clothe you, all goodness to supply you, and all happiness to crown you.

Thomas Brooks

God does not deliberate or consult, but has once for all decreed before the creation of the world what he will do.

John Calvin

Nothing that is attempted in opposition to God can ever be successful.

John Calvin

Satan ... can do nothing without the command of God, to whose dominion he is subject.

John Calvin

God has sovereign right to dispose of us as he pleases. We ought to acquiesce in all that God does with us and to us.

William Carey

Events of all sorts creep and fly exactly as God pleases.

William Cowper

Men, like stars, appear on the horizon at the command of God.

J. H. Merle d'Aubigné

God casts the die, not the dice.

Albert Einstein

That my times are in God's hand is a fact whether I realize and experience it or not.

E. F. Hallock

Things do not happen in this world — they are brought about.

Will Hays

God is in the facts of history as surely as he is in the march of the seasons.

John Lanahan

There is no question of a compromise between the claims of God and the claims of culture, or politics, or anything else.

C. S. Lewis

Where a God who is totally purposive and totally foreseeing acts upon a nature which is totally interlocked, there can be no accidents or loose ends, nothing whatever of which we can safely use the word 'merely'. Nothing is 'merely a by-product' of anything else.

C. S. Lewis

The devil is God's devil.

Martin Luther

There is no situation so chaotic that God cannot from that situation create something that is surpassingly good.

Handley C. G. Moule

God is the great Unanswerable.

Stuart Olyott

To deny the sovereignty of God is to deny God.

T. P. Osborne

Once for all, let us rid our minds of the idea that things are as they are because God cannot help it.

J. I. Packer

To know that nothing happens in God's world apart from God's will may frighten the godless, but it stabilizes the saints.

J. I. Packer

God always has the last word.

James Philip

God acts as he does because he is what he is.

William S. Plumer

Man does what he can, and God what he will.

John Ray

The kingdom of God is not a democracy. When the Lord speaks ... he utters his law unilaterally. He does not rule by referendum.

R. C. Sproul

No doctrine in the whole Word of God has more excited the hatred of mankind than the truth of the absolute sovereignty of God.

C. H. Spurgeon

Opposition to divine sovereignty is essentially atheism.

C. H. Spurgeon

There is no attribute of God more comforting to his children than the doctrine of divine sovereignty.

C. H. Spurgeon

God in his wisdom is making evil men as well as good men; adverse things as well as favourable things work for the bringing forth of his glory in the day when all shall be fulfilled in him.

A. W. Tozer

The whole history of the world is discovered to be but a contest between the wisdom of God and the cunning of Satan and fallen men. The outcome of the contest is not in doubt.

A. W. Tozer

Monarchs have their times and their turns, their rises and their ruin.

John Trapp

God would never permit any evil if he could not bring good out of evil.

Thomas Watson

GOD — Wisdom

God knows best what is best. Why then should we question him?

Anon.

The truth is that God in his wisdom, to make and keep us humble and to teach us to walk by faith, has hidden from us almost everything that we should like to know about the providential purposes which he is working out in the churches and in our own lives.

J. I. Packer

God is not in the slightest degree baffled or bewildered by what baffles and bewilders us ... he is either a present help, or he is not much help at all.

J. B. Phillips

God's wisdom is that attribute of God whereby he produces the best possible results with the best possible means.

H. B. Smith

None of us has the ability to fool God.

A. W. Tozer

GOD — Wrath

The wrath of God is not ignoble. Rather, it is too noble, too just, too perfect — it is this that bothers us.

James Montgomery Boice

The love of God has no meaning apart from Calvary. And Calvary has no meaning apart from the holy and just wrath of God.

Jerry Bridges

The wrath of God is as pure as the holiness of God. When angry he is perfectly angry. When he is displeased there is every reason he should be.

Stuart Briscoe

There is nothing impersonal about God's wrath; it is the necessary response of his holiness to persistent wickedness.

F. F. Bruce

God has an endless variety of scourges for punishing the wicked.

John Calvin

God giveth his wrath by weight, but his mercy without measure.

Thomas Fuller

When we merely *say* that we are bad, the 'wrath' of God seems a barbarous doctrine; as soon as we *perceive* our badness, it appears inevitable, a mere corollary from God's goodness.

C. S. Lewis

The essence of God's action in wrath is to *give men what they choose,* in all its implications: nothing more, and equally nothing less.

J. I. Packer

Those who are under the rule of sin are also under the wrath of God.

J. I. Packer

A God who cannot be angry is a God who cannot love.

James Philip

There are more references (in the Bible) to the anger, fury and wrath of God than there are to his love and tenderness.

A. W. Pink

A God of love who has no wrath is no God. He is an idol of our own making as much as if we carved him out of stone.

R. C. Sproul

It is the cross ... that reveals the most violent and mysterious outpouring of the wrath of God that we find anywhere in Scripture.

R. C. Sproul

If God be against you, who can be for you?

C. H. Spurgeon

The God of the Bible is as severe as if he were unmerciful, and just as if he were not gracious; and yet he is as gracious and as merciful as if he were not just.

C. H. Spurgeon

The most terrible warning to impenitent men in all the world is the death of Christ. For if God spared not his own Son, on whom was only laid *imputed* sin, will he spare sinners whose sins are their own?

C. H. Spurgeon

The wrath of God does not end with death.

C. H. Spurgeon

Not only is it right for God to display anger against sin, I find it impossible to understand how he could do otherwise.

A. W. Tozer

GODHEAD
(See also: God)

The doctrine of the Trinity is the differentiating doctrine of the Christian faith.

D. Martyn Lloyd-Jones

It needs to be stressed that the eternal relationship between the Father and the Son in no way suggests that one is senior and the other junior.

Stuart Olyott

The proper study of the Christian is the Godhead. The highest science, the loftiest speculation, the mightiest philosophy, which can ever engage the attention of a child of God is the name, the nature, the person, the work, the doings, and the existence of the great God whom he calls the Father.

C. H. Spurgeon

GODLINESS

(See also: Christlikeness; Holiness)

The rich are not always godly, but the godly are always rich.

Anon.

It is impossible to practise godliness without a constant, consistent and balanced intake of the Word of God in our lives.

Jerry Bridges

There is no higher compliment that can be paid to a Christian than to call him godly.

Jerry Bridges

The truly godly person is not interested in becoming rich.

He possesses inner resources which furnish riches far beyond that which earth can offer.

Jerry Bridges

Righteousness flows from only one principle — the fear of God.

John Calvin

There is a certain secret majesty in holy discipline and in sincere godliness.

John Calvin

The difference between worldliness and godliness is a renewed mind.

Erwin W. Lutzer

The godly man's dearest wish is to exalt God with all that he is in all that he does.

J. I. Packer

The way to be truly happy is to be truly human, and the way to be truly human is to be truly godly.

J. I. Packer

If society is to be awakened one day from its deep slumber, it will only be done by Christians who have first woken up themselves to the full splendour of their privilege and who have taken seriously the call to live wholly and entirely for God.

Maurice Roberts

GOOD DEEDS

(See also: Faith — and Deeds; Fruitfulness; Holiness — and Justification)

Better do it than wish it done.
Anon.

Deeds are fruit, words are leaves.
Anon.

In our good works nothing is our own.
John Calvin

Do good until it is an unconscious habit of life and you do not know you are doing it.
Oswald Chambers

Learn the luxury of doing good.
Oliver Goldsmith

It is not enough to do good. One must do it in the right way.
John Morley

Do what you can with what you have where you are.
Theodore D. Roosevelt

The reward of a good action lies in having done it.
Seneca

Good works, as they are called, in sinners are nothing but splendid sins.
C. H. Spurgeon

If you can save yourselves by your works, go and do so, fools that you are, for you might as well hope to drink dry the Atlantic.
C. H. Spurgeon

Unpractical religion is unscriptural religion.
James Wolfendale

GOODNESS

(See also: Ethics; Morality; Virtue)

Don't compare your goodness with that of other men; compare it with the goodness of the Man of Galilee.
Anon.

Goodness is like praise to God.
Anon.

He that is good is free, though he be a slave; he that is evil is a slave, though he be a king.
Augustine

Goodness is kindness in action.
Jerry Bridges

The good have no need of an advocate.
Phocion

It is chiefly in being good persons ourselves that we help others.

Elton Trueblood

GOSPEL

(See also: Evangelism; Soul-Winning)

If you believe what you like in the gospel, and reject what you don't like, it is not the gospel you believe, but yourself.

Augustine

The gospel is not so much a miracle as a marvel, and every line is suffused with wonder.

Roland Bainton

Christ's gospel is the sceptre of his kingdom.

John Calvin

The Spirit of God, from whom the doctrine of the gospel comes, is its only true interpreter.

John Calvin

The whole gospel is contained in Christ.

John Calvin

Whenever the gospel is preached it is as if God himself came into the midst of us.

John Calvin

There is nothing attractive about the gospel to the natural man; the only man who finds the gospel attractive is the man who is convicted of sin.

Oswald Chambers

The law and the gospel are allies, not enemies.

Walter J. Chantry

The gospel is good news. But Jesus never said it was easy news.

Charles Colson

Religion is the story of what a sinful man tries to do for a holy God; the gospel is the story of what a holy God has done for sinful men.

Roy Gustafson

Any man touched by Jesus Christ is good publicity for the gospel.

Vance Havner

The gospel makes some people sad, some mad and some glad. It is better that people should go out of church mad than merely go out, neither sad, mad, nor glad.

Vance Havner

The gospel does not abrogate God's law, but it makes men love it with all their hearts.

J. Gresham Machen

127

A gospel that elevates man and dethrones God is not the gospel.

Will Metzger

The world has many religions; it has but one gospel.

George Owen

The nature of the gospel is that it divides.

Richard Owen Roberts

The man who does not glory in the gospel can surely know little of the plague of sin that is within him.

J. C. Ryle

The revelation of the gospel is to a world that is already under indictment for its universal rejection of God the Father.

R. C. Sproul

If our Lord's bearing our sin for us is not the gospel, I have no gospel to preach.

C. H. Spurgeon

The heart of the gospel is redemption, and the essence of redemption is the substitutionary sacrifice of Christ.

C. H. Spurgeon

When we preach Christ crucified, we have no reason to stammer, or stutter, or hesitate, or apologize; there is nothing in the gospel of which we have any cause to be ashamed.

C. H. Spurgeon

GOSSIP
(See also: Rumour; Slander; Speech)

Gossip is nature's telephone.

Sholem Aleichem

A gossip's mouth is the devil's mailbag.

Anon.

A gossip usually makes a mountain out of a molehill by adding some dirt.

Anon.

Gossip is like mud thrown against a clean wall; it may not stick, but it leaves a mark.

Anon.

Gossip is what no one claims to like but what everybody enjoys.

Joseph Conrad

A lie has no leg, but a scandal has wings.

Thomas Fuller

Gossip is the lack of a worthy theme.

Elbert Green Hubbard

A gossip is one who talks to you about others; a bore is one who talks to you about himself; and a brilliant conversationalist is one who talks to you about yourself.

Lisa Kirk

Never report what may hurt another unless it be a greater hurt to conceal it.

William Penn

When tempted to gossip, breathe through your nose.

T. N. Tiemeyer

GRACE — the Christian's indebtedness to

God owes us nothing.

Anything this side of hell is pure grace.

Anon.

Men may fall by sin, but cannot raise up themselves without the help of grace.

John Bunyan

There is not a day, nor a duty; not a day that you live, nor a duty that you do, but will need that mercy should come after to take away your iniquity.

John Bunyan

God's grace turns out men and women with a strong family likeness to Jesus Christ, not milksops.

Oswald Chambers

We can never be blessed until we learn that we can bring nothing to Christ but our need.

Vance Havner

We have a constant dependence upon God. All our natural actions depend upon his providence, all our spiritual actions upon his grace.

Matthew Henry

A man is not a Christian unless he can say with Paul, 'I am what I am by the grace of God.'

D. Martyn Lloyd-Jones

Were it not for the grace of God there would be no such thing as a Christian.

D. Martyn Lloyd-Jones

The human mind without grace is a nest of wickedness swarming with thoughts of evil.

William S. Plumer

The church of Christ is little better than a great hospital. We ourselves are all, more or less, weak, and all daily need the skilful treatment of the heavenly Physician. There will be no complete cures until the resurrection day.

J. C. Ryle

Grace is not like the tide, that ebbs and flows, that we know when it will come again when we see it go.

Richard Sibbes

Any blessing which is bestowed by the Father upon his undeserving children must be considered to be an act of grace.

David Smith

God never owes us grace.

R. C. Sproul

The God of the Bible is as severe as if he were unmerciful, and just as if he were not gracious; and yet he is as gracious and as merciful as if he were not just.

C. H. Spurgeon

The greatest, highest and most practical truth of our life is that we are *recipients*.

William Still

Grace finds us beggars but leaves us debtors.

Augustus Toplady

GRACE — Common Grace

Common grace places everyone continually in God's debt — and the debt grows with every moment of life.

Common grace is an omnipresent operation of divine mercy, which reveals itself everywhere where human hearts are found to beat, and which spreads its blessing upon these human hearts.

Abraham Kuyper

All common grace is earlier grace. Its commonness lies in its earliness. It pertains not merely to the lower dimensions of life. It pertains to all dimensions, and to these dimensions in the same way at all stages of history.

Cornelius Van Til

The essence of common grace is the restraint of the process of sin.

Cornelius Van Til

Every time you draw your breath you suck in mercy.

Thomas Watson

GRACE — Daily

The will of God can never lead you where the grace of God cannot keep you.

Anon.

No folly is greater than to suppose that God is optional for daily living.
Edmund P. Clowney

I would rather make bricks without straw than try to live the Sermon on the Mount in my own strength.
D. Martyn Lloyd-Jones

God crowns grace with grace.
Richard Sibbes

There is within our nature that which would send the best saint to hell if sovereign grace did not prevent.
C. H. Spurgeon

We need restraining grace as well as saving grace.
William Tiptaft

No human frailty need be a hindrance to God's infinite grace.
David Watson

GRACE — Essence

In the Bible there are three distinctive meanings of grace; it means the mercy and active love of God; it means the winsome attractiveness of God; it means the strength of God to overcome.
Charles L. Allen

Grace is a certain beginning of glory in us.
Thomas Aquinas

God gives where he finds empty hands.
Augustine

Mercy is God's favour that holds back from us what we deserve. Grace is God's favour that gives us what we do not deserve.
Rolfe Barnard

Grace is but glory begun, and glory is but grace perfected.
Jonathan Edwards

Grace often grows strongest where conviction of sin has pierced deepest.
Sinclair Ferguson

Grace is love that gives, that loves the unlovely and the unlovable.
Oswald C. Hoffman

God gives his gifts where he finds the vessel empty enough to receive them.
C. S. Lewis

Grace is God's contradiction of human pride.
David Silversides

131

Grace is love that cares and stoops and rescues.

> *John R. W. Stott*

Grace is omnipotence acting redemptively.

> *Geoff Thomas*

GRACE — and Heaven

If you would lay up a treasure of glory in heaven, lay up a treasure of grace in your hearts.

> *John Mason*

Grace tried is better than grace, it is more than grace, it is glory in its infancy.

> *Samuel Rutherford*

If you have one grain of grace, you must die to know how rich you are.

> *William Tiptaft*

What a mercy to have a religion that will do to die by.

> *William Tiptaft*

The way to heaven lies not over a toll-bridge, but over a free bridge.

> *Augustus M. Toplady*

The more we grow in grace the more we shall flourish in glory.

> *Thomas Watson*

GRACE — and Salvation

Grace and election are the essence and mystery of history.

> *Augustine*

The sinner, apart from grace, is unable to be willing and unwilling to be able.

> *W. E. Best*

Justice is getting what you deserve; mercy is not getting what you deserve; grace is getting what you do not deserve.

> *Stuart Briscoe*

Law and love have no quarrel. The conflict arises between law and grace as a way of salvation.

> *Walter J. Chantry*

Grace first inscribed my name
In God's eternal book:
'Twas grace that gave me to the
   Lamb,
Who all my sorrows took.

> *Philip Doddridge*

We will never properly understand the work of God which takes place in the Christian life unless we first of all have some kind of grasp of why we need the grace of God.

> *Sinclair Ferguson*

Grace is to corruption as water is to fire.

John Flavel

In God's economy, emptying comes before filling, confession before forgiveness and poverty before riches.

Billy Graham

God excludes none if they do not exclude themselves.

William Guthrie

If the 'grace' you have received does not help you to keep the law, you have not received grace.

D. Martyn Lloyd-Jones

A man must completely despair of himself in order to become fit to obtain the grace of Christ.

Martin Luther

In a God-centred gospel, grace is central.

Will Metzger

The law tells me how crooked I am. Grace comes along and straightens me out.

D. L. Moody

There is nothing more offensive to man's self-esteem than a gospel of salvation by the grace of God, and by that grace alone.

T. P. Osborne

No man ever believes with a true and saving faith unless God inclines his heart; and no man when God does incline his heart can refrain from believing.

Blaise Pascal

Grace that cannot be seen is no grace at all.

J. C. Ryle

To come to the end of your resources is a happy state, for then you grow desperate, and desperate men find God.

Hugh Silvester

The first link between my soul and Christ is not my goodness but my badness, not my merit but my misery, not my riches but my need.

C. H. Spurgeon

GRACE — Supremacy

Grace comes into the soul as the morning sun into the world; first a dawning, then a light; and at last the sun in his full and excellent brightness.

Thomas Adams

Nothing can be done aright without grace.

John Bunyan

Faith and prayer may be means for procuring us an interest in the grace of God, but the source whence it flows is not within but without us.

John Calvin

Whatever is laudable in our works proceeds from the grace of God.

John Calvin

The ultimate test of our spirituality is the measure of our amazement at the grace of God.

D. Martyn Lloyd-Jones

Grace is the sum and substance of New Testament faith.

J. I. Packer

This one word 'grace' contains within itself the whole of New Testament theology.

J. I. Packer

A little grace is better than many gifts.

J. C. Ryle

Grace in the heart of man is an exotic. It is a new principle from without, sent down from heaven and implanted in his soul.

J. C. Ryle

Grace is stronger than circumstances.

J. C. Ryle

Abounding sin is the terror of the world, but abounding grace is the hope of mankind.

A. W. Tozer

God is always previous, God is always there first, and if you have any desire for God, and for the things of God, it is God himself who put it there.

A. W. Tozer

GRATITUDE
(See also: Thanksgiving)

Don't grumble because you don't get what you want; be grateful that you don't get what you deserve.

Anon.

It is only with gratitude that life becomes rich.

Dietrich Bonhoeffer

There is nothing quite so stirring in the matter of moving us to pray as being thankful to God for what he has done for us and with us.

E. F. Hallock

So much has been given to me,
I have no time to ponder over
that which has been denied.
Helen Keller

Gratitude is a duty which ought
to be paid, but which none have
a right to expect.
Jean Jacques Rousseau

The essence of Christian ethics
is gratitude.
R. C. Sproul

God is pleased with gratitude;
he gets so little of it.
William Tiptaft

GREATNESS

He is genuinely great who considers himself small and cares
nothing about high honours.
Thomas à Kempis

Great men never know they are
great; small men never know
they are small.
Anon.

Kindness is the true revealer of
a person's greatness.
Anon.

Greatness is a matter, not of
size, but of quality, and it is
within the reach of every one of
us.
Sidney Greenberg

Nothing can make a man truly
great but being truly good and
partaking of God's holiness.
Matthew Henry

The man who disciplines himself stands out and has the mark
of greatness upon him.
D. Martyn Lloyd-Jones

The true hallmark of greatness
is simplicity. It is little minds
that are complicated and involved.
D. Martyn Lloyd-Jones

One of the marks of true greatness is the ability to develop
greatness in others.
J. C. MacAulay

Seek not greatness, but seek
truth, and you will find both.
Horace Mann

Really great men have a curi-
ous feeling that the greatness is
not in them but through them.
John Ruskin

All greatness is unconscious.
Walter Scott

The great of this world are
those who simply loved God
more than others did.
A. W. Tozer

GREED

(See also: Covetousness; Gluttony)

No gain satisfies a greedy mind.

Anon.

Greed and ambition ... the two sources from which stems the corruption of the whole of the ministry.

John Calvin

That we shall carry nothing out of this world is a sentence better known than trusted, otherwise I think men would take more care to live well than to die rich.

John P. K. Henshaw

Nearly all those evils in the world which people put down to greed or selfishness are really far more the result of pride.

C. S. Lewis

Poverty wants much; greed everything.

Publilius Syrus

Most men pray more for full purses than for pure hearts.

Thomas Watson

GROWTH

God will do everything that we cannot do in order that we may live, but will do nothing that we can do in order that we may grow.

Anon.

Why stay we on earth except to grow?

Robert Browning

All our progress and perseverance are from God.

John Calvin

We Christians are miserable indeed if we grow old in making no improvement.

John Calvin

Measure your growth in grace by your sensitiveness to sin.

Oswald Chambers

It is only when men begin to worship that they begin to grow.

Calvin Coolidge

You can't do anything about the length of your life, but you can do something about its width and depth.

Evan Esar

The more a Christian grows in grace the more aware he becomes of the need for purity of heart.

Owen French

There is no formula to teach us how to arrive at maturity, and there is no grammar for the language of the inner life.

Dag Hammarskjold

God would have us not merely 'take a stand', he would have us walk. Too many have taken a stand and are still standing; for years they have made no progress.

Vance Havner

The best of all tests of growth is a man's attitude to God.

D. Martyn Lloyd-Jones

There is no better test of growth than that a man desires God because he is God.

D. Martyn Lloyd-Jones

The quest for excellence is a mark of maturity. The quest for power is childish.

Max Lucado

A Christian is never in a state of completion but always in a process of becoming.

Martin Luther

There are no short cuts to spiritual maturity. It takes time to be holy.

Erwin W. Lutzer

All growth that is not towards God is growing to decay.

George MacDonald

Maturity begins to grow when you can sense your concern for others outweighing your concern for yourself.

John MacNaughton

Progress is a tide. If we stand still we will surely be drowned.

Harold Mayfield

God never put anyone in a place too small to grow in.

Henrietta Mears

Growth is the only evidence of life.

John Henry Newman

We may lay it down as an elemental principle of religion that no large growth in holiness was ever gained by one who did not take time to be often alone with God.

Austin Phelps

The mature believer is a searching believer.

John Powell

When a Christian ceases to grow he begins to decay.

Clate Risley

None of us can come to the highest maturity without enduring the summer heat of trials.

C. H. Spurgeon

God wants us to be victors, not victims; to grow, not grovel; to soar, not sink; to overcome, not to be overwhelmed.

William A. Ward

We shall never graduate this side of heaven.

David Watson

GUIDANCE

(See also: Will of God)

Christ leads me through no darker rooms than he went through before.

Richard Baxter

The answer to decision-making is not putting the Lord to the test by ascribing arbitrary significance to events in his providence ... God has not authorized us to make oracles of events.

Edmund P. Clowney

Always try the suggestions or impressions that you may at any time feel by the unerring rule of God's most holy Word.

Jonathan Edwards

One erroneous principle, than which scarce any has proved more mischievous to the present glorious work of God, is a notion that it is God's manner in these days to guide his saints, at least some that are more eminent, by inspiration, or immediate revelation.

Jonathan Edwards

God is an ever-present Spirit guiding all that happens to a wise and holy end.

David Hume

A glimpse of the next three feet of road is more important than a view of the horizon.

C. S. Lewis

However you define guidance you must resist anything that moves it in the direction of new revelation from God.

Sam Logan

All the biblical narratives of God's direct communications with men are on the face of it exceptional, and the biblical method of personal guidance is quite different.

J. I. Packer

Be prepared for God to direct you to something you do not like, and teach you to like it!

J. I. Packer

If God restored David after his adultery with Bathsheba and murder of Uriah, and Peter after his threefold denial of Christ, we should have no doubt that he can and will restore Christians who err through making honest mistakes about his guidance.

J. I. Packer

Scripture gives us no more warrant constantly to expect 'hotline', 'voice-from-the control-tower' guidance than to expect new authoritative revelations to come our way for the guidance of the whole church.

J. I. Packer

The fundamental mode whereby our rational Creator guides his rational creatures is by rational understanding and application of his written Word.

J. I. Packer

The truth is that God in his wisdom, to make and keep us humble and to teach us to walk by faith, has hidden from us almost everything that we should like to know about the providential purposes which he is working out in the churches and in our own lives.

J. I. Packer

God Almighty, to reserve to himself the sole right of instructing us, and to prevent our solving the difficulties of our own being, has hid the knot so high, or, to speak more properly, so low, that we cannot reach it.

Blaise Pascal

In the light of God, human vision clears.

James Philip

God made the moon as well as the sun; and when he does not see fit to grant us the sunlight, he means us to guide our steps by moonlight.

Richard Whately

Deep in your heart it is not guidance that you want so much as a guide.

John White

GUILT

(See also: Depravity; Man — a Sinner; Sin; Sinful Nature)

A guilty conscience needs no accuser.

Anon.

Who was the guilty? Who brought this upon thee?
Alas, my treason, Lord Jesus, hath undone thee.

'Twas I, Lord Jesus, I it was
    denied thee;
I crucified thee!
Johann Heermann

There smites nothing so sharp,
nor smelleth so sour, as shame.
William Langland

All men stand condemned, not
by alien codes of ethics, but by
their own, and all men therefore are conscious of guilt.
C. S. Lewis

We have no choice but to be
guilty. God is unthinkable if we
are innocent.
Archibald MacLeish

We need not be ashamed of that
now, which we are sure we
shall not repent of when we
come to die.
John Mason

Every guilty person is his own
hangman.
Seneca

GULLIBILITY

You can have such an open
mind that it is too porous to
hold a conviction.
George Crane

A dog that follows everybody
is no good to anybody.
Vance Havner

Incredible as it may seem, there
are still people who believe
what they read in the newspapers.
D. Martyn Lloyd-Jones

HABIT

Habits are like cork or lead.
They tend to keep you up or
hold you down.
Anon.

It is but a step from
companionship to slavery
when one associates with vice.
Hosea Ballou

Every man has his besetting
sin.
Cicero

The second half of a man's life
is made up of the habits he
acquired during the first half.
Fyodor Dostoyevski

A young sinner will be an old
devil.
William Gurnall

The strength of a man's virtues
should not be measured by his

special exertions, but by his habitual acts.

Blaise Pascal

The miller does not observe the noise of his own mill.

C. H. Spurgeon

How hard it is to pray against besetting sins!

William Tiptaft

HAPPINESS

(See also: Joy)

A happy life depends on a good conscience.

John Calvin

While all men seek after happiness, scarcely one in a hundred looks for it from God.

John Calvin

The enjoyment of God is the only happiness with which our souls can be satisfied.

Jonathan Edwards

The search for happiness is one of the chief sources of unhappiness.

Eric Hoffer

True happiness is not attained through self-gratification, but through fidelity to a worthy purpose.

Helen Keller

The end of life is not to be happy, nor to achieve pleasure and avoid pain, but to do the will of God, come what may.

Martin Luther King

A right to happiness doesn't, for me, make much more sense than a right to be six feet tall, or to have a millionaire for your father, or to get good weather whenever you want to have a picnic.

C. S. Lewis

Seek for happiness and you will never find it. Seek righteousness and you will discover you are happy. It will be there without your knowing it, without your seeking it.

D. Martyn Lloyd-Jones

Pleasure-seeking is a barren business; happiness is never found till we have the grace to stop looking for it, and to give our attention to persons and matters external to ourselves.

J. I. Packer

It is a barren life that holds only happiness.

Frances J. Roberts

The greatest happiness you can have is knowing that you do not necessarily require happiness.

William Saroyan

Wise men and women in every major culture have maintained that the secret of happiness is not in getting more but in wanting less.

Philip Slater

Happiness does not depend on the actual number of blessings we manage to scratch from life, but on our attittude towards them.

Alexandr Solzhenitsyn

Happier to be chained in a dungeon with a Paul than reign in the palace with an Ahab.

C. H. Spurgeon

Whoever thinks of finding happiness in this world will be a day's march behind.

William Tiptaft

Happiness is the spiritual experience of living every minute with love, grace and gratitude.

Denis Waitley

HATRED
(See also: Anger; Passion)

Violent hatred sinks us below those we hate.

Anon.

Hatred is nothing more than inveterate anger.

John Calvin

Hatred is like fire — it makes even light rubbish deadly.

George Eliot

Animosity cloaked in piety is a demon even if it sits in church praising the Creator.

Calvin Miller

Life is too short for hate.

George Peppard

I will not permit any man to narrow and degrade my soul by making me hate him.

Bokker T. Washington

HEART
(See also: Soul)

A man's heart is right when he wills what God wills.

Thomas Aquinas

To my fellow men a heart of love; to my friends a heart of loyalty; to my God a heart of flame; to myself a heart of steel.

Augustine

The recesses of the heart are so hidden that no judgement can be formed by any human being.

John Calvin

The essence of the virtue and vice of dispositions of the heart and acts of the will lies not in their cause but in their nature.

Jonathan Edwards

The more a Christian grows in grace the more aware he becomes of the need for purity of heart.

Owen French

The basic needs of the human heart never change. The answers to that need never change.

William G. Hughes

It is the heart which experiences God and not the reason.

Blaise Pascal

Keep your heart with all diligence and God will look after the universe.

A. W. Tozer

HEAVEN — the Christian's Eternal Home
(See also: Eternal Security; Eternity)

All the places in heaven and hell are reserved.

There are no tourists in heaven.

In heaven to be even the least is a great thing, for all will be great.

Thomas à Kempis

If God were not willing to forgive sin heaven would be empty.

Anon.

It is not the Christian doctrine of heaven that is a myth, but the humanist dream of utopia.

Roy Clements

I've wrestled on towards heaven,
'Gainst storm and wind and tide;
Now, like a weary traveller
That leans upon his guide,
Amid the shades of evening,
While sinks life's lingering sand,
I hail the glory dawning
From Immanuel's land.

Anne Ross Cousin

This world is the land of the dying; the next is the land of the living.

Tryon Edwards

Christians are not citizens of earth trying to get to heaven, but citizens of heaven making their way through this world.

Vance Havner

The church will outlive the universe; in it the individual person will outlive the universe. Everything that is joined to the

143

immortal Head will share his immortality.

C. S. Lewis

We must ... I'm afraid recognize that, as we grow older, we become like old cars — more and more repairs and replacements are necessary. We must look forward to the fine new machines (latest resurrection model) which are waiting for us, we hope, in the Divine garage!

C. S. Lewis

Worship alone of all the activities of the believer will continue in heaven and will occupy the redeemed host for ever.

Robert G. Rayburn

I wonder, many times, that ever a child of God should have a sad heart, considering what his Lord is preparing for him.

Samuel Rutherford

Eternal life does not begin with death, it begins with faith.

Samuel Shoemaker

He is sure of heaven who is sure of Christ.

C. H. Spurgeon

I have a strong appetite for heaven.

C. H. Spurgeon

Many may outlive me on earth, but they cannot outlive me in heaven.

George Whitefield

HEAVEN — Glory

Heaven would be hardly be heaven if we could define it.

W. E. Biederwolf

Take the deepest enchantment that you have ever known, the loftiest ecstasy that you have ever felt. Take that moment when you felt most totally alive. Then intensify that instant a millionfold, and perhaps you will be getting within range of imagining what heaven is like.

Roy Clements

If the fire of hell is not literal, it is worse than actual fire; and if the gates of the Celestial City are not actual gold, they are far finer.

Vance Havner

Heaven is not a state of mind. Heaven is reality itself.

C. S. Lewis

Heaven will be a world of sanctified excitement.

Maurice Roberts

If sin or evil could ever enter into heaven we could never truly enjoy a moment's peace there.

Maurice Roberts

I suspect that every saved soul in heaven is a great wonder, and that heaven is a vast museum of wonders of grace and mercy, a palace of miracles, in which everything will surprise everyone who gets there.

C. H. Spurgeon

If this world with its fading pleasures is so much admired, what must heaven be, which God praises!

William Tiptaft

HEAVEN — God's Presence

In heaven, God will never hide his face and Satan will never show his.

Heaven is the perfectly ordered and harmonious enjoyment of God and of one another in God.

Augustine

I do not go to heaven to be advanced, but to give honour to God.

David Brainerd

Hell is to be eternally in the presence of God. Heaven is to be eternally in the presence of God, *with a Mediator.*

R. A. Finlayson

How can we expect to live with God in heaven if we love not to live with him on earth?

John Mason

HEAVEN — Perfection

Believers will swim for ever in an ocean of joy.

Thomas Boston

We shall have everything we desire and desire everything we have.

Richard Brooks

There are three things which the true Christian desires in respect to sin: justification, that it might not condemn; sanctification, that it may not reign; and glorification, that it may not be.

Richard Cecil

I do not know much about heaven. Nobody does. But I can guarantee one thing. Nobody there is ever bored.

Roy Clements

In heaven it is always autumn. God's mercies are ever in their maturity.

John Donne

One hour in heaven and we shall be ashamed we ever grumbled.

Vance Havner

Heaven is a day without a cloud to darken it and without a night to end it.

John Mason

In heaven there is the presence of all good and the absence of all evil.

John Mason

Beyond this vale of tears
There is a life above;
Unmeasured by the flight of
    years,
And all that life is love.

James Montgomery

Heaven is a state of holiness, which only persons with holy tastes will appreciate, and into which only persons of holy character can enter.

J. I. Packer

'Difficulty' is not a word to be found in the dictionary of heaven.

C. H. Spurgeon

There can be no grief in heaven any more than there can be joy in hell.

Thomas Watson

HEAVEN — Preparation for

The Christian should never look ahead without looking up.

To believe in heaven is not to run away from life; it is to run towards it.

Joseph D. Blinco

Make it the business of life to prepare for heaven.

Esther Burr

We ought to apply our minds to meditation upon a future life, so that this world may become cheap to us.

John Calvin

When we learn to hold the world with a loose grip we are learning to take hold of the world to come with a firm grip.

Sinclair Ferguson

The child is willing who calls to be put to bed.

William Gurnall

A continual looking forward to the eternal world is not a form of escapism or wishful thinking, but one of the things a Christian is meant to do.

C. S. Lewis

The more spiritual we are, the more we shall think about heaven.

D. Martyn Lloyd-Jones

Basic to New Testament ethics is the belief that Christians should live on earth in the light of heaven, should make decisions in the present with their eye on the future, and should avoid behaving here in a way that would jeopardize their hope of glory hereafter.

J. I. Packer

There is only one attitude possible for us if we mean to get to heaven. We must wage a ceaseless warfare against sin within us all the days of our life.

Maurice Roberts

Holy living trains Christians for heaven. The nearer we live to God while we live, the more shall we be to dwell for ever in his presence when we die.

J. C. Ryle

Eternal life does not begin with death; it begins with faith.

Samuel Shoemaker

The person who cannot look forward to God's dessert will have a tough time munching his way through the turnip greens and the rolled oats porridge now.

Paul B. Smith

HELL

(See also: Eternity; Judgement; Satan)

There are no quiet corners in hell.

The roads to hell are all downhill.

To appreciate justly and fully the gospel of eternal salvation we must believe, thoroughly believe, the doctrine of eternal damnation.

J. L. Dagg

Damnation: continual dying.

John Donne

Eternal death is not the cessation of existence, but rather the loss of that life of fellowship with God which alone is worthy of the name.

D. Edmond Hiebert

I willingly believe that the damned are, in one sense, successful, rebels to the end; that the doors of hell are locked on the *inside*.

C. S. Lewis

147

The reason why so many fall into hell is because so few think of it.

John Mason

They that will not feel the punishment in the threatening shall feel the threatening in the punishment.

John Mason

Hell is full of God's glory, as well as heaven, and the sinner shall show it forth in his perdition no less truly than the saint in his salvation.

Thomas V. Moore

Sin is but hell in embryo; hell is but sin in fulfilment.

Thomas V. Moore

I do not know if there is a more dreadful word in the English language than that word 'lost'.

C. H. Spurgeon

I greatly fear that the denial of the eternity of future punishment is one wave of an incoming sea of infidelity.

C. H. Spurgeon

In hell there is no hope. They have not even the hope of dying.

C. H. Spurgeon

The wrath of God does not end with death.

C. H. Spurgeon

Think lightly of hell and you will think lightly of the cross.

C. H. Spurgeon

Hell is the highest reward that the devil can offer you for being a servant of his.

Billy Sunday

If there is no hell, a good many preachers are obtaining money under false pretences!

Billy Sunday

Hell will be the ugliest place in all of creation.

A. W. Tozer

Hell is full of hard hearts; there is not one soft heart there.

Thomas Watson

HERESY

An error is the more dangerous the more truth it contains.

Henri Amiel

Almost all the corruptions of doctrines flow from the pride of men.

John Calvin

Error, preached as truth, has contributed to the delusion of multitudes who are lost.
Iain H. Murray

It is the oldest stratagem of Satan to disfigure the truth by misrepresentation.
Iain H. Murray

Error does not advertise its coming to the soul. It sidles in, and breeds inward and secret infidelity for long before it becomes evident to others.
James Philip

To commit theological error is to commit sin.
R. C. Sproul

Serious piety is the best defence against wicked doctrines.
Thomas Wilson

HISTORY

History teaches us the mistakes we are going to make.
Anon.

The biblical view of history is not cyclical, it is linear. It has a definite beginning, with God's creation of the universe, and it is building to a final climax.
John Benton

The farther back you look, the farther forward you are likely to see.
Winston Churchill

The history of the world should purport to be the annals of the government of the great King.
J. H. Merle d'Aubigné

History is little more than the crimes, follies and misfortunes of mankind.
Edward Gibbon

History is the long story of man trying to be God.
Vance Havner

We learn from history that we do not learn from history.
Georg Hegal

The whole course of history is represented (in Scripture) as the development of the plan and purpose of God; and yet human history is little else than the history of sin.
Charles Hodge

History is a story written by the finger of God.
C. S. Lewis

History can be understood only in terms of God's kingdom.
D. Martyn Lloyd-Jones

149

Consciousness of the past alone makes us understand the present.

Herbert Luethy

The history of man is his attempt to escape his own corruption.

Daniel Mullis

The purpose of the historian is not to construct a history from preconceived notions and to adjust it to his own liking, but to reproduce it from the best evidence and to let it speak for itself.

Philip Schaff

We must never set theology and history over against each other, since Scripture refuses to do so.

John R. W. Stott

HOLINESS — Definition
(See also: Christlikeness; Godliness)

Sanctification is that gracious and continuous operation of the Holy Spirit by which he delivers the justified sinner from the pollution of sin, renews his whole nature in the image of God, and enables him to perform good works.

Louis Berkhof

Holiness is not an experience you have; holiness is keeping the law of God.

D. Martyn Lloyd-Jones

If regeneration is a work of new creation, sanctification is a work of new formation. If regeneration is a new birth, sanctification is a new growth.

J. I. Packer

Sanctification is a process by which, because we love God, we become like him.

Joseph Pipa

Wrong views about holiness are generally traceable to wrong views about human corruption.

J. C. Ryle

HOLINESS — Essence

Never be tempted to think that you can achieve in a moment's crisis what God has said can only happen by a lifetime's process.

Show me someone who hates sin and I will show you someone who loves holiness.

Richard Alderson

Holiness does not produce cranks.

John Benton

Holiness does not consist in mystic speculations, enthusiastic fervours, or uncommanded austerities; it consists in thinking as God thinks and willing as God wills.

John Brown

The holiest person is ... one who is most conscious of what sin is.

Oswald Chambers

Holiness is much more than a set of rules against sin. Holiness must be seen as the opposite of sin.

Charles Colson

Holiness is the only possible response to God's grace.

Charles Colson

Holy living is loving God.

Charles Colson

Holiness has love for its essence, humility for its clothing, the good of others as its employment, and the honour of God as its end.

Nathanael Emmons

Holiness depends less upon what we do than how we do it.

Frederick W. Faber

How little people know who think that holiness is dull.

C. S. Lewis

The essence of true holiness is conformity to the nature and will of God.

Samuel Lucas

Holiness is not freedom from temptation, but power to overcome temptation.

G. Campbell Morgan

Sanctification is not mystical passivity, as our use of the slogan 'let go and let God' has too often implied, but it is active moral effort energized by prayerful and expectant faith.

J. I. Packer

Holiness is persevering obedience.

C. H. Spurgeon

HOLINESS — Importance

God is much more concerned about our holiness than our happiness, much more about our character than our comfort.

Holiness is to be the driving ambition of the Christian.

Without holiness there is no wholeness, no spiritual happiness — and no heaven.

Holiness is the everyday business of every Christian.
Charles Colson

God saved us to make us holy, not happy. Some experiences may not contribute to our happiness, but all can be made to contribute to our holiness.
Vance Havner

Holiness is the distinguishing mark of the Christian.
Michael Howell

If you do not desire to be holy I do not see that you have any right to think that you are a Christian.
D. Martyn Lloyd-Jones

The New Testament way of handling sanctification is never an appeal, it is a command.
D. Martyn Lloyd-Jones

Sanctification is the main course of the Christian life.
Joseph Pipa

Sanctification will not get us to heaven but we cannot go to heaven without it.
Joseph Pipa

True holiness flows from the soundness of a man's doctrine.
Robert A. Richey

Holiness is better than morality. It goes beyond it. Holiness affects the heart. Holiness respects the motive. Holiness regards the whole nature of man.
C. H. Spurgeon

The gifts which I feel I should crave beyond every other boon is holiness, pure and immaculate holiness.
C. H. Spurgeon

HOLINESS —
and Justification
(See also: Faith — and Deeds; Good Deeds)

The God who declares us righteous in Christ by imputation will make us holy by imparting that righteousness.
Richard Alderson

Any Christian who is not earnestly pursuing holiness in every aspect of his life is flying in the face of God's purpose in saving him.
Jerry Bridges

It is as dangerous to rest on a justification unattended with holiness as it is to rest on a justification that has works for its basis.

William S. Plumer

There is no time lapse between our justification and the beginning of our sanctification ... As soon as we truly believe, at that very instant, the process of becoming pure and holy is under way, and its future completion is certain.

R. C. Sproul

Christ promises to save his people from their sins, not in their sins.

C. H. Spurgeon

Grace can be no more concealed than fire.

Thomas Watson

Purity is the end of our election.

Thomas Watson

HOLINESS — Man's Part

All we have to do is to be holy; and we are to be holy in all we do.

We do not strive to be holy in order to be saved; that is legalism. We do not strive to be holy in order to prove we are saved; that is bondage. We seek to be holy because that is

God's purpose in saving us and because we have come to be thankful to him.

John Benton

Men make more haste to get their afflictions removed than their hearts sanctified; but this is not the work God looks for.

Thomas Case

There is no detour to holiness. Jesus came to the resurrection through the cross, not around it.

Leighton Ford

Righteousness is a commitment to a relationship.

Don Garlington

The old mystics tried to make themselves holier by hiding from society; but living in a hole does not make you holier!

Vance Havner

Holiness is not something to be received in a meeting; it is a life to be lived and to be lived in detail.

D. Martyn Lloyd-Jones

It is a great deal better to live a holy life than to talk about it. Lighthouses do not ring bells and fire cannon to call attention to their shining — they just shine!

D. L. Moody

153

To live in the light of eternity and the coming day of God is the surest way of promoting the work of sanctification in our hearts.

James Philip

HOLINESS — Rewards

When there shall be universal holiness there shall also be universal happiness.

Thomas V. Moore

Many of us would pursue holiness with far greater zeal and eagerness if we were convinced that the way of holiness is the way of life *and peace.* And that is precisely what it is; there is life and peace no other way.

J. I. Packer

We are becoming what we shall be eternally.

Samuel E. Waldron

HOLY SPIRIT

(See also: Godhead)

Fulness of the Spirit is not a press-button panacea; it is the growing experience of those who hunger and thirst after righteousness.

He never sins against the Holy Ghost that fears he has sinned against the Holy Ghost.

William Bridge

God does not bestow his Spirit on his people in order to set aside the use of his Word, but rather to render it fruitful.

John Calvin

The gift of the Spirit was a fruit of the resurrection of Christ.

John Calvin

The Spirit of God, from whom the doctrine of the gospel comes, is its only true interpreter.

John Calvin

There is one thing we cannot imitate; we cannot imitate being full of the Holy Ghost.

Oswald Chambers

The Spirit-filled life is no mystery revealed to a select few, no goal difficult of attainment. To trust and to obey is the substance of the whole matter.

Victor Edman

One might as well try to catch sunbeams with a fishhook as to lay hold of God's revelation unassisted by the Holy Spirit.

Vance Havner

Paul speaks of being absent from the body and present with the Lord. But being present in the body does not mean being absent from the Lord; for he lives in all who believe, and these bodies are the temples of the Holy Spirit.

Vance Havner

Satan has scored a point in making us so afraid of extremism about the Holy Spirit — which abounds indeed — that we may miss the true in our fear of the false. We can be so wary of getting out on a limb that we never go up the tree!

Vance Havner

The Holy Spirit is the only authenticator of Christianity.

Arthur P. Johnson

We could not pray at all were it not for the Holy Spirit.

D. Martyn Lloyd-Jones

The Spirit is the source of all our natural gifts.

Donald MacLeod

The work of the Holy Spirit is as needful as that of Christ.

William MacLeod

God commands us to be filled with the Spirit, and if we are not filled it is because we are living beneath our privileges.

D. L. Moody

Scripture places no limitation upon the Spirit's work of glorifying Christ and extending his kingdom.

Iain H. Murray

(The Holy Spirit) has not promised to reveal new truths, but to enable us to understand what we read in the Bible; and if we venture beyond the pale of Scripture we are upon enchanted ground and exposed to all the illusions of imagination and enthusiasm.

John Newton

The mind of the unregenerate man can easily hear and mentally comprehend the facts set forth in the gospel, but only the Spirit of God can make the inward man experience the spiritual power of those truths.

John G. Reisinger

We may depend upon it as a certainty that where there is no holy living there is no Holy Ghost.

J. C. Ryle

The Holy Spirit is always in, with and by the Word.

Philipp Spener

If you could pray the best prayer in the world without the Holy Spirit, God would have nothing to do with it.

C. H. Spurgeon

The Spirit who convicts us is also the Spirit who consoles.

C. H. Spurgeon

Unless the Spirit of God convinces the judgement and constrains the will, man has no heart to believe in Jesus unto eternal life.

C. H. Spurgeon

The only way to arrive at faith in the Holy Spirit is along the road of self-despair.

John R. W. Stott

The Spirit-filled life is not a special, deluxe edition of Christianity. It is part and parcel of the total plan of God for his people.

A. W. Tozer

HONESTY
(See also: Truth)

Where is there dignity unless there is honesty?

Cicero

The only basis for real fellowship with God and man is to live out in the open with both.

Roy Hession

Honesty is the first chapter in the book of wisdom.

Thomas Jefferson

I have not observed men's honesty to increase with their riches.

Thomas Jefferson

If faith does not make a man honest, it is not an honest faith.

C. H. Spurgeon

HOPE
(See also: Eternal Security; Future; Heaven)

Hope is grief's best music.

Anon.

Hope is the foundation of patience.

John Calvin

The word hope I take for faith; and indeed hope is nothing else but the constancy of faith.

John Calvin

When hope animates us there is a vigour in the whole body.

John Calvin

Hope means expectancy when things are otherwise hopeless.
G. K. Chesterton

There can be no hope without faith in Christ, for hope is rooted in him alone. Faith without hope would, by itself, be empty and futile.
Ernst Hoffmann

Hope teaches endurance and an eager anticipation of that which will become reality.
Simon J. Kistemaker

True faith is never found alone; it is accompanied by expectation.
C. S. Lewis

The world hopes for the best, but Jesus Christ offers the best hope.
John Wesley White

HUMANISM

Humanism can motivate neither morality nor life itself.
Gordon H. Clark

The very first temptation that ever came to man and woman was to be a humanist.
Brian H. Edwards

Humanism is caught in an inescapable relativism. If we are ever to discover the clue to the meaning of reality, history, and life itself, it must come to us from beyond the flux of the human situation.
Clark H. Pinnock

Modern humanism celebrates the importance of man while whistling in the dark.
R. C. Sproul

Modern secular humanism is one of the stupidest beliefs ever concocted.
R. C. Sproul

HUMILITY — Blessings

Humility is to the Christian what ballast is to the ship; it keeps him in his proper position and regulates all his thoughts and feelings.
Archibald Alexander

God is closest to those whose hearts are broken.
Anon.

Humility is the beginning of true intelligence.
John Calvin

157

Humility, after the first shock, is cheerful virtue.

> *C. S. Lewis*

Only those who see themselves as utterly destitute can fully appreciate the grace of God.

> *Erwin W. Lutzer*

The less a person strives for himself, the more God will be his champion.

> *John Trapp*

Humility solders Christians together in peace.

> *Thomas Watson*

HUMILITY — Characteristics

He is genuinely great who considers himself small and cares nothing about high honours.

> *Thomas à Kempis*

I did nothing that I might not have done better.

> *Richard Baxter*

Humility is not thinking meanly of oneself, but rather it means not thinking of oneself at all.

> *Vance Havner*

He whose garments are the whitest will best perceive the spots upon them.

> *C. H. Spurgeon*

If pride and madness go together, so do humility and sanity.

> *John R. W. Stott*

HUMILITY — Essence

If you sincerely desire to hide your good actions, pride will not harm you.

> *Augustine*

Humility is not simply feeling small and useless — like an inferiority complex. It is sensing how great and glorious God is, and seeing myself in that light.

> *Sinclair Ferguson*

Humility is the ability to see ourselves as God describes us.

> *Henry Jacobsen*

If anyone would like to acquire humility, I can, I think, tell him the first step. The first step is to realize that one is proud.

> *C. S. Lewis*

The way to become poor in spirit is to look at God.

> *D. Martyn Lloyd-Jones*

Humility is a most strange thing. The moment that you think you have acquired it is just the moment you have lost it.

Bernard Meltzer

Humility is to make a right estimate of oneself.

C. H. Spurgeon

Poverty of spirit is a kind of self-annihilation.

Thomas Watson

The poor in spirit are divorced from themselves.

Thomas Watson

HUMILITY — False

There is nothing more awful than conscious humility; it is the most satanic type of pride.

Oswald Chambers

If any man tells me that he is humble, I know him to be profoundly proud.

C. H. Spurgeon

HUMILITY — Importance

One test of a person's strength is his knowledge of his weakness.

Anon.

Much more of true religion consists in deep humility, brokenness of heart and an abasing sense of barrenness and want of grace and holiness than most who are called Christians imagine.

David Brainerd

Nothing but the pure knowledge of God can teach us humility.

John Calvin

I believe every Christian man has a choice between being humble and being humbled.

C. H. Spurgeon

Humility is the sweet spice that grows from poverty of spirit.

Thomas Watson

Till we are poor in spirit we are not capable of receiving grace.

Thomas Watson

HYPOCRISY
(See also: Formalism)

Spoken faith is not necessarily saving faith.

Nothing is more amiable than true modesty, and nothing more contemptible than false. The one guards virtue, the other betrays it.

Joseph Addison

I will have nought to do with a man who can blow hot and cold with the same breath.

Aesop

A clean glove often hides a dirty hand.

Anon.

A hypocrite preaches by the yard but practises by the inch.

Anon.

Keeping up appearances is the most expensive thing in the world.

A. C. Benson

Hypocrites are so stupid that they do not feel their sores.

John Calvin

A bad man is worse when he pretends to be a saint.

Oswald Chambers

If the devil ever laughs, it must be at hypocrites; they are the greatest dupes he has.

C. C. Colton

Men defend nothing more violently than the pretensions they live by.

Allen Drury

A man can be outwardly conformed to the Christian way of life while he is inwardly conformed to the spirit of this world.

Sinclair Ferguson

Religion is the best armour in the world, but the worst cloak.

Thomas Fuller

How difficult it is to avoid having a special standard for oneself!

C. S. Lewis

Of all bad men religious bad men are the worst.

C. S. Lewis

The most exhausting thing in life is being insincere.

Anne Morrow Lindbergh

We play the game; God keeps the score.

Erwin W. Lutzer

There are many who agree with God in principle but not in practice.

Richard Owen Roberts

Nothing devalues the truth more quickly than the counterfeit.

R. C. Sproul

Of all things in the world that stink in the nostrils of men, hypocrisy is the worst.

C. H. Spurgeon

Hypocrites cannot sail in stormy weather.
Thomas Watson

Hypocrites love a cheap religion.
Thomas Watson

The hypocrite's tongue may be silver, yet his heart stone.
Thomas Watson

The white devil is the worst.
Thomas Watson

IDOLATRY

All who forsake the Word fall into idolatry.
John Calvin

Every one of us is, from his mother's womb, expert in inventing idols.
John Calvin

Satan doesn't care what we worship, as long as we don't worship God.
D. L. Moody

The method of the evil one is to obsure himself behind some other object of worship.
G. Campbell Morgan

You do not have to make a graven image picturing God as a man to be an idolator; a false mental image is all that is needed to break the second commandment.
J. I. Packer

Whatsoever our trust is most in, that is our god.
Richard Sibbes

The most basic sin found in the world is that of idolatry.
R. C. Sproul

While it is intimidating to bow down in awe before the powerful God of the Bible, it is utterly pointless to bow politely to false gods of our own making.
R. C. Sproul

IGNORANCE

An empty sack cannot stand upright.
Anon.

Education is never as expensive as ignorance.
Anon.

The mind is never so enlightened that there are no remains of ignorance, nor the heart so established that there are no misgivings.
John Calvin

It is debatable which is causing us more harm — hot-headed

ignorance or cold-hearted intellectualism.

Vance Havner

We know things about God, but our real trouble is our ignorance about God himself — what he really is, and what he is to his people.

D. Martyn Lloyd-Jones

The more I advance, the more clearly I perceive that the greatest human knowledge amounts to a more pompous proof of our ignorance, by showing us how little we know about anything.

John Newton

As creatures, we have no right or reason to expect that at every point we shall be able to comprehend the wisdom of our Creator.

J. I. Packer

Everybody is ignorant — only on different subjects.

Will Rogers

Half our fears are the result of ignorance.

C. H. Spurgeon

Grace cannot reign where ignorance reigns.

Thomas Watson

Ignorance is Satan's stronghold.

Thomas Watson

IMMORTALITY
(See also: Destiny; Eternity; Heaven)

The human body is formed for immortality ... By sinking into death it does not utterly perish.

John Calvin

Immortal souls were not created for merely mortal ends.

C. H. Spurgeon

He sins against this life who slights the next.

Edward Young

IMPATIENCE

Ignorance of the providence of God is the cause of all impatience.

John Calvin

Adversity borrows its sharpest sting from our impatience.

George Horne

The nicest people are often the most impatient.

D. Martyn Lloyd-Jones

The Almighty is working on a great scale and will not be hustled by our peevish impetuosity.

W. Graham Scroggie

IMPENITENCE

God is irreconcilable to the impenitent.

John Calvin

The essence of original sin is to hate God.

R. C. Sproul

INCARNATION —
Jesus Christ
(See also: Virgin Birth)

The incarnation of Christ is the clearest affirmation of the truth that man is created in the image of God.

Lawrence Adams

Filling the world he lies in a manger!

Augustine

Christ voluntarily took upon him everything that is inseparable from human nature.

John Calvin

The incarnation was a necessary means to an end, and the end was the putting away of the sin of the world by the offering of the body of Christ.

Thomas Hewitt

The Christian story is precisely the story of one grand miracle.

C. S. Lewis

Christmas is the day that holds all time together.

Alexander Smith

He that made man was made man.

C. H. Spurgeon

The glory of the incarnation is that it presents to our adoring gaze not a humanized God or a deified man, but a true God-man — one who is all that God is and at the same time all that man is: one on whose almighty arm we can rest, and to whose human sympathy we can appeal.

Benjamin B. Warfield

INDOLENCE

He who kills time kills opportunities.

Anon.

It costs the devil little trouble to catch the lazy man.

Anon.

No one ever climbed the ladder of success with his hands in his pockets.

Anon.

The lazier a man is the more he plans to do tomorrow.

Anon.

An *idle* man and a *Christian* are names which do not harmonize.

Albert Barnes

Laziness breeds a love of amusement.

Richard Baxter

To do nothing is nothing less than to do some harm.

Chrysostom

While God assists our weakness, he does not intend to encourage our laziness.

Henry Dove

Despise an idle mind.

Jim Elliff

Laziness grows on people; it begins in cobwebs and ends in iron chains.

M. Hale

Do not so contemplate eternity that you waste today.

Vance Havner

Idleness is the devil's workshop.

Vance Havner

The field left idle returns to weeds and thorns.

Vance Havner

The slothful desire the gains which the diligent get, but they hate the pains which the diligent take.

Matthew Henry

The way to be nothing is to do nothing.

Nathaniel Howe

Determine never to be idle ... It is wonderful how much may be done if we are always doing.

Thomas Jefferson

Idle Christians are not tempted of the devil so much as they tempt the devil to tempt them.

C. H. Spurgeon

It is an abomination to let the grass grow up to your knees and do nothing towards making it into hay. God never sent a man into the world to be idle.

C. H. Spurgeon

Enthusiasm and persistence can make an average person superior; indifference and lethargy can make a superior person average.

William A. Ward

The greatest failure is the failure to try.

William A. Ward

Beware of idleness. Satan sows most of his seed in fallow ground.

Thomas Watson

Religion gives no warrant for idleness ... a Christian must mind not only heaven, but his calling.

Thomas Watson

INFLUENCE
(See also: Example)

A crooked stick will have a crooked shadow.

Anon.

We are the salt of the earth, not the sugar, and our ministry is truly to cleanse and not just to change the taste.

Vance Havner

Your influence is negative or positive, never neutral.

Henrietta Mears

The entire ocean is affected by a pebble.

Blaise Pascal

A little man may cast a long shadow.

C. H. Spurgeon

INGRATITUDE

Forgetfulness of God's benefits is a sort of madness.

John Calvin

Ingratitude is very frequently the reason why we are deprived of the light of the gospel, as well as of other divine favours.

John Calvin

When we become thankless we become sinners against God and man.

E. F. Hallock

Every virtue divorced from thankfulness is maimed and limps along the spiritual road.

John Henry Jowett

Alas for that capital crime of the Lord's people — barrenness in praises!

John Livingstone

I fear that what will surprise us most, when we see our Lord, will be the extent of our own ingratitude.

E. B. Pusey

It must make the devils themselves marvel to see us able to receive a pardon and a title to everlasting glory with scarcely more than a few cold syllables of gratitude to God.

Maurice Roberts

It is *sad* when there is nothing for which we feel grateful to God, but it is *serious* when there *is* something and we fail to show gratitude, and it is *tragic* when we are so busy asking for more that we forget to thank him for what we have received.

William Still

INJUSTICE

If you are suffering from a bad man's injustice, forgive him lest there be two bad men.

Augustine

Those who commit injustice bear the greatest burden.

Hosea Ballou

Injustice anywhere is a threat to justice everywhere.

Martin Luther King

Injustice never rules for ever.

Seneca

INTEGRITY

The three most important ingredients in Christian work are integrity, integrity, integrity.

Charles Colson

Integrity without knowledge is weak and useless, and knowledge without integrity is dangerous and dreadful.

Samuel Johnson

Integrity is the first step to true greatness.

Charles Sommons

If we cannot be believed on our word, we are surely not to be trusted on our oath.

C. H. Spurgeon

A guileless mind is a great treasure; it is worth any price.

A. W. Tozer

JEALOUSY
(See also: Envy)

Jealousy is a blister on the heels of friendship.

Anon.

Jealousy sees too much.

Anon.

166

JESUS CHRIST — Ascension

Christ was taken up into heaven, not to enjoy blessed rest at a distance from us, but to govern the world for the salvation of all believers.

John Calvin

Christ's ascension into heaven was the real commencement of his reign.

John Calvin

Astronauts sink into insignificance beside this ascension!

Vance Havner

He hath left with us the earnest of the Spirit, and taken from us the earnest of our flesh, which he hath carried into heaven as a pledge that the whole shall follow after.

Tertullian

JESUS CHRIST — Death
(See also: Atonement; Cross; Forgiveness by God)

The death of Jesus was not a proposition for sinners but a plan of salvation.

Christ suffered in his soul the dreadful torments of a person condemned and irretrievably lost.

John Calvin

If Christ's soul had experienced no punishment he would have been only a Redeemer for the body.

John Calvin

Jesus Christ never died for our good works. They were not worth dying for. But he gave himself for our sins, according to the Scriptures.

Martin Luther

A dying Christ is the last resort of the believer.

C. H. Spurgeon

God had condemned sin before, but never so efficiently as in the death of his Son.

C. H. Spurgeon

Christ's death, as it were, uncovered God so that man might have a vision of the glory that shone upon his face.

R. V. G. Tasker

JESUS CHRIST — Deity and Humanity

Jesus neither laid aside his deity when he came to earth nor his humanity when he returned to heaven.

167

As the print of the seal on the wax is the express image of the seal itself, so Christ is the express image — the perfect representation — of God.

Ambrose

A man who can read the New Testament and not see that Christ claims to be more than a man can look all over the sky at high noon on a cloudless day and will not see the sun.

W. E. Biederwolf

With the exception of being sinful, everything that can be said about a man can be said about Jesus Christ.

James Montgomery Boice

The nature of Christ's existence is mysterious, I admit; but this mystery meets the wants of man. Reject it and the world is an inexplicable riddle; believe it, and the history of our race is satisfactorily explained.

Napoleon Bonaparte

He who ... does not perceive Christ to be God ... is blind amidst the brightness of noonday.

John Calvin

The characteristics of God Almighty are mirrored for us in Jesus Christ. Therefore if we want to know what God is like we must study Jesus Christ.

Oswald Chambers

As to his deity he had no mother, and as to his humanity he had no father.

Robert Clarke

Christ was God, not because he was virgin born. He was virgin born because he was God.

Robert Clarke

Christ is the image of God — no feature absent, none misplaced and none impaired in fulness or dimmed in lustre.

John Eadie

All that Jesus was and taught and did is but a revealing of the eternal God.

E. F. Hallock

The Son of God did not unite himself with a human person, but with a human nature.

Charles Hodge

Christians believe that Jesus Christ is the Son of God because he said so. The other evidence about him has convinced them that he was neither a lunatic nor a quack.

C. S. Lewis

The union between God and nature in the person of Christ admits no divorce.

C. S. Lewis

If Christ is divested of his deity, there remains no help against God's wrath and no rescue from his judgement.

Martin Luther

The doctrine that Jesus Christ had a true human nature is probably the single most important article of the Christian faith.

Donald MacLeod

We do not believe that God has added, or ever will add, anything to his revelation in his Son.

C. B. Moss

The fact that Jesus will sit upon the throne of judgement will be the consternation of his enemies and the consolation of his people.

John Murray

The eternal generation of the Son in no way implies inferiority.

Stuart Olyott

Christ is the aperture through which the immensity and magnificence of God can be seen.

J. B. Phillips

It is an infallible proof of our Lord's divinity that he may be addressed in prayer.

C. H. Spurgeon

Jesus is not the child of eternity, but the Father of it.

C. H. Spurgeon

If Jesus Christ was a product of evolution, how is it that no better man has since appeared, after nineteen centuries?

W. H. Griffith Thomas

We know how God would act if he were in our place — he has been in our place.

A. W. Tozer

The incarnation of the Son of God was not a diminishing of his deity, but an acquiring of manhood.

Verna Wright

JESUS CHRIST — Glory

The Word of God became flesh;
The Son of God became Man;
The Lord of all became a servant;
The Righteous One was made sin;
The Eternal One tasted death;
The Risen One now lives in men;

169

The Seated One is coming again!

Anon.

The whole gospel is contained in Christ.

John Calvin

Who can deny that Jesus of Nazareth, the incarnate Son of the Most High God, is the eternal glory of the human race?

Benjamin Disraeli

Christ has outlasted the empire that crucified him nineteen centuries ago. He will outlast the dictators who defy him now.

Ralph W. Sockman

God is more glorified in the person of his Son than he would have been by an unfallen world.

C. H. Spurgeon

There was never a sinner half as big as Christ is as a Saviour.

C. H. Spurgeon

The act of incarnation was not a temporary arrangement which ended with Christ's death and resurrection but, as the Scriptures make evident, his human nature continues for ever.

John F. Walvoord

To rob the divine nature of God of a single attribute would destroy his deity, and to rob man of a single attribute would result in the destruction of a true humanity. It is for this reason that the two natures of Christ cannot lose or transfer a single attribute.

John F. Walvoord

Without question the crucial issue in biblical theology is the deity of Christ, and disregard or question of this central doctrine of the Bible leads to inevitable chaos in theology as a whole.

John F. Walvoord

All that man as man is, that Christ is to eternity.

Benjamin B. Warfield

JESUS CHRIST — Humility

No other man has ever humbled himself so greatly; and no man has ever been more exalted as a result.

Nothing is so sweet and beautiful, yet to ambitious men so surprising, as the humility of the Lord Jesus.

Walter J. Chantry

JESUS CHRIST — Intercession

God can listen to no prayers without the intercession of Christ.

John Calvin

There is no way of obtaining favour from God but through the intercession of Christ.

John Calvin

See where before the throne he stands,
And pours the all-prevailing prayer,
Points to his side, and lifts his hands,
And shows that I am graven there.

Charles Wesley

JESUS CHRIST — Life and Influence

Jesus Christ disturbs everything he confronts.

Rolfe Barnard

Jesus walking on the earth is far more important than man walking on the moon.

James Irwin

Jesus' miracles are decisive evidence for all time of who he is and what power he has.

J. I. Packer

Jesus was the very King of meekness.

A. W. Pink

Christ's deeds and examples are commandments of what we should do.

John Wycliffe

JESUS CHRIST — Lordship

The whole of Satan's kingdom is subject to the authority of Christ.

John Calvin

There is nothing holier, or better, or safer, than to content ourselves with the authority of Christ alone.

John Calvin

Jesus will not be a Saviour to any man who refuses to bow to him as Lord.

Walter J. Chantry

No repentance is true repentance which does not recognize Jesus as Lord over every area of life.

John C. Chapman

If Christ is Lord of all, Christians must recapture their sense of moral outrage.

Charles Colson

171

If Christ's lordship does not disrupt our own lordship, then the reality of our conversion must be questioned.

Charles Colson

Jesus Christ demands more complete allegiance than any dictator who ever lived. The difference is, he has the right to.

Vance Havner

Salvation is not a cafeteria where you take what you want and leave the rest. You cannot take Christ as Saviour and refuse him as Lord and be saved.

Vance Havner

You cannot receive Christ in bits and pieces.

D. Martyn Lloyd-Jones

Jesus Christ is everywhere; he is behind everything we see if only we have eyes to see him; and he is the Lord of history if only we penetrate deep enough beneath the surface.

Charles Malik

Christ is the great central fact in the world's history. To him everything looks forward or backward. All the lines of history converge upon him.

C. H. Spurgeon

The keys of providence swing at the girdle of Christ.

C. H. Spurgeon

Nobody can call himself a Christian who does not worship Jesus.

John R. W. Stott

JESUS CHRIST — Love

The man who knows the love of Christ in his heart can do more in one hour than the busy type of man can do in a century.

D. Martyn Lloyd-Jones

There is no higher priority in the believer's life than to delight himself in the love of Christ.

Maurice Roberts

The distinguishing mark of a Christian is his confidence in the love of Christ, and the yielding of his affections to Christ in return.

C. H. Spurgeon

JESUS CHRIST — Perfection

Fallen human nature has neither grace nor truth in it, but the human nature of Christ was full of grace and truth.

W. E. Best

Only a perfect righteousness can stand in the judgement, and the Christian can have such righteousness only outside himself and in the perfection of Christ.

John Calvin

Every virtue known to man is found in Jesus.

Michael Green

We can say that Christ was 'made sin' but we cannot say that he was made sinful.

Donald MacLeod

Our Lord Jesus Christ called himself the Truth, not the Custom.

Tertullian

Jesus Christ is made up of all sweets and delights. He himself is all that is desirable. He is light to the eye, honey to the taste, joy to the heart.

Thomas Watson

JESUS CHRIST — Power

We marvel, not that Christ performed miracles, but rather that he performed so few. He who could have stormed the citadels of men with mighty battalions of angels let men spit on him and crucify him.

Oswald Chambers

Jesus Christ is God's everything for man's total need.

Richard Halverson

Jesus Christ is the divine Physician and Pharmacist, and his prescriptions are never out of balance.

Vance Havner

It is not your hold of Christ that saves, but his hold of you!

C. H. Spurgeon

The highest sin and the deepest despair together cannot baffle the power of Jesus.

C. H. Spurgeon

JESUS CHRIST — Teaching

The essential teachings of Jesus ... were literally revolutionary and will always remain so if they are taken seriously.

Herbert J. Miller

We shall never understand anything of our Lord's preaching and ministry unless we continually keep in mind what exactly and exclusively his errand was in this world.

Alexander Whyte

JESUS CHRIST —
Uniqueness

The strange thing about Jesus is that you can never get away from him.

Anon.

To search for wisdom apart from Christ means not simply foolhardiness but utter insanity.

John Calvin

In a civilization like ours, I feel that everyone has to come to terms with the claims of Jesus Christ upon his life, or else be guilty of inattention or of evading the question.

C. S. Lewis

The more you know about Christ, the less you will be satisfied with superficial views of him.

C. H. Spurgeon

JOY
(See also: Happiness)

It is a poor heart that never rejoices.

Anon.

True Christian joy is both a privilege and a duty.

Jerry Bridges

There is nothing in afflictions which ought to disturb our joy.

John Calvin

Joy is the gigantic secret of the Christian.

G. K. Chesterton

Laughter adds richness, texture and colour to otherwise ordinary days. It is a gift, a choice, a discipline and an art.

Tim Hansel

The joy of the Lord is not to be confused with the religious levity that has no root or depth.

Vance Havner

The joy of the Christian is a holy joy; the happiness of the Christian is a serious happiness.

D. Martyn Lloyd-Jones

Great joys, like griefs, are silent.

Shackerley Marmion

Laughter is the music of life.

William Osler

Joy is a condition that is experienced, but it is more than a feeling; it is, primarily, a state of mind.

J. I. Packer

Joy is at the heart of satisfied living.

J. I. Packer

Joy is not an accident of temperament or an unpredictable providence; joy is a matter of choice.

J. I. Packer

The secret of joy for believers lies in the fine art of Christian thinking.

J. I. Packer

The word 'joy' is too great and grand to be confused with the superficial things we call happiness.

Kirby Page

Next to Christ I have one joy, to preach Christ my Lord.

Samuel Rutherford

Joy is delight at God's grace which enables us to endure our trials.

George Seevers

Nothing gives believers more joy than to see God glorified.

R. C. Sproul

Better to have a Christian's days of sorrows than a wordling's joys.

C. H. Spurgeon

Joy in God is the happiest of all joys.

C. H. Spurgeon

Sorrow for sin should be the keenest sorrow; joy in the Lord should be the loftiest joy.

C. H. Spurgeon

The greatest joy of a Christian is to give joy to Christ.

C. H. Spurgeon

We never better enjoy ourselves than when we most enjoy God.

Benjamin Whichcote

JUDGEMENT
(See also: Destiny; Eternity; Heaven; Hell)

We shall stand before the judgement seat of Christ on the basis of our performance, not our profession.

We will go past the judgement seat of Christ in single file.

God does not pay weekly, but he pays at the end.

Anon.

Nothing has contributed more powerfully to wean me from all that held me down to earth than the thought, constantly dwelt upon, of death and of the last judgement.

Augustine

There is nothing that tends more to check a foolish eagerness for display than to reflect that we have to deal with God.

John Calvin

Man cannot cover what God would reveal.

Thomas Campbell

He whose throne is built on justice and righteousness will see that righteousness prevails. That is why sin must, and will, be punished.

John C. Chapman

Secular sanctions do not work. Morality needs the divine sanction of a judgement day.

Gordon H. Clark

As the king of terrors leaves us, so the day of terror will find us.

John Mason

We must fall into the arms of Christ or into the flames of hell.

John Mason

God will be glorified in the punishment of sin as well as in the reward of obedience.

Thomas V. Moore

God's will is done no less in the condemnation of unbelievers than in the salvation of those who put faith in the Lord Jesus.

J. I. Packer

The coming day of judgement is a doctrine that has been abused, misunderstood and often used to manipulate people. But correctly understood in the context of God's character and justice, it is a doctrine full of comfort for Christians.

Frank Retief

There are simply too many atrocities in the history of our world for there to be no day of judgement.

Frank Retief

There will be no possibility of standing before Christ but by standing in Christ.

William Secker

If you are not seeking the Lord, judgement is at your heels.

C. H. Spurgeon

It is shocking to reflect that a change in the weather has more effect on some men's lives than the dread alternative of heaven or hell.

C. H. Spurgeon

JUSTICE

Without justice, what are kingdoms but great banditries?
Augustine

When we speak of justice in the
biblical sense we ... are talking
about meeting need wherever it
exists and particularly where it
exists most helplessly.
Jay Poppinga

Belief in a just God is not optional.
John Rowland

JUSTIFICATION
(See also: Faith — and Deeds;
Holiness — and Justification)

Justification by faith is the
hinge on which all true religion
turns.
John Calvin

The scriptural doctrine of
justification by faith alone,
without any manner of
goodness or excellency of
ours, does in no wise diminish
either the necessity or benefit
of a sincere evangelical
obedience.
Jonathan Edwards

When God justifies the ungodly, he does not declare that
the sinner is innocent, but that
satisfaction for his sins has
been made, and that, as a believer in the Lord Jesus Christ,
he has a title to eternal life — a
title which is founded in justice.
Ernest F. Kevan

Evangelical obedience is fully
a condition of justification but
not a cause of justification.
Sam Logan

A Christian man is free from all
things; he needs no works in
order to be justified and saved,
but receives these gifts in abundance from his faith alone.
Martin Luther

I have preached justification by
faith so often, and I feel sometimes that you are so slow to
receive it that I could almost
take the Bible and bang it about
your heads.
Martin Luther

We may rest assured that we
are in the domain of error if we
in any way divorce justification and sanctification.
William S. Plumer

177

KINDNESS

(See also: Love for others; Mercy to others)

Speak your kind words soon, for you never know how soon it will be too late.

Anon.

If you're naturally kind you attract a lot of people you don't like.

William Feather

As perfume to the flower, so is kindness to speech.

Katherine Francke

A part of kindness consists in loving people more than they deserve.

Joseph Joubert

Be kind; everyone you meet is fighting a hard battle.

Ian MacLaren

Constant kindness can accomplish much. As the sun makes ice melt, kindness causes misunderstanding, mistrust and hostility to evaporate.

Albert Schweitzer

Kindness is a hard thing to give away. It keeps coming back to the giver.

Ralph Scott

KINGDOM OF GOD

The throne of God outlives the dissolution of the world.

Stephen Charnock

The principles of the kingdom of God cannot be woven by unregenerated men into the pattern of our pagan society. The blueprints of the age to come cannot be forced upon this present world.

Vance Havner

He who is the King of the kingdom of heaven is at the same time the Father of its citizens.

William Hendriksen

The kingdom of God is not a value system.

Donald MacLeod

Everyone wants the kingdom of God, but few want it first.

Charles L. Venable

KNOWLEDGE

(See also: Education; Mind; Reason)

Knowledge fills a large brain; it merely inflates a small one.

Anon.

It is not good to know more unless we do more with what we already know.

R. K. Bergethon

Knowledge of nature and atheism are incompatible. To know nature is to know that there must be a God.

Edward G. Bulwer-Lytton

All knowledge must come from him who made us in his image.

Edmund P. Clowney

Knowledge cannot save us, but we cannot be saved without knowledge.

John Donne

However paradoxical it seems to our natural minds, it is one of the facts of spiritual reality that practical Christian living is based on understanding and knowledge.

Sinclair Ferguson

Because some things do not make sense to us now does not mean they will never make sense.

Vance Havner

It is debatable which is causing us more harm — hot-headed ignorance or cold-hearted intellectualism.

Vance Havner

Things which don't make sense to our ordinary reasoning can make sense to our spiritual understanding.

Vance Havner

One of the things that distinguishes man from the other animals is that he wants to know things, wants to find out what reality is like, simply for the sake of knowing.

C. S. Lewis

The more I advance, the more clearly I perceive that the greatest human knowledge amounts to a more pompous proof of our ignorance, by showing us how little we know about anything.

John Newton

Not only do we know God through Jesus Christ, we only know ourselves through Jesus Christ.

Blaise Pascal

Knowledge is indispensable to Christian life and service ... Knowledge is given us to be used, to lead us to higher worship, greater faith, deeper holiness, better service.

John R. W. Stott

The natural man must know in order to believe; the spiritual man must believe in order to know.

A. W. Tozer

All human knowledge is only fragmentary. All of us who call ourselves students of nature possess only portions of natural science.

Rudolph Virchow

The knowledge of which we make no use will only serve to condemn us.

Thomas Wilson

KNOWLEDGE OF GOD

(See also: Revelation)

Who has God has all; who has him not has less than nothing.

Anon.

That knowledge of God that does not produce a love to him and a desire to be like him is not true knowledge.

Esther Burr

The true knowledge of God corresponds to what faith discovers in the written Word.

John Calvin

Faith is not on this side of knowledge but beyond it.

John Donne

Everything in the Christian life depends upon an adequate understanding of who God is.

Ronald Dunn

If we seek God for our own good and profit, we are not seeking God.

Meister Eckhart

The recognition of who God is is a lifelong process.

Elizabeth Elliot

Knowing God is your single greatest privilege as a Christian.

Sinclair Ferguson

There is no such thing as genuine knowledge of God that does not show itself in obedience to his Word and will.

Sinclair Ferguson

When you come to knowing God, the initiative lies on his side. If he does not show himself, nothing you can do will enable you to find him.

C. S. Lewis

If we want to know God and to be blessed of God, we must start by worshipping him.

D. Martyn Lloyd-Jones

He that is made in the image of God must know him or be desolate.

George MacDonald

What a vast difference there is between knowing God and loving him!

Blaise Pascal

The larger the God we know, the larger will be our faith. The secret of power in our lives is to know God and expect great things from him.

A. B. Simpson

If you wish to know God you must know his Word.

C. H. Spurgeon

The knowledge of God is the great hope of sinners.

C. H. Spurgeon

Our greatest claim to nobility is our created capacity to know God, to be in personal relationship with him, to love him and to worship him. Indeed, we are most truly human when we are on our knees before our Creator.

John R. W. Stott

God is never found accidentally.

A. W. Tozer

The Christian is strong or weak depending upon how closely he has cultivated the knowledge of God.

A. W. Tozer

The heart that knows God can find God anywhere.

A. W. Tozer

The wisest person in the world is the person who knows the most about God.

A. W. Tozer

To know God is at once the easiest and the most difficult thing in the world.

A. W. Tozer

We can never know who or what we are till we know at least something of what God is.

A. W. Tozer

We can seek God and find him! God is knowable, touchable, hearable, seeable, with the mind, the hands, the ears and the eyes of the inner man.

A. W. Tozer

The Christian is a God-explorer.

Tom Wells

LAW OF GOD

Those who go against the grain of God's laws shouldn't complain when they get splinters.

Anon.

Love is not perfected, except as the fulfilling of the law.
Theodore Beza

Without law, love is blind.
Samuel Bolton

Those only are worthy students of the law who come to it with a cheerful mind, and are so delighted with its instruction as to account nothing more desirable or delicious than to make progress therein.
John Calvin

Law and love have no quarrel. The conflict arises between law and grace as a way of salvation.
Walter J. Chantry

Law makes love practical. Love which is unexpressed will die.
Walter J. Chantry

Love makes the law enjoyable. Anyone who loves God delights in keeping his precepts.
Walter J. Chantry

The cross means nothing apart from the law.
Walter J. Chantry

The law and the gospel are allies, not enemies.
Walter J. Chantry

We cannot understand the Ten Commandments apart from Jesus Christ. If we view them as a list of 'don'ts' from which we may infer a corresponding list of 'dos', we forget the Lord who spoke the words from Sinai and the context in which he spoke them. God's commandments call his people to acknowledge him as their Saviour and Lord.
Edmund P. Clowney

All the decrees of God are harmonious.
Jonathan Edwards

We have not learned the commandments until we have learned to do them.
Vance Havner

If God had wanted us to have a permissive society he would have given us the Ten Suggestions instead of the Ten Commandments.
M. M. Hershman

The Ten Commandments are not a set of dos and don'ts; rather, for the Christian, they are rules for thankful living.
Simon J. Kistemaker

The law was not meant to be praised, it was meant to be practised.
D. Martyn Lloyd-Jones

The gospel does not abrogate God's law, but it makes men love it with all their hearts.

J. Gresham Machen

The law tells me how crooked I am. Grace comes along and straightens me out.

D. L. Moody

The law of God is the royal law of liberty, and liberty consists in being captive to the Word and law of God. All other liberty is not liberty but the thraldom of servitude to sin.

John Murray

Law is needed as love's eyes; love is needed as law's heartbeat. Law without love is Pharisaism; love without law is antinomianism.

J. I. Packer

Law and order are infinitely important because they are the expression of the character of God.

James Philip

The law of God is no other than a transcript of his most holy mind, and ... whoever loves one must love the other.

Thomas Robinson

I cannot find a syllable in [the Apostle's] writings which teach that any one of the Ten Commandments is done away ... I believe that the coming of Christ's gospel did not alter the position of the Ten Commandments one hair's breadth.

J. C. Ryle

The law is meant to lead the sinner to faith in Christ by showing the impossibility of any other way.

C. H. Spurgeon

The law stirs the mud at the bottom of the pool and proves how foul the waters are.

C. H. Spurgeon

There is no healing a man till the law has wounded him, no making him alive till the law has slain him.

C. H. Spurgeon

To convince and condemn is all the law can do.

C. H. Spurgeon

Keep close to the law if thou wilt keep close to Christ.

John Wesley

The commands of God are all designed to make us more happy than we can possibly be without them.

Thomas Wilson

LEADERSHIP

A bad servant will not make a good master.

Anon.

A leader has been defined as one who knows the way, goes the way and shows the way.

Anon.

The pursuit of power can separate the most resolute of Christians from the true nature of Christian leadership.

Charles Colson

Leadership is a serving relationship that has the effect of facilitating human development.

Ted Ward

LEGALISM

Legalism is always unloving.

Robert M. Horn

Legalism is man's misuse of God's law.

Robert M. Horn

Legalism is self-righteousness. It is the belief that God is satisfied with our attempt to obey a moral code.

Erwin W. Lutzer

LIBERALISM

Ecumenical advocates appear to have forgotten that the more important question to be asked today is not what will fill the churches but what emptied them in the first place ... When the critics emptied the Bible of its meaning they emptied the churches of their members.

Brian H. Edwards

This is exactly where a liberal attitude to the Bible leads us: there is no final authority, no reliable words of Christ, no test by which we shall be judged, and nothing to obey.

Brian H. Edwards

Many modern critics are to the Word of God what blow-flies are to the food of men: they cannot do any good, and unless relentlessly driven away they do great harm.

C. H. Spurgeon

LIBERTY

No man has a right to do as he pleases unless he pleases to do right.

Anon.

The modern cry 'Less creed and more liberty' is a degeneration from the vertebrate to the jellyfish.

B. H. Carroll

True freedom is not liberty to do as you want. That is licence, or anarchy. True freedom is the liberty to do as you *ought*.

Roy Clements

This is liberty: to know that God alone matters.

Donald Haukey

Freedom comes by filling your mind with God's thoughts.

Erwin W. Lutzer

The only perfect freedom is serving God.

Malcolm Muggeridge

We find freedom when we find God; we lose it when we lose him.

Paul Sherer

It is a positive and very hurtful sin to magnify liberty at the expense of doctrine.

Walter Shurden

The only freedom that man ever has is when he becomes a slave to Jesus Christ.

R. C. Sproul

The important thing about a man is not where he goes when he is compelled to go, but where he goes when he is free to go where he will.

A. W. Tozer

We are free to choose, but not free to choose the consequences of our choice, for those are determined by the eternal purpose and laws of God.

Spiros Zodhiates

LIFE

Life is a one-way street.

Bernard Berenson

Live your life and forget your age.

Frank Bering

Life is but a day at most.

Robert Burns

One life — a little gleam of time between two eternities.

Thomas Carlyle

Life is not measured by length but by depth. Birthdays tell us how long we have been on the road, not how far we have travelled.

Vance Havner

Life is only lived wisely to the extent that it is spent in preparation for the eternity which follows.

Dave Hunt

The most important thing in life is to live your life for something more important than your life.

William James

The end of life is not to be happy, nor to achieve pleasure and avoid pain, but to do the will of God, come what may.

Martin Luther King

Actually it seems to me that one can hardly say anything either bad enough or good enough about life.

C. S. Lewis

The longest life is a lingering death.

John Mason

One can live on less when he has more to live for.

S. S. McKenny

Let God have your life; he can do more with it than you can.

D. L. Moody

The seven ages of man: spills, drills, thrills, bills, ills, pills, wills.

Richard J. Needham

We are here to add what we can to life, not to get what we can from it.

William Osler

For the Christian, all of life is sacred.

Paul B. Smith

The meaning of earthly existence is not, as we have grown used to thinking, in prosperity, but in the development of the soul.

Alexandr Solzhenitsyn

We should employ our passions in the service of life, not spend life in the service of our passions.

Richard Steele

Let us endeavour so to live that when we come to die even the undertaker will be sorry.

Mark Twain

No one can live well until they can die well.

David Watson

O Lord, let me not live to be useless!

John Wesley

There is nothing that arises more spontaneously from man's nature than the question about life's meaning.

Rheinallt Nantlais Williams

Life is the childhood of our immortality.

Johann Wolfgang

LITERATURE

The oldest books in the world are still only just out to those who have not read them.

Samuel Butler

Next to acquiring good friends, the best acquisition is that of a good book.

C. C. Colton

The worst thing about new books is that they keep us from reading the old ones.

Joseph Joubert

You really lose a lot by never reading books again.

C. S. Lewis

Nothing substitutes for what can be found when we master books.

Gordon MacDonald

I divide all readers into two classes: those who read to remember and those who read to forget.

Willia Lyons Phelps

The printed page never flinches, it never shows cowardice; it is never tempted to compromise. The printed page never gets tired; it never gets disheartened.

Ernest C. Reisinger

The printed page travels cheaply — you can be a missionary for the price of a stamp.

Ernest C. Reisinger

Everything in this modern world is somehow inexplicably geared to inducing sleep in our souls ... This is one reason why the modern Christian must keep up his spiritual and theological reading. We need to read for dear life.

Maurice Roberts

A man may usually be known by the books he reads as well as by the company he keeps.

Samuel Smiles

Reading is to the mind what exercise is to the body.

Richard Steele

Books are the treasured wealth of the world, the fit inheritance of generations and actions.

Henry David Thoreau

The things you read will fashion you by slowly conditioning your mind.

A. W. Tozer

The man who does not read good books has no advantage over the man who cannot read at all.

Mark Twain

The value of a book is not determined by its cost but by its use.

Jerry Walker

The most effective political and religious movements have always known the power of the printed page. What men think is largely determined by what they read.

David Watson

LONELINESS

There is none more lonely than the man who loves only himself.

Abraham Ibn Esra

Loneliness is inner emptiness. Solitude is inner fulfilment.

Richard Foster

One of the worst things about loneliness is that you can't run away from it.

Vance Havner

LORD'S DAY

Sunday clears away the rust of the whole week.

Joseph Addison

In the absence of any divine instruction to the contrary, we may assume that the fourth commandment is still binding on us.

Gleason Archer

He keeps the Sunday badly who does no good works. Rest from bad works ought to be perpetual.

Augustine

God, by giving the sabbath, has given fifty-two springs in every year.

Samuel Taylor Coleridge

The law of the sabbath is still binding on us today.

Matthew Henry

A well-spent sabbath we feel to be a day of heaven upon earth ... we love to rise early on that morning, and to sit up late, that we may have a long day with God.

Robert Murray M'Cheyne

If the sabbath is the Lord's Day, it ought to be suffused with the joy derived from and correspondent with the resurrection joy of the Lord.

John Murray

As a rule there is a general flight of steps down from 'no sabbath' to 'no God'.

J. C. Ryle

Love to our heavenly Father is seen by loving his day.

Thomas Watson

The commandment of keeping the sabbath was not abrogated with the ceremonial law, but is purely moral, and the observation of it is to be continued to the end of the world.

Thomas Watson

Blessed be God for the day of rest and religious occupation wherein earthly things assume their true size.

William Wilberforce

LOVE FOR CHRIST

(See also: Communion with Christ; Meditation; Prayer)

If we love Christ our devotion will not remain a secret.

Anon.

True love for Christ will mean hatred of sin.

John Benton

If we love Christ much, surely we shall trust him much.

Thomas Brooks

If you claim to love Christ and yet are living an unholy life, there is only one thing to say about you. You are a bare-faced liar!

D. Martyn Lloyd-Jones

You must love Christ with a sincere love, with a new love, with an entire love, with a superlative love; and you must love him for himself, and not anything you get from him.

James Renwick

A man who loves his wife will love her letters and her photographs because they speak to him of her. So if we love the Lord Jesus, we shall love the Bible because it speaks to us of him.

John R. W. Stott

No man can be a true disciple of Christ who gives his friends a preference to Christ in the affections of his heart.

Kennedy Sunkuthu

LOVE FOR GOD
(See also: Communion with God; Meditation; Prayer)

It is but right that our hearts should be on God, when the heart of God is so much on us.
Richard Baxter

Love for God is not love for him at all unless it expresses itself in a practical way.
John Benton

We ought to love our Maker for his own sake, without either hope of good or fear of pain.
Miguel de Cervantes

A true love to God must begin with a delight in his holiness, and not with a delight in any other attribute.
Jonathan Edwards

O Jesus, Jesus, dearest Lord!
Forgive me if I say,
For very love, thy sacred name
A thousand times a day.
Frederick W. Faber

God cares not for phrases but for affections.
Joseph Hall

Christian love, either towards God or towards man, is an affair of the will.
C. S. Lewis

Every Christian would agree that a man's spiritual health is exactly proportional to his love for God.
C. S. Lewis

There is no better test of growth than that a man desires God because he is God.
D. Martyn Lloyd-Jones

Self-love may lead us to prayers, but love to God excites us to praises.
Thomas Manton

I ought to have loved God always. It is of his mere mercy that I love him now.
Handley C. G. Moule

What a vast difference there is between knowing God and loving him!
Blaise Pascal

The man who loves God is in an unassailable position.
J. B. Phillips

We must give our Lord our love or that love will go somewhere else. We are so created that we must love something or other.
C. H. Spurgeon

You may rest quite certain that if you love God it is a fruit, not a root.

C. H. Spurgeon

The great of this world are those who simply loved God more than others did.

A. W. Tozer

To adore God means we love him with all the powers within us.

A. W. Tozer

Our love of God will always be according to our knowledge of him and his perfections.

Daniel Wilson

LOVE FOR OTHERS — Definition

(See also: Kindness; Mercy to Others)

Love is not affectionate feeling, but a steady wish for the loved person's ultimate good as far as it can be obtained.

C. S. Lewis

LOVE FOR OTHERS — Importance

Faith and love must be inseparable companions. There is a necessary connection between them. Faith without love is no living grace, and love without faith is no saving grace.

Francis Burkitt

Whatever is devoid of love is of no account in the sight of God.

John Calvin

You can give without loving, but you cannot love without giving.

Amy Carmichael

There is no greater opportunity to influence our fellowman for Christ than to respond with love when we have been unmistakably wronged.

James C. Dobson

Our understanding of what it means to be human affects how we treat other people.

R. C. Sproul

LOVE FOR OTHERS — Measure

If my heart is right with God, every human being is my neighbour.

Oswald Chambers

Religion that does not glow with love is unsatisfactory.

Richard Glover

Love rules his kingdom without a sword.

> *Robert Herrick*

LOVE FOR OTHERS — Practical

Love never asks, 'How much must I do?', but 'How much can I do?'

> *Frederick Agar*

People will not care what you know until they know that you care.

> *Anon.*

Respect is what we owe; love is what we give.

> *Philip James Bailey*

Love rolls up its sleeves.

> *Robert Cook*

True love is always costly.

> *Billy Graham*

He who does not love sinners cannot pray aright for them.

> *C. H. Spurgeon*

LUST

Lust is like rot in the bones.

> *Anon.*

Lust and reason are enemies.

> *Solomon Ben Gabirol*

Lust is felt even by fleas and lice.

> *Martin Luther*

LUXURY

Many are so devoted to luxury in all their senses that their mind lies buried.

> *John Calvin*

Luxury is more deadly than any foe.

> *Juvenal*

On the soft bed of luxury most kingdoms have died.

> *Edward Young*

LYING
(See also: Dishonesty)

A clean glove often hides a dirty hand.

> *Anon.*

We lie loudest when we lie to ourselves.

> *Eric Hoffer*

Every liar is a child of the devil, and will be sent home to his father.

> *C. H. Spurgeon*

MALICE

Malice never spoke well.
William Camden

Malice has a strong memory.
Thomas Fuller

Nothing on earth consumes a man more quickly than resentment.
Friedrich Nietzsche

MAN — Dignity

Man is indeed lost, but that does not mean he is nothing.
Francis Schaeffer

Man's dignity is derived and dependent, not intrinsic.
R. C. Sproul

We are not autonomous czars over slime; we are vice-regents over a divine creation.
R. C. Sproul

Our greatest claim to nobility is our created capacity to know God, to be in personal relationship with him, to love him and to worship him. Indeed, we are most truly human when we are on our knees before our Creator.
John R. W. Stott

I am greater than the stars for I know that they are up there, and they do not know that I am down here.
William Temple

If this is God's world, there are no unimportant people.
George Thomas

MAN — a Failure

Our world is filled with self-absorbed, frightened, hollow people.
Charles Colson

I haven't any language weak enough to depict the weakness of my spiritual life. If I weakened it enough it would cease to be language at all. As when you try to turn the gas-ring a little lower still, it merely goes out.
C. S. Lewis

Never, never pin your whole faith on any human being; not if he is the best and wisest in the whole world. There are lots of nice things you can do with sand; but do not try building a house on it.
C. S. Lewis

The real trouble about fallen man is not the strength of his pleasure but the weakness of his reason.

C. S. Lewis

Man in sin is a pygmy fighting against Almighty God — like a fly pitting itself against atomic power!

D. Martyn Lloyd-Jones

The state of the world today is nothing but an appalling monument to human failure.

D. Martyn Lloyd-Jones

If God should call me into judgement before him, according to the strictness of his perfect law, for the best duty I ever performed, and for nothing else, I must be condemned as a transgressor; for when weighed in these exact balances, it would be found wanting.

Thomas Scott

The best of men are still men at their best.

C. H. Spurgeon

The weakness of man sets the stage for the display of God's strength.

Janice Wise

MAN — God's Creation and Concern

The incarnation of Christ is the clearest affirmation of the truth that man is created in the image of God.

Lawrence Adams

Godly self-respect is possible when we realize that we are created in the image of God, that we are accepted by God solely on the merits of Jesus Christ.

Jerry Bridges

We are here for God's designs, not for our own.

Oswald Chambers

Man is a creature, because he is made by God. But he is a unique creature, because he is made like God.

Edmund P. Clowney

Man can only find meaning for his existence in something outside himself.

Viktor Frankl

We have come from somewhere and are going somewhere. The great Architect of the universe never built a stairway that leads to nowhere.

Robert Milkman

Man can be truly understood only in the light of God and his purpose for mankind.

Bruce Milne

All men are by nature equal, made of the same earth by the same Creator, and however we deceive ourselves, as dear to God is the poor peasant as the mighty prince.

Plato

Man is heaven's masterpiece.

Francis Quarles

Immortal souls were not created for merely mortal ends.

C. H. Spurgeon

We human beings have both a unique dignity as creatures made in God's image and a unique depravity as sinners under his judgement.

John R. W. Stott

God is not greater for our being, nor would he be less if we did not exist. That we do exist is altogether of God's free determination, not by our desert nor by divine necessity.

A. W. Tozer

MAN — a Religious Being

Man does not have a soul, he is a soul.

James Barr

The idea of a Deity impressed upon the mind of man is indelible.

John Calvin

The soul is a never-ending sigh after God.

Theodore Christlieb

The human self was never created for any other purpose than to manifest the divine Self.

Norman P. Grubb

God designed the human machine to run on himself. He himself is the fuel our spirits were designed to burn, or the food our spirits were designed to feed on. There is no other.

C. S. Lewis

Our whole being by its very nature is one vast need: incomplete, preparatory, empty yet cluttered, crying out for him who can untie things that are now knotted together and tie up things that are still dangling loose.

C. S. Lewis

There can be no greater glory for man than to glorify God.

J. I. Packer

I could not bear to be an 'ignoramus' or an 'agnostic' about God! I must have a God. I cannot do without him.

C. H. Spurgeon

MAN — a Sinner
(See also: Depravity; Guilt; Sin; Sinful Nature)

By obeying the serpent, Adam and Eve made themselves the friends of Satan and the enemies of God.

Edmund P. Clowney

Man is God's natural enemy.

Jonathan Edwards

We are members of a spoiled species.

C. S. Lewis

Even if we never did anything wrong, we should still be sinners.

D. Martyn Lloyd-Jones

The natural man is always play-acting, always looking at himself and admiring himself.

D. Martyn Lloyd-Jones

The whole case of the Bible is that the trouble with man is not intellectual (in the mind) but moral (in the heart).

D. Martyn Lloyd-Jones

The world is beautiful, but has a disease called man.

Friedrich Nietzsche

Man is the greatest miracle and the greatest problem on this earth.

David Sarnoff

It is one of the axioms of theology that if a man be lost God must not be blamed for it; and it is also an axiom of theology that if a man be saved, God must have the glory for it.

C. H. Spurgeon

Man is a reeking mass of corruption.

C. H. Spurgeon

Man is a suicide. Our sin slays the race. We die because we have sinned. How this should make us hate sin!

C. H. Spurgeon

Man is the only animal that blushes — and the only animal that needs to!

Mark Twain

A wicked man may search the records of hell for his pedigree.
Thomas Watson

By nature we are strangers to God, swine not sons.
Thomas Watson

MARRIAGE
(See also: Family Life)

Marriage is a perpetual test of character.
Anon.

All the troubles men find in marriage they ought to impute to sin.
John Calvin

Marriage is a covenant consecrated by God.
John Calvin

It is not marriage that fails, it is people that fail.
Harry Emerson Fosdick

A successful marriage demands a divorce: a divorce from your own self-love.
Paul Frost

A pertinent question for millions would be: 'Is there a *home* in your house?'
Vance Havner

The cause of broken marriages is selfishness in one form or another.
Vance Havner

Anyone can build a house; we need the Lord for the creation of a home.
John Henry Jowett

The woman was made for the man, yet not as his slave-girl, but his queen.
Meredith Kline

It takes two to make a marriage a success and only one to make it a failure.
Herbert Samuel

MARTYRDOM
(See also: Persecution)

The martyr is made by his cause, not by his punishment.
John Calvin

If they are blessed who die in the Lord, are they not blessed who die for the Lord?
Thomas Watson

Never have any princes been so famous for their victories as the martyrs were for their sufferings.
Thomas Watson

The hypocrite makes faith a cloak; the martyr makes it a shield.
Thomas Watson

MATERIALISM
(See also: Money; Possessions; Prosperity; Riches; Wealth)

Materialism is suicidal.
Michael Griffiths

The more you have to live *for*, the less you need to live *on*. Those who make acquisition their goal never have enough.
Sydney Harris

Materialism, open or disguised, is the logical result of thinking that above and beyond this world there is nothing else.
Stephen Olford

The genius of modern civilization, if it is allowed to run its present course to perfection, will bring mankind to the point at which there is everything to live with and nothing to live for.
Maurice Roberts

Materialism is organized emptiness of the spirit.
Franz Werfel

MEANNESS

A miser is ever in want.
Anon.

Some people don't let the left hand know what the right hand is giving because they don't want to embarrass the right hand.
Anon.

When it comes to helping others some people stop at nothing.
Anon.

Many people will always be poor because they never give to the cause of God.
C. H. Spurgeon

The miser does no one any good, but he treats himself worst of all.
Publilius Syrus

MEDITATION
(See also: Communion with God; Love for God; Prayer)

Memorization is the first step to meditation.
Jerry Bridges

Continual meditation on the Word is not ineffectual ... God, by one and another promise, establishes our faith.

John Calvin

Merely having an open mind is nothing. The object of opening the mind, as of opening the mouth, is to shut it again on something solid.

G. K. Chesterton

Meditation is the soul's chewing.

William Grimshaw

Speed-reading may be a good thing, but it was never meant for the Bible. It takes calm, thoughtful, prayerful meditation on the Word to extract its deepest nourishment.

Vance Havner

When we are too busy to sharpen the axe, we are too busy.

Vance Havner

The mind grows by what it feeds on.

Josiah Holland

Meditation is a serious intention of the mind whereby we come to search out the truth and settle it effectively upon the heart.

Thomas Hooker

There is such a thing as sacred idleness.

George MacDonald

If it is the will of the Holy Ghost that we attend to the soul, certainly it is not his will that we neglect the mind.

Charles Malik

True contemplation is not a psychological trick but a theological grace.

Thomas Merton

Sustained imaginative reflection is, if I am not mistaken, so rare today that few of us understand its power to motivate, and are not ourselves motivated by it.

J. I. Packer

Meditation is the grand means of our growth in grace; without it, prayer itself is an empty service.

Charles Simeon

The heart is heated by meditation and cold truth is melted into passionate action.

Donald S. Whitney

MEEKNESS
(See also: Humility; Self-Crucifixion)

Meekness is a matter of grace, not genetics.

Meekness is having a teachable spirit.
> *Ronald Dunn*

Meekness is a jewel polished by grace.
> *Sinclair Ferguson*

The meek man is the one who has stood before God's judgement and abdicated all his supposed 'rights'. He has learned, in gratitude for God's grace, to submit himself to the Lord and to be gentle with sinners.
> *Sinclair Ferguson*

Meekness does not mean indolence.
> *D. Martyn Lloyd-Jones*

Meekness is compatible with great strength.
> *D. Martyn Lloyd-Jones*

Jesus was the very King of meekness.
> *A. W. Pink*

Meekness is the opposite of self-will towards God and of ill-will towards men.
> *A. W. Pink*

Meekness is the self-imposed restraint exercised by Christians so that Christ may be glorified in their lives.
> *Frank Retief*

Meekness is looking to yourself in the light of God's law.
> *George Seevers*

MEMORY

God gave us memories that we might have roses in December.
> *James M. Barrie*

Each man's memory is his private literature.
> *Aldous Huxley*

The memory should be a storehouse, not a lumber-room.
> *John Jewel*

MERCY FROM GOD
(See also: Forgiveness by God)

When all thy mercies, O my God,
My rising soul surveys,
Transported with the view, I'm lost
In wonder, love and praise.
> *Joseph Addison*

Sin's misery and God's mercy are beyond measure.
> *Anon.*

God leads us to eternal life not by our merits but according to his mercy.

Augustine

What a world this would be if God sat on a throne of justice only, and if no mercy were ever to be shown to men!

Albert Barnes

Remembrance of past mercies is a great stimulus to present faith.

Jerry Bridges

When we come to election, we see nothing but mercy on every side.

John Calvin

I have been a man of great sins, but he has been a God of great mercies, and now, through his mercies, I have a conscience as sound and quiet as if I had never sinned.

Donald Cargill

God giveth his wrath by weight, but his mercy without measure.

Thomas Fuller

If God dealt with people today as he did in the days of Ananias and Sapphira, every church would need a morgue in the basement.

Vance Havner

God's mercy is never given at the expense of his justice.

Gordon J. Keddie

No man acts with true wisdom till he fears God and hopes in his mercy.

William S. Plumer

Everything that comes from God to his children, it is a mercy.

Richard Sibbes

The God of the Bible is as severe as if he were unmerciful; and as just as if he were not gracious; and yet he is as gracious and as merciful as if he were not just.

C. H. Spurgeon

You never have to drag mercy out of Christ, as money from a miser.

C. H. Spurgeon

Every misery that I miss is a new mercy.

Izaac Walton

Every time you draw your breath you suck in mercy.

Thomas Watson

The tree of mercy will not drop its fruits unless shaken by the hand of prayer.

Thomas Watson

God of all mercy is a God unjust.

Edward Young

MERCY TO OTHERS
(See also: Forgiveness of Others;
Kindness; Love for Others)

In helping others we benefit
ourselves; we heal our own
wounds in binding up those of
others.

Ambrose

Nowhere do we imitate God
more than in showing mercy.

Albert Barnes

Mercy imitates God and disap-
points Satan.

Chrysostom

Our presence in a place of need
is more powerful than a thousand sermons.

Charles Colson

It will not bother me in the hour
of death to reflect that I have
been 'had for a sucker' by any
number of imposters; but it
would be a torment to know
that one had refused even one
person in need.

C. S. Lewis

MIND
(See also: Education; Knowledge;
Reason; Thoughts)

The head begins to swell when
the mind stops growing.

Anon.

If we have not quiet in our
minds, outward comfort will
do no more for us than a golden
slipper on a gouty foot.

John Bunyan

You can have such a open mind
that it is too porous to hold a
conviction.

George Crane

Despise an idle mind.

Jim Elliff

The quiet mind is richer than a
crown.

Robert Greene

The human mind is like an
umbrella — it functions best
when open.

Walter Gropius

A mind at leisure from itself
beats all rest cures.

Vance Havner

Rule your mind or it will rule
you.

Horace

The difference between world-liness and godliness is a re-newed mind.
Erwin W. Lutzer

The human mind without grace is a nest of wickedness swarm-ing with thoughts of evil.
William S. Plumer

One of the highest and noblest functions of man's mind is to listen to God's Word, and so to read his mind and think his thoughts after him.
John R. W. Stott

A guileless mind is a great treasure; it is worth any price.
A. W. Tozer

MIRACLES

God is not in a rut, unable to do anything new or different.

The Christian faith cannot stand without miracles.
E. H. Andrews

Miracles must never be sep-arated from the Word.
John Calvin

We marvel, not that Christ per-formed miracles, but rather that he performed so few. He who could have stormed the citadels of men with mighty battalions of angels let men spit upon him and crucify him.
Oswald Chambers

It is not safe to define a miracle as something which cannot be understood; for, at that rate, what can be understood?
Francis Champneys

It is absurd for Christians to constantly seek new demon-strations of God's power, to expect a miraculous answer to every need, from curing in-grown toenails to finding park-ing spaces; this only leads to faith in miracles rather than the Maker.
Charles Colson

A miracle is God doing what only God can do.
Ronald Dunn

Miracles, in both the Old and New Testaments, had only one main purpose, and that was to reveal God.
Brian H. Edwards

Some say that to believe the Bible miracles would mean in-tellectual suicide for them. If all who complain that way did commit such suicide, it would not be a major disaster!
Vance Havner

203

The average run-of-the-mill Christian today believes that God can do miracles, but few think he will in any given case.

Vance Havner

The Christian life itself is a miracle, and every phase of it ought to bear the mark of the supernatural.

Vance Havner

By definition, miracles must of course interrupt the usual course of nature; but if they are real they must, in the very act of doing so, assert all the more the unity and self-consistency of total reality at some deeper level.

C. S. Lewis

Do not attempt to water Christianity down. There must be no pretence that you can have it with the supernatural left out. So far as I can see Christianity is precisely the one religion from which the miraculous cannot be separated.

C. S. Lewis

I am in no way committed to the assertion that God has never worked miracles through and for pagans, or never permitted created supernatural beings to do so.

C. S. Lewis

The Christian story is precisely the story of one grand miracle, the Christian assertion being that what is beyond all space and time, what is uncreated, eternal, came into nature, into human nature, descended into his own universe, and rose again, bringing nature up with him. It is precisely one great miracle. If you take that away there is nothing specifically Christian left.

C. S. Lewis

The mind which asks for a non-miraculous Christianity is a mind in process of relapsing into mere 'religion'.

C. S. Lewis

The miracles in fact are a re-telling in small letters of the very same story which is written across the whole world in letters too large for some of us to see.

C. S. Lewis

Miracles are not meant to be understood, they are meant to be believed.

D. Martyn Lloyd-Jones

If the ministry of Jesus had been merely signs and wonders, it would have been sterile within a generation.

R. C. Lucas

The New Testament without the miracles would be far easier to believe. But the trouble is, would it be worth believing?
J. Gresham Machen

We are not to require 'signs', but we are to regard signs. They are not given to produce faith, but to inform faith.
Ian MacPherson

We may define a miracle, then, as an event brought about by the immediate agency of God, in contrast with his ordinary method of working.
H. D. McDonald

The attempt to deny miracles in principle can succeed only by assuming the conclusion as one of the premises.
Bruce Milne

The only way we can know whether an event can occur is to see whether in fact it has occurred. The problem of 'miracles', then, must be solved in the realm of historical investigation, not in the realm of philosophical speculation.
John W. Montgomery

Jesus' miracles are decisive evidence for all time of who he is and what power he has.
J. I. Packer

A miracle would not be a miracle if it could be explained!
J. C. Ryle

The greatest of all miracles is the salvation of a soul.
C. H. Spurgeon

Bare inexplicableness cannot be accepted as the sufficient criterion of the miraculous.
Benjamin B. Warfield

No event can be really miraculous which has implications inconsistent with fundamental religious truth.
Benjamin B. Warfield

The connection of alleged miracles with erroneous doctrine invalidates their claim to be genuine works of God.
Benjamin B. Warfield

We believe in a wonder-working God, but not in a wonder-working church.
Benjamin B. Warfield

If God exists, miracles are not merely logically possible, but really and genuinely possible at every moment.
Merald Westphal

MISTAKES

The person who never makes a mistake never makes anything.
Anon.

We must never overlook the untold benefits that can be derived from mistakes. A person should never hesitate to own he has been in the wrong, which is but saying in other words that he is wiser today than he was yesterday, because of his mistake.
Anon.

The only real mistake is the one from which we learn nothing.
John Powell

Many people would learn from their mistakes if they weren't so busy denying them.
Harold J. Smith

Our mistakes won't irreparably damage our lives unless we let them.
James Sweaney

MODESTY

Nothing is more amiable than true modesty, and nothing more contemptible than the false. The one guards virtue, the other betrays it.
Joseph Addison

Let us learn to lay upon ourselves the restraint of modesty.
John Calvin

MONEY

(See also: Materialism; Possessions; Prosperity; Riches; Wealth)

Money is in some respects like fire; it is a very excellent servant, but a terrible master.
P. T. Barnum

Money will buy a pretty good dog, but it won't buy the wag of his tail.
Josh Billings

We cannot serve God and mammon, for as the thoughts of the one rise up, the other goes down.
Donald Cargill

In the battle of faith, money is usually the last stronghold to fall.
Ronald Dunn

If a person gets his attitude towards money straight, it will help straighten out almost every other area in his life.
Billy Graham

Few things eat into the soul as devastatingly as the love of money.
James Philip

206

MORALITY

(See also: Ethics; Goodness; Virtue)

Give ten thoughts to the question what will God think of it, before one to what men will think of it.

J. W. Alexander

A breakdown in moral order leads to a breakdown in civil order.

Frederick Catherwood

Morality is not only correct conduct on the outside, but correct thinking within where only God can see.

Oswald Chambers

Morality without sanctions is a morality without obligations.

Gordon H. Clark

If Christ is Lord of all, Christians must recapture their sense of moral outrage.

Charles Colson

The moment you say that one set of moral ideas can be better than another, you are, in fact, measuring them both by a standard ... comparing them both with some Real Morality, admitting that there is such a thing.

C. S. Lewis

Morality is always higher than law.

Alexandr Solzhenitsyn

The moral character of the soul depends upon its central object.

David Thomas

A man may be wonderfully moralized, yet but a tame devil.

Thomas Watson

Morality may damn as well as vice. A vessel may be sunk with gold as well as with dung.

Thomas Watson

Morality does not make a Christian, yet no man can be a Christian without it.

Thomas Wilson

MOTIVE

Man sees your action, but God your motives.

Thomas à Kempis

God considers not the action, but the spirit of the action.

Peter Abelard

Devotion to God is the only acceptable motive for actions that are pleasing to God.

Jerry Bridges

To be absolutely honest, I can't ever be certain what motivates me. Jeremiah tells us that nothing is more deceitful than the human heart — and he's right.

Charles Colson

I cannot, by direct moral effort, give myself new motives. After the first few steps in the Christian life we realize that everything which really needs to be done in our souls can be done only by God.

C. S. Lewis

'Actions speak louder than words', but, with God, motives speak louder than either.

Arthur Neil

A good end cannot sanctify evil means; nor must we ever do evil that good may come of it.

William Penn

We should often be ashamed of our best actions were the world witness to the motives which produce them.

François Rochefoucauld

It is not what a man does that determines whether his work is sacred or secular, it is why he does it.

A. W. Tozer

MURMURING

A grouch always looks as if he were weaned on a pickle.

Anon.

Discontent generally arises more from our desires than from our wants.

Anon.

Murmuring is a time-destroying sin.

Thomas Brooks

If we growl all day we shouldn't be surprised if we end up dog tired at night!

Vance Havner

One hour in heaven and we shall be ashamed we ever grumbled.

Vance Havner

Complaining about our lot in life might seem quite innocent in itself, but God takes it personally.

Erwin W. Lutzer

God's people may groan, but they may not grumble.

C. H. Spurgeon

Ten minutes' praying is better than a year's murmuring.

C. H. Spurgeon

MYSTERY

A religion that is small enough for our understanding is not great enough for our need.
Arthur J. Balfour

With God there are mysteries but no mistakes.
Michael Griffiths

All the scriptural imagery (harps, crowns, gold, etc.) is, of course, a merely symbolic attempt to express the inexpressible ... People who take these symbols literally might as well think that when Christ told us to be like doves, he meant that we were to lay eggs.
C. S. Lewis

Reason's last step is the recognition that there are an infinite number of things that are beyond it.
Blaise Pascal

Even though there is no final answer to the mystery of evil prospering in the world, the overriding consideration that more than offsets everything else is God's unchanging love and care.
James Philip

NATURE
(See also: Creation; Evolution)

Knowledge of nature and atheism are incompatible. To know nature is to know that there must be a God.
Edward G. Bulwer-Lytton

All the powers of nature prove the greatness of the God of nature, from whom they are derived and on whom they depend.
Matthew Henry

The world is charged with the grandeur of God.
Gerard Manley Hopkins

There are no laws of nature, only customs of God.
C. Kingsley

Because God created the natural — invented it out of his love and artistry — it demands our reverence.
C. S. Lewis

We find ourselves in a world of transporting pleasures, ravishing beauties, and tantalizing possibilities, but all constantly being destroyed, all coming to nothing. Nature has all the air of a good thing spoiled.
C. S. Lewis

The universe is centred on neither the earth nor the sun. It is centred on God.

Alfred Noyes

Everywhere I find the signature, the autograph of God.

Joseph Parker

Nature has some perfections in order to show that she is the image of God, and some defects to show that she is only his image.

Blaise Pascal

If a watch proves the existence of a watchmaker but the universe does not prove the existence of a great architect, then I consent to be called a fool.

François M. Voltaire

NEGLIGENCE
(See also: Sin of Omission)

We can easily lose by negligence what we have laboured to acquire by grace.

Thomas à Kempis

Neglect destroys men.

C. H. Spurgeon

No talent can survive the blight of neglect.

Edgar A. Whitney

OBEDIENCE — Blessing

In the mysterious chemistry of God's mercy, a man's very obedience is made a blessing to him.

It is not wrong to feel good about ourselves, but this should be a by-product of obedience which is motivated by a desire to please God.

Jerry Bridges

It is only by obedience that we understand the teaching of God.

Oswald Chambers

The Christian life begins with obedience, depends on obedience, and results in obedience.

Charles Colson

Obedience is the key that unlocks the door to every profound spiritual experience.

Dorothy Kerin

Obedience is the road to freedom.

C. S. Lewis

Obedience is not only the touchstone of all progress in the Christian life, it is our only safe course.

James Philip

To obey God's will is to find the fulfilment of our lives.

David Watson

OBEDIENCE — Characteristics

Obedience to God should never be conditioned by our convenience of comfort.

Wicked men obey from fear; good men from love.

Aristotle

The beginning and perfection of lawful worship is readiness to obey.

John Calvin

When God designs to forgive us he changes our hearts and turns us to obedience by his Spirit.

John Calvin

Only when confidence wavers does obedience hesitate.

Ronald Dunn

Obedience is submitting to the lover of our souls.

Ken Myers

OBEDIENCE — Importance

Becoming a Christian does not alter the fact that I am still a created being under obligation to obey.

Richard Alderson

Only he who believes is obedient; only he who is obedient believes.

Dietrich Bonhoeffer

God does not give us his power so that we might feel good about ourselves; he gives us his power so that we can obey him for his sake, for his glory.

Jerry Bridges

No man will actually obey God but he who loves him.

John Calvin

Obedience is the end of our calling.

John Calvin

The basis of true religion is obedience.

John Calvin

Obedience is what we were made for.

Roy Clements

211

It is not what we do that matters, but what a sovereign God chooses to do through us. God doesn't want our success; he wants us. He doesn't demand our achievements; he demands our obedience.

Charles Colson

What God wants from his people is obedience, no matter what the circumstances, no matter how unknown the outcome.

Charles Colson

To obey is the proper office of a rational soul.

Michel E. de Montaigne

The scriptural doctrine of justification by faith alone, without any manner of goodness or excellency of ours, does in no wise diminish either the necessity or benefit of a sincere evangelical obedience.

Jonathan Edwards

There is no such thing as genuine knowledge of God that does not show itself in obedience to his Word and will.

Sinclair Ferguson

One of the reasons people find it hard to be obedient to the commands of Christ is that they are uncomfortable taking orders from a stranger.

Gary Gulbranson

God uses broken things: broken soil and broken clouds to produce rain; broken grain to produce bread; broken bread to feed our bodies. He wants our stubbornness broken into humble obedience.

Vance Havner

To know God is to know that our obedience is due to him.

C. S. Lewis

Evangelical obedience is fully a condition of justification but not a cause of justification.

Sam Logan

God's commands carry no RSVP — man indeed has the *power* to refuse the divine summons, but not the *right*.

R. C. Sproul

Though the heavens should fall through our doing right, we are not to sin in order to keep them up.

C. H. Spurgeon

It is the simplest things that are most difficult to understand and accept, and one of those which seems in my experience to have been most difficult for people to understand and accept has been the fact that the Lord demands of his servants, each and every one of them, to listen to him only and obey his will implicitly, irrespective of what it costs.

William Still

True faith commits us to obedience.

A. W. Tozer

OLD AGE

Age: the only thing that comes to us without effort.

Anon.

We Christians are miserable indeed if we grow old in making no improvement.

John Calvin

The passions of the young are vices in the old.

Joseph Joubert

If you will be cherished when you are old, be courteous while you are young.

John Lyly

There is more felicity on the far side of baldness than young men can possibly imagine.

Logan Pearsall Smith

OPINION

All too often we think we are standing on principle when in reality we may be only insisting on our opinion.

Jerry Bridges

Opinion is a mean between knowledge and ignorance.

Plato

OPPORTUNITIES

The reason some people don't recognize opportunity is that it usually comes disguised as hard work.

Anon.

A wise man will make more opportunities than he finds.

Francis Bacon

Small opportunities are often the beginning of great enterprises.

Demosthenes

PAIN
(See also: Sickness; Suffering; Trials)

We cannot learn without pain.

Aristotle

213

Pain can either make us better or bitter.

Tim Hansel

I'd rather hobble into heaven than walk into hell!

D. Martyn Lloyd-Jones

God uses chronic pain and weakness, along with other afflictions, as his chisel for sculpting our lives.

J. I. Packer

The weaker we feel, the harder we lean. And the harder we lean, the stronger we grow spiritually, even while our bodies waste away.

J. I. Packer

Pain makes man think.

John Patrick

I am trying, if I can, to find a joy in rheumatism, but I cannot get up to it yet. I have found a joy when it is over — I can reach that length — and I can and do bless God for any good result that may come of it; but when the pain is on me, it is difficult to be joyous about it, and so I conclude that my sanctification is very incomplete.

C. H. Spurgeon

Those who wear the shoe know best where it pinches.

C. H. Spurgeon

If I ever wonder about the appropriate 'spiritual' response to pain and suffering, I can note how Jesus responded to his own: with fear and trembling, with loud cries and tears.

Philip Yancey

PASSION
(See also: Anger; Hatred; Zeal)

When your temper boils over, you are usually in hot water.

Anon.

Fanaticism is the false fire of an overheated mind.

William Cowper

A frenzy is worse than a fever.

Thomas Watson

Passion unmans a man.

Thomas Watson

PATIENCE

A delay is better than a disaster.

Anon.

A handful of patience is worth more than a bushel of brains.

Anon.

Patience is the companion of wisdom.

Augustine

Patience achieves more than force.

Edmund Burke

Hope is the foundation of patience.

John Calvin

Patience is the fruit and proof of faith.

John Calvin

Where there is no patience, there is not even a spark of faith.

John Calvin

Never cut what you can untie.

Joseph Joubert

Teach us, O Lord, the discipline of patience, for to wait is often harder than to work.

Peter Marshall

The times we find ourselves having to wait on others may be the perfect opportunities to train ourselves to wait on the Lord.

Joni Eareckson Tada

The deep and due consideration of the infinite patience of God towards us will greatly promote the patience of *our* spirits, and transform us into the same image.

John Trapp

A Christian without patience is like a soldier without arms.

Thomas Watson

Patience makes a Christian invincible.

Thomas Watson

PEACE

Great tranquillity of heart is his who cares for neither praise nor blame.

Thomas à Kempis

Peace rules the day when Christ rules the mind.

Anon.

Where there is peace, God is.

Anon.

Peace is to the soul what health is to the body: a sign of balance and order.

Guy Appéré

Peace is a free gift and flows from the pure mercy of God.

John Calvin

Peace is not to be purchased by the sacrifice of truth.

John Calvin

Peace is not packaged in pills.

Vance Havner

God is able to give us peace when our lives are going to pieces.

James F. Lewis

Five great enemies to peace: greed, ambition, envy, anger and pride.

Petrarch

If you are to have peace with God there must be war with Satan.

C. H. Spurgeon

We must not be so in love with the golden crown of peace as to pluck off the jewels of truth.

Thomas Watson

The fewer the desires, the more peace.

Joseph Wilson

PENITENCE

(See also: Confession; Contrition; Conviction of Sin; Repentance)

He truly bewails the sins he has committed who never commits the sins he has bewailed.

Augustine

Men never entertain a real hatred towards sin unless God illuminates their minds and changes their hearts.

John Calvin

It is with a true penitent as with a wounded man. He comes to the surgeon and shows him all his wounds.

Thomas Watson

PERFECTION

Those who aim at perfection, and persevere, will come much nearer to it than those whose laziness and despondency make them give it up as unattainable.

Philip D. S. Chesterfield

I have met with some of these 'perfectly sanctified' gentlemen, but I could have spoilt their perfection simply by treading on their corns; and I believe I have done so, for they seem to be immensely cross when I have denied their proud boast.

C. H. Spurgeon

Perfection in the flesh is a lie: I believe it to be one of the grossest falsehoods ever palmed on foolish minds.

C. H. Spurgeon

All the perfection we can arrive at in this life is sincerity.

Thomas Watson

PERSECUTION
(See also: Martyrdom)

The purest church is the church under the cross.
J. H. Merle d'Aubigne

Never expect to find this world anything better than a wilderness.
Jonathan Edwards

It is unnatural for Christianity to be popular.
Billy Graham

If you are under any illusions about the attitude of this world towards Jesus Christ, try really living for him for a week and you will find out!
Vance Havner

Let a man really dare to be a New Testament Christian and take Christ seriously, beginning next Monday morning, and he will wake up to the fact that he is a sheep among wolves.
Vance Havner

Wherever you see persecution, there is more than a probability that truth is on the persecuted side.
Hugh Latimer

Persecution often does in this life what the last great day will do completely — separate the wheat from the tares.
James Milner

The Word of God never yet prospered in the world without opposition.
Iain H. Murray

If you were not strangers here the hounds of the world would not bark at you.
Samuel Rutherford

Persecution is the legacy bequeathed by Christ to his people.
Thomas Watson

Put the cross in your creed.
Thomas Watson

The weight of glory makes persecution light.
Thomas Watson

To have two heavens is more than Christ had. Was the head crowned with thorns and do we think to be crowned with roses?
Thomas Watson

PERSEVERANCE

Endurance and perseverance are qualities we would all like

217

to possess, but we are loath to go through the process that produces them.

Jerry Bridges

Endurance is the ability to stand up under adversity; perseverance is the ability to progress in spite of it.

Jerry Bridges

True grace always produces vigilance rather than complacency; it always produces perseverance rather than indolence.

Jerry Bridges

All our progress and perseverance are from God.

John Calvin

We persevere through faith and never apart from it.

Sinclair Ferguson

By perseverance the snail reached the ark.

C. H. Spurgeon

Perseverance is the hallmark of a genuine interest in Christ.

Geoffrey B. Wilson

PHILOSOPHY

The highest philosophy is often a judicious suspense of judgement.

Michael Faraday

Good philosophy must exist ... because bad philosophy needs to be answered.

C. S. Lewis

If a philosophy of life cannot help me to die, then in a sense it cannot help me to live.

D. Martyn Lloyd-Jones

The ordinary Christian knows and understands more about life than the greatest philosopher who is not a Christian.

D. Martyn Lloyd-Jones

It is poor philosophy to say we will believe nothing unless we can understand everything!

J. C. Ryle

Philosophy and science are good servants of Christ, but they are poor guides when they rule out the Son of God.

Augustus H. Strong

Philosophy and science have not always been friendly towards the idea of God, the reason being that they are dedicated to the task of accounting for things and are impatient with anything that refuses to give an account of itself.

A. W. Tozer

PIETY

Piety is the root of charity.
John Calvin

Serious piety is the best defence against wicked doctrines.
Thomas Watson

PLEASURES

The difference between false pleasure and true is just this: for the true, the price is paid before you enjoy it; for the false, after you enjoy it.
John Foster

There is no earthly pleasure whereof we may not surfeit; of the spiritual we can never have enough.
Joseph Hall

A man never makes a bigger fool of himself than when he settles down in Sodom for personal advantage.
Vance Havner

Let me rather have that fire which is rewarded with heaven than those pleasures which shall be rewarded with fire.
John P. K. Henshaw

There is no earthly comfort in the long run.
C. S. Lewis

In the order of creation, pleasures are meant to serve as pointers to God.
J. I. Packer

Keeping our heads despite the pull of pleasure is as hard a task as any for the affluent believer.
J. I. Packer

The quest for one's own pleasure in some shape or form is the rule and driving force of the egocentric life.
J. I. Packer

POPULARITY
(See also: Fame)

Popularity is fleeting, fickle and futile.

A dish around which I see too many people doesn't tempt me.
Julien Green

The more one pleases everybody, the less one pleases profoundly.
Stendhal

219

POSSESSIONS

(See also: Materialism; Money; Prosperity; Riches; Wealth)

If we have not quiet in our minds, outward comfort will do no more for us than a golden slipper on a gouty foot.

John Bunyan

Possession pampers the mind.

William Hazlitt

Every possession is a trust.

Roy L. Smith

All that we possess is qualified by what we are.

John Spalding

That only is worth my having which I can have for ever. That only is worth my grasping which death cannot tear out of my hand.

C. H. Spurgeon

One day we stand to lose everything except those qualities that have eternal value.

David Watson

POVERTY

Better to be poor than wicked.

Anon.

Better to be a child of God in poverty than a child of Satan in riches.

C. H. Spurgeon

We must lose things to know the value of them. It is a dry well which makes people know the value of water.

William Tiptaft

A piece of bread with God's love is angel's food.

Thomas Watson

POWER

Greatness lies not in being strong, but in the right use of strength.

Anon.

When God is our strength, it is strength indeed; when our strength is our own, it is only weakness.

Augustine

The greater the power the more dangerous the abuse.

Edmund Burke

Power intoxicates men. When a man is intoxicated by alcohol he can recover, but when intoxicated by power he seldom recovers.

James F. Byrnes

Power can corrupt us in Christian service as easily as it can corrupt those in political service.

Charles Colson

The pursuit of power can separate the most resolute of Christians from the true nature of Christian leadership.

Charles Colson

Power will intoxicate the best hearts as wine the strongest heads. No man is wise enough, nor good enough, to be trusted with unlimited power.

C. C. Colton

The lust for power is not rooted in strength but in weakness.

Erich Fromm

Nearly all men can stand adversity, but if you want to test a man's character, give him power.

Abraham Lincoln

The quest for excellence is a mark of maturity. The quest for power is childish.

Max Lucado

Only those who do not desire power are fit to hold it.

Plato

There is no stronger test of a man's character than power and authority.

Plutarch

He who has great power should use it lightly.

Seneca

The weaker we feel, the harder we lean on God. And the harder we lean, the stronger we grow.

Joni Eareckson Tada

No power has such a commanding influence over us as the power of love.

David Thomas

PRAISE
(See also: Worship)

Too often we forget to thank God for answered prayer. Praise is the proper punctuation mark for an answered prayer.

Anon.

I have never sufficiently praised the Lord, and never can.

Andrew Bonar

The servants of the Lord are to sing his praises in this life to the world's end; and in the next life world without end.

John Boys

The most holy service that we can render to God is to be employed in praising his name.

John Calvin

There is not a corner in heaven or on earth where God is not praised.

John Calvin

Praise shall conclude that work which prayer began.

William Jenkyn

In commanding us to glorify him, God is inviting us to enjoy him.

C. S. Lewis

A line of praises is worth a leaf of prayer, and an hour of praises is worth a day of fasting and mourning!

John Livingstone

The music of praise arises out of a fixed heart, a heart settled on God.

John MacArthur

Praise, to be acceptable to God, must come from a heart devoted to him.

Albertus Magnus

Self-love may lead us to prayers, but love to God excites us to praises.

Thomas Manton

Praising energizes and renews praying.

J. I. Packer

Have we not more cause to praise God than to pray? Surely, for we have many things to thank him for, which we never ask for.

A. W. Pink

God deserves every imaginable praise from his creatures, whether heathens or Christians, and the more men praise him the greater will be their happiness.

Charles Simeon

God does not need praise by men, but he knows that when men cease to praise him they begin to praise one another excessively.

Isaac Bashevis Singer

While we cannot comprehend God in his fulness, we can know enough about him through his revelation to praise him appropriately.

R. C. Sproul

Praise is the rent which God requires for the use of his mercies.

C. H. Spurgeon

The whole life of the Christian should be a psalm, of which the contents should be summed up in this sentence, 'Bless the Lord, O my soul: and all that is within me, bless his holy name.'

C. H. Spurgeon

Our glorifying of God should be a good, loud brag about him.

Billy Strachan

Oh, how I wish I could adequately set forth the glory of that One who is worthy to be the object of our worship!

A. W. Tozer

The motion of our praise must be the motion of our pulse, which beats as long as life lasts.

Thomas Watson

Though nothing can add to God's essential glory, yet praise exalts him in the eyes of others.

Thomas Watson

PRAYER — Answers

Too often we forget to thank God for answered prayer. Praise is the proper punctuation mark for an answered prayer.

Anon.

The hand of faith never knocked in vain at the door of heaven. Mercy is as surely ours as if we had it, if we have but faith and patience to wait for it.

Francis Burkitt

There is nothing meritorious in our prayers ... Whenever God hears them, it is in exercise of his free goodness.

John Calvin

Never make the blunder of trying to forecast the way God is going to answer your prayer.

Oswald Chambers

Keep praying, but be thankful that God's answers are wiser than your prayers!

William Culbertson

Surely he who feeds the ravens when they cry will not starve his children when they pray.

Joseph Hall

If there be anything under heaven that I am as sure as I am of the demonstrations of mathematics, it is the fact that God answers prayer.

C. H. Spurgeon

When I pray coincidences happen, and when I do not, they don't.

William Temple

I should not think lightly of that man's religion who gets answers to prayer.

William Tiptaft

PRAYER — Earnestness

In prayer it is better to have a heart without words, than words without a heart.

John Bunyan

That is but poor prayer which is only one of words.

John Bunyan

The best prayers have often more groans than words.

John Bunyan

I am convinced that nothing in Christianity is so rarely attained as a praying heart.

Charles G. Finney

Self-examination is the high road to prayer.

D. Martyn Lloyd-Jones

Do not reckon you have prayed until you have pleaded, for pleading is the very marrow of prayer.

C. H. Spurgeon

He who prays without fervency does not pray at all.

C. H. Spurgeon

I know of no better thermometer to your spiritual temperature than this, the measure of the intensity of your prayer.

C. H. Spurgeon

Only that prayer which comes from our heart can get to God's heart.

C. H. Spurgeon

The habit of prayer is good, but the spirit of prayer is better.

C. H. Spurgeon

God the Father understands prayers which are sighed rather than said, because he searches our hearts and can read our thoughts.

John R. W. Stott

PRAYER — Essence

When you kneel to pray, don't give orders — report for duty!

Anon.

Prayer is weakness leaning on omnipotence.

W. S. Bowden

Prayer is not only our approach to God, but also his approach to us.

E. F. Hallock

We can never be blessed until we learn that we can bring nothing to Christ but our need.
Vance Havner

Prayer is a ladder on which thoughts mount to God.
Abraham J. Heschel

Prayer is exhaling the spirit of man and inhaling the spirit of God.
Edwin Keith

If you have never had any difficulty in prayer, it is absolutely certain that you have never prayed.
D. Martyn Lloyd-Jones

Prayer is not monologue but dialogue. God's voice in response to mine is its most essential part.
Andrew Murray

Prayer is not some mystic reasoning after the unknown; it is response to the God who speaks in Scripture, the God who personally acts in the lives of his people.
Iain H. Murray

True prayer is born out of brokenness.
Frances J. Roberts

A prayer which only contains thanksgiving and profession, and asks nothing, is essentially defective. It may be suitable for an angel, but it is not suitable for a sinner.
J. C. Ryle

To pray is to expose the shores of the mind to the incoming tide of God.
Ralph W. Sockman

Prayer is the pulse of the renewed soul; and the constancy of its beat is the test and measure of the spiritual life.
Octavius Winslow

PRAYER — and Faith
(See also: Faith — and Prayer)

Pray not for crutches but for wings.
Phillips Brooks

The man who prays without faith has a radical defect in his character.
H. W. Fulford

Many a person is praying for rain with his tub the wrong side up.
Sam Jones

Dear Lord, never let me be afraid to pray for the impossible.

Dorothy Shellenberger

When faith sets prayer on work, prayer sets God on work.

Thomas Watson

PRAYER — and Fasting

Since this is a holy exercise both for the humbling of men and for their confession of humility, why should we use it less than the ancients did?

John Calvin

Fasting is the voluntary denial of a normal function for the sake of intense spiritual activity.

Richard Foster

Fasting is calculated to bring a note of urgency and importance into our praying, and to give force to our pleading in the court of heaven. The man who prays with fasting is giving heaven notice that he is truly in earnest.

Arthur Wallis

Few disciplines go against the flesh and the mainstream of culture as this one.

Donald S. Whitney

Without a purpose, fasting can be a miserable, self-centred experience.

Donald S. Whitney

PRAYER — a Gift

Of all the blessings of Christian salvation none is greater than this, that we have access to God in prayer.

D. Martyn Lloyd-Jones

We could not pray at all were it not for the Holy Spirit.

D. Martyn Lloyd-Jones

Only the prayer which comes from God can go to God.

C. H. Spurgeon

PRAYER — Hindrances

There is a great difference between praying to God about something and mentioning it to him in passing.

It is strange that in our praying we seldom ask for a change of character, but always a change in circumstances.

Anon.

Too many people pray like little boys who knock at doors, then run away.

Anon.

Doubtful prayer is no prayer at all.

John Calvin

If you seek your own advantage or blessing through God you are not really seeking God at all.

Meister Eckhart

A heap of unmeaning words only smothers the words of devotion.

J. Hamilton

The sin of failing to come to God in prayer is one of the most common offences a Christian commits.

Simon J. Kistemaker

I fancy we may sometimes be deterred from small prayers by a sense of our own dignity rather than of God's.

C. S. Lewis

What a fearful canopy the prayers that do not get beyond the atmosphere would make if they turned brown with age!

George MacDonald

Satan is far more anxious to keep us off our knees than he is to keep us off our feet!

Ivor Powell

Prayer without faith! What sort of prayer is it? It is the prayer of a man who does not believe in God.

C. H. Spurgeon

Public prayer is no evidence of piety. It is practised by an abundance of hypocrites. But private prayer is a thing for which the hypocrite has no heart.

C. H. Spurgeon

Prayer is good, but when used as a substitute for obedience, it is naught but a blatant hypocrisy, a despicable Pharisaism.

C. T. Studd

How hard it is to pray against besetting sins!

William Tiptaft

PRAYER — and Holy Living

Our lives must be as holy as our prayers.

Andrew Murray

If we are not right, our prayers cannot be.

James Philip

It is what we *are* when we pray our prayers that counts with God.

James Philip

227

The cardinal element in true prayer is no mere outward ritual but the inward, moral state of the one who prays.
James Philip

Our prayers are only as powerful as our lives. In the long pull we pray only as well as we live.
A. W. Tozer

PRAYER — Importance

The place for prayer is everywhere.

Kneel before you leap.
George H. Allen

Prayer is the key of the morning and the bolt of the night.
Anon.

Many of us cannot reach the mission fields on our feet, but we can reach them on our knees.
T. J. Bach

To clasp the hands in prayer is the beginning of an uprising against the spirit of the world.
Karl Barth

Prayer honours God, acknowledges his being, exalts his power, adores his providence, secures his aid.
E. M. Bounds

If man is man and God is God, to live without prayer is not merely an awful thing, it is an infinitely foolish thing.
Phillips Brooks

Prayer is the chief exercise of faith.
John Calvin

What an awful place is the Christian's closet. The whole Trinity is about it every time he kneels.
Edward Griffin

Prayer is a divine imperative because God desires fellowship with his redeemed children.
E. F. Hallock

Prayerlessness is a sin against God and it is a sin that can find no excuse.
E. F. Hallock

The Bible is permeated by prayer.
E. F. Hallock

When we do not pray, we work against God.
E. F. Hallock

The measure of any Christian is his prayer life.
Vance Havner

Prayer is the breath of the newborn soul, and there can be no Christian life without it.
Rowland Hill

Everything we do in the Christian life is easier than prayer.
D. Martyn Lloyd-Jones

Ultimately there is no better index of one's spiritual state and condition than one's prayers.
D. Martyn Lloyd-Jones

To pray well is the better half of study.
Martin Luther

Prayer is the barometer of the church.
Thomas V. Moore

Prayer is the pulse of life.
Andrew Murray

Men who know their God are before anything else men who pray.
J. I. Packer

Anything is a blessing which makes us pray.
C. H. Spurgeon

As artists give themselves to their models, and poets to their classical pursuits, so must we addict ourselves to prayer.
C. H. Spurgeon

He that is never on his knees on earth shall never stand upon his feet in heaven.
C. H. Spurgeon

I always feel that there is something wrong if I go without prayer for even half an hour in the day.
C. H. Spurgeon

If you cannot go to the house of the Lord, go to the Lord of the house.
C. H. Spurgeon

It is a good rule never to look into the face of man in the morning till you have looked into the face of God.
C. H. Spurgeon

Neglect of private prayer is the locust which devours the strength of the church.
C. H. Spurgeon

Prayer has become as essential to me as the heaving of my lungs and the beating of my pulse.
C. H. Spurgeon

Prayer is the breath of faith. Prayer meetings are the lungs of the church.
C. H. Spurgeon

Remember that prayer is your best means of study.

C. H. Spurgeon

A prayerless man is a careless man.

William Tiptaft

I want to be begging mercy every hour.

William Tiptaft

PRAYER — Length

We may pray most when we say least, and we may pray least when we say most.

Augustine

Some people's prayers need to be cut off at both ends and set on fire in the middle.

D. L. Moody

It is better ... that the hearers should wish the prayer had been longer, than spend half or a considerable part of the time in wishing it was over.

John Newton

God does not, it seems to us, frequently yield up his blessing to us till we have spent a reasonable length of time in his presence.

Maurice Roberts

Time spent with God in the secret place is never the cause of spiritual inefficiency.

Maurice Roberts

PRAYER — Power

He stands best who kneels most.

Anon.

If your day is hemmed with prayer it is less likely to become unravelled.

Anon.

Within God's limitations prayer is unlimited.

E. F. Hallock

Prayer may not get us what we want, but it will teach us to want what we need.

Vance Havner

When a man makes alliance with the Almighty, giants look like grasshoppers.

Vance Havner

When prayers are strongest, mercies are nearest.

Edward Reynolds

All our perils are as nothing, so long as we have prayer.

C. H. Spurgeon

I could no more doubt the efficacy of prayer than I could disbelieve in the law of gravitation.

C. H. Spurgeon

PRAYER — and the Promises of God

(See also: Promises of God)

Theology and prayer are inextricably intertwined.

Richard Bewes

God loves to be consulted.

Charles Bridges

Prayer is only true when it is within the compass of God's Word.

John Bunyan

Prayer flows from doctrine.

John Calvin

True prayer is rooted in the promises and covenants of God, in his past achievements, in his ability to do immeasurably more than all we ask or imagine.

Bob Cotton

That which God abundantly makes the subject of his promises, God's people should abundantly make the subject of their prayers.

Jonathan Edwards

Prayer is receiving what God has promised.

E. F. Hallock

We cannot expect too little from man, nor too much from God.

Matthew Henry

We are to pray only for what God has promised, and for the communication of it unto us in that way whereby he will work it and effect it.

John Owen

Every prayer is an inverted promise ... If God teaches us to pray for any good thing, we may gather by implication the assurance that he means to give it.

C. H. Spurgeon

PRAYER — Unanswered

God can never be expected to undertake a cause which is unworthy of defence.

John Calvin

I have learned that God's silence to my questions is not a door slammed in my face. I may not have the answers — but I do have him.

Dave Dravecky

God is not a cosmic bellboy for whom we can press a button to get things.

> *Harry Emerson Fosdick*

God has not always answered my prayers. If he had, I would have married the wrong man — several times!

> *Ruth Bell Graham*

If God had granted all the silly prayers I've made in my life, where would I be now?

> *C. S. Lewis*

It is quite useless knocking at the door of heaven for earthly comfort; it's not the sort of comfort they supply there.

> *C. S. Lewis*

Prayer is request. The essence of request, as distinct from compulsion, is that it may or may not be granted. And if an infinitely wise Being listens to the requests of finite and foolish creatures, of course he will sometimes refuse them.

> *C. S. Lewis*

If you can't pray a door open, don't pry it open.

> *Lyell Rader*

PRAYER — and the Will of God

What God sovereignly decrees in eternity, men will always demand in time.

> *Anon.*

God's sovereignty does not negate our responsibility to pray, but rather makes it possible to pray with confidence.

> *Jerry Bridges*

We ask what we think to be best; God gives what he knows to be best.

> *William Burkitt*

God always answers us in the deeps, never in the shallows of our soul.

> *Amy Carmichael*

The marvellous and supernatural power of prayer consists not in bringing God's will down to us, but in lifting our will up to his.

> *Robert Law*

Don't pray to escape trouble. Don't pray to be comfortable in your emotions. Pray to do the will of God in every situation. Nothing else is worth praying for.

> *Samuel Shoemaker*

Every true prayer is a variation on the theme 'Thy will be done.'

John R. W. Stott

Prayer is not a convenient device for imposing our will upon God, or bending his will to ours, but the prescribed way of subordinating our will to his.

John R. W. Stott

Father, I wait thy daily will;
Thou shalt divide my portion still;
Grant me on earth what seems thee best,
Till death and heaven reveal the rest.

Isaac Watts

PREACHING AND PREACHERS — Aim

The purpose of preaching must always be the first condition that decrees its character ... and what is preaching for? The answer comes without hesitation. It is for men's salvation.

Phillips Brooks

Our people do not so much have to have their heads stored as to have their hearts touched, and they stand in the greatest need of that sort of preaching which has the tendency to do this.

Jonathan Edwards

A true pastor must not only feed the flock, he must warn the flock. He must not only be zealous but jealous.

Vance Havner

It is a mark of a prophet to make men face sin.

Vance Havner

The task of the preacher is to comfort the afflicted and afflict the comfortable.

Vance Havner

We are here to preach sin black, hell hot, judgement certain, eternity long and salvation free.

Vance Havner

The history of ministers proves that the Saviour has never withheld his blessing from the labours of those whose supreme object, whose first, last, and absorbing desire has been the salvation of their fellow-men.

D. P. Kidder

I can forgive the preacher almost anything if he gives me a sense of God.

D. Martyn Lloyd-Jones

Preaching is not a specific form or method of proclamation. Preaching is verbalizing the gospel. Beyond that we cannot be more specific.

Donald MacLeod

We are not called upon to invent the message, nor to decorate the message, but to proclaim God's Word.

Donald MacLeod

God will either give you what you ask, or something far better.

Robert Murray M'Cheyne

I wish I could be cut in pieces to preach the gospel, and that every drop of blood might tell it to my perishing fellow-men.

C. H. Spurgeon

We have done nothing for sinners until, by the power of the Holy Ghost, we bring them to faith; and we only reckon that our preaching is useful to saints as we see them increase in faith.

C. H. Spurgeon

PREACHING AND PREACHERS — Christ the Message

The sermon which is the richest, most profitable, instruc-

tive and edifying is the one which is fullest of the Lord Jesus Christ.

John R. de Witt

Great sermons lead the people to praise the preacher. Good preaching leads the people to praise the Saviour.

Charles G. Finney

Next to Christ I have one joy, to preach Christ my Lord.

Samuel Rutherford

A sermon without Christ as its beginning, middle and end is a mistake in conception and a crime in execution.

C. H. Spurgeon

Across my pulpit and my tabernacle shall be the mark of the blood; it will disgust the enemy, but it will delight the faithful. Substitution seems to me to be the soul, the life of the gospel, the essence of the gospel; therefore must it be ever in the front.

C. H. Spurgeon

As for me, I know no other gospel, and let this tongue be dumb rather than it should ever preach any other. Substitution is the very marrow of the whole Bible, the soul of salvation, the essence of the gospel; we ought to saturate all our sermons with it, for it is the life-blood of a gospel ministry.

C. H. Spurgeon

I do not think a man ought to hear a minister preach three sermons without learning the doctrine of atonement.

C. H. Spurgeon

I wish that our ministry — and mine especially — might be tied and tethered to the cross.

C. H. Spurgeon

If a man can preach one sermon without mentioning Christ's name in it, it ought to be his last, certainly the last that any Christian ought to go to hear him preach.

C. H. Spurgeon

More and more I am jealous lest any views upon prophecy, church government, politics, or even systematic theology should withdraw one of us from glorying in the cross of Christ.

C. H. Spurgeon

Preach nothing down but the devil, nothing up but the Christ.

C. H. Spurgeon

When we preach Christ crucified, we have no reason to stammer, or stutter, or hesitate, or apologize; there is nothing in the gospel of which we have any cause to be ashamed.

C. H. Spurgeon

When we preach Jesus Christ, oh! then we are not putting out the plates, and the knives and the forks, for the feast, but we are handing out the bread itself.

C. H. Spurgeon

PREACHING AND PREACHERS — Dangers

Of all the defects of utterance I have ever known, the most serious is having nothing to utter.

J. W. Alexander

A preacher should never say 'Finally' — and certainly not more than once.

Anon.

Greed and ambition ... the two sources from which stems the corruption of the whole of the ministry.

John Calvin

It is too common a fault that men desire to be taught in an ingenious and witty style.

John Calvin

235

Teachers ... have no plague more to be dreaded than ambition.

John Calvin

We would expect that when men claim to teach the Scriptures, they would imitate the meek and humble Jesus rather than the ostentatious entertainers.

Walter J. Chantry

A lot of preaching misses the mark because it proceeds from the love of preaching, not love of people.

Vance Havner

A preacher who is too big for a little crowd would be too little for a big crowd.

Vance Havner

I trust I am not one who pounds because he can't expound.

Vance Havner

If you want to be popular, preach happiness; if you want to be unpopular, preach holiness.

Vance Havner

Some sermons are all garnish, with not enough meat and potatoes to feed one soul for one day.

Vance Havner

The pastor is called upon to feed the sheep ... He is certainly not to become an entertainer of goats.

William G. Hughes

I am convinced that the first panic-stricken rush into the arms of the waiting commentators is the death of any originality a man may possess.

George Johnstone Jeffrey

I would say that a dull preacher is a contradiction in terms; if he is dull he is not a preacher.

D. Martyn Lloyd-Jones

Sentimentalism is out for the true preacher of the Word.

R. C. Lucas

When people say, 'What a wonderful messenger', I have problems.

Donald MacLeod

Don't talk down to your congregation. They are not there.

F. R. Maltby

No man preaches his sermon well to others if he does not first preach it to his own heart.

John Owen

Every preacher who trims himself to suit everybody will soon whittle himself away.

J. Harold Smith

An idler has no right in the pulpit.

C. H. Spurgeon

Better abolish pulpits than fill them with men who have no experimental knowledge of what they teach.

C. H. Spurgeon

Good sermons need not be long, and bad ones ought not to be.

C. H. Spurgeon

If I could be an orator, I would not be. The game of eloquence, with the souls of men for the counters, and eternity for the table, is the most wicked sport in the world.

C. H. Spurgeon

If I thought I could save every soul in this place, or do any other stupendous thing by making the slightest compromise with my conscience, I dare not in the sight of the living God do it.

C. H. Spurgeon

It is a terribly easy matter to be a minister of the gospel and a vile hypocrite at the same time.

C. H. Spurgeon

Nonsense does not improve by being bellowed.

C. H. Spurgeon

The way of salvation is far too important a matter to be the theme of oratorical displays. The cross is far too sacred to be made a pole on which to hoist the flags of our fine language.

C. H. Spurgeon

It is unmercifulness to souls to preach so as not to be understood.

Thomas Watson

PREACHING AND PREACHERS — Divine Calling

Christ appoints pastors to his church, not to rule but to serve.

John Calvin

The sublimest calling which man can attain on earth is that of preaching the Word of God.

J. H. Merle d'Aubigné

God is on the lookout today for a man who will be quiet enough to get a message from him, brave enough to preach it, and honest enough to live it.

Vance Havner

A man sent to preach is a man whose mind is constantly turning to this one thing.

Iain H. Murray

The ministry is the most honourable employment in the world. Jesus Christ has graced this calling by his entering into it.

Thomas Watson

PREACHING AND PREACHERS — Doctrine

Preach doctrine, preach all the doctrine that you know, and learn forever more and more; but preach it always not that men may believe it, but that men may be saved by believing it.

Phillips Brooks

Preaching is the communication of truth by man to man. It has in it two essential elements, truth and personality. Neither of those can it spare and still be preaching.

Phillips Brooks

All the authority that is possessed by pastors ... is subject to the Word of God.

John Calvin

The only way you can speak for God with certainty is to speak from the Bible.

Charles Colson

Authority is inherent in truth.

Henry C. Fish

We must persuade by teaching; we must never teach by persuasion.

William Gurnall

If a preacher is not doctrinally ready to preach, he is not ready.

Vance Havner

It has not dawned upon most of us that we do not need some new thing so much as some old things that would be new if anybody tried them!

Vance Havner

The very fact that the truth is not popular is all the more reason for preaching it ... It is not our responsibility to make it acceptable; it is our duty to make it available.

Vance Havner

What feeds the souls of men is not our trimmings but God's truth.

Vance Havner

Preaching which is nothing but evangelistic is obviously inadequate. Preaching, on the other hand, which is never evangelistic is equally inadequate.

D. Martyn Lloyd-Jones

What is preaching? Logic on fire! Eloquent reason!

D. Martyn Lloyd-Jones

The devil receives his marching orders when the church begins to preach the truth.

> *R. C. Lucas*

Anybody going into the ministry who is not committed to expository preaching is cutting his own throat.

> *John MacArthur*

If a minister is not sure about his message, let him keep quiet till he is sure about it.

> *C. H. Spurgeon*

If people do not like the doctrine of grace, give them all the more of it.

> *C. H. Spurgeon*

We must not stand on the Bible to preach, but we must preach with the Bible above our heads.

> *C. H. Spurgeon*

PREACHING AND PREACHERS — Earnestness

No man can be a great preacher without great feeling.

> *J. W. Alexander*

When people sleep in church, maybe it's the preacher we should wake up.

> *Anon.*

Something of the quality of enthusiasm must be in every man who preaches. He who lacks it cannot be a preacher.

> *Phillips Brooks*

Heart preaching inflames the spirit to worship; head preaching smothers the glowing embers.

> *Richard Foster*

Some preachers ought to put more fire into their sermons or more sermons into the fire.

> *Vance Havner*

It is not enough that what we say comes from the heart, but it must come from a composed heart, and not from a sudden heat or passion.

> *Matthew Henry*

It is not to be doubted that many a well-meant and otherwise good sermon has been wholly inefficient for lack of that energy of purpose which is necessary to impress other minds.

> *D. P. Kidder*

The difference between the preaching that does nothing and the preaching that does something is the difference between preaching *before* people and preaching *to* people.

> *G. Campbell Morgan*

239

A burning heart will soon find for itself a flaming tongue.

C. H. Spurgeon

A sermon wept over is more acceptable with God than one gloried over.

C. H. Spurgeon

I dread getting to be a mere preaching machine, without my heart and soul being exercised in this solemn duty.

C. H. Spurgeon

Each sermon or study should be preached as if it was the first and last.

William Still

We are not diplomats but prophets, and our message is not a compromise but an ultimatum.

A. W. Tozer

Zeal in the ministry is as proper as fire on the altar.

Thomas Watson

Give me one hundred preachers who fear nothing but sin and desire nothing but God, and I care not a straw whether they be clergymen or laymen, such alone will shake the gates of hell and set up the kingdom of God on earth.

John Wesley

PREACHING AND PREACHERS — Glory of Preaching

Preaching is the most amazing, the most thrilling activity that one can ever be engaged in, because of all that it holds out for all of us in the present, and because of the glorious endless possibilities in an eternal future.

D. Martyn Lloyd-Jones

No church can rise higher than its pulpit.

Conrad Mbewe

Draw a circle around my pulpit and you have hit the spot where I am nearest heaven.

C. H. Spurgeon

What I receive for my ministry is not a tenth of what I could readily earn in an engagement infinitely less laborious and harassing than my present position; although, be it added, I would not leave my ministry for ten thousand worlds.

C. H. Spurgeon

It is one thing to learn the technique and mechanics of preaching; it is quite another to preach a sermon which will draw back the veil and make the barriers fall that hide the face of God.

> *James S. Stewart*

A successful preacher wears two crowns: a crown of righteousness in heaven and a crown of rejoicing here upon earth.

> *Thomas Watson*

PREACHING AND PREACHERS — and the Holy Spirit

No one is a true pastor whom the Lord does not rule by his Spirit.

> *John Calvin*

A ministry that is college-trained but not Spirit-filled works no miracles.

> *Samuel Chadwick*

The preacher is to be a free man, not bound by study and his script. The curriculum has to be left in the hands of the Holy Spirit.

> *Tony Sargent*

All the hope of our ministry lies in the Spirit of God operating on the spirits of men.

> *C. H. Spurgeon*

It were better to speak six words in the power of the Holy Ghost than to preach seventy years of sermons without the Spirit.

> *C. H. Spurgeon*

PREACHING AND PREACHERS — Humility

The gospel minister should be heard, and not seen.

> *Maurice Roberts*

Only once did God choose a completely sinless preacher.

> *Alexander Whyte*

PREACHING AND PREACHERS — Life of the Preacher

A good example is the best sermon.

> *Anon.*

If it be not your daily business to study your own hearts and to subdue corruption and to walk with God, if you make not this a work to which you constantly attend, all will go wrong and you will starve your hearers.

> *Richard Baxter*

If the parsonage does not show the pattern as well as the doctrine, exhortations from thence will only excite the ridicule of the ungodly, and confirm them in their habits of sin.

Charles Bridges

The minister's life is the people's looking-glass, by which they usually dress themselves.

William Burkitt

A message prepared in the mind reaches a mind; a message prepared in a life reaches a life.

Bill Gothard

The devil will let a preacher prepare a sermon if that will keep him from preparing himself.

Vance Havner

The man in whose thought and prayer God ever looms greater knows that in the ministry no man is his competitor.

George Johnstone Jeffrey

A minister's study should be an upper room and not a lounge.

John Henry Jowett

Let the preacher beware of any affectation of feeling which he does not possess. Instead let him seek first to experience deeply within his own soul the power of divine grace, and then to make every sermon its organ of communication to the souls of others.

D. P. Kidder

The preacher must first and foremost be a spiritual man.

Donald MacLeod

There is no heartache to a minister like the heartache of his own heart.

Al Martin

My people's greatest need is for my own holiness.

Robert Murray M'Cheyne

It must be obvious that the most important ingredient of the minister's sermon is his character.

S. E. McNair

When you tell me what a man is in the pulpit, you must also tell me what he is out of it, or I shall not know his size.

John Newton

Men may refuse to see the truth of our arguments, but they cannot evade the evidence of a holy life.

J. C. Ryle

The life of the preacher should be a magnet to draw men to Christ.

C. H. Spurgeon

The inner man makes the preacher.

James S. Stewart

PREACHING AND PREACHERS — Love

A loveless preacher is a lifeless preacher.

When love is felt, the message is heard.

Jim Vaus

PREACHING AND PREACHERS — Prayer

Every minister ought to know that if the prayer meetings are neglected all his labours are in vain.

Charles Finney

If our lives and ministry are to count for anything today we must solemnly resolve to make time for God.

Vance Havner

The preacher who has not learned to curtain off a big corner of his time to stock up on bread from heaven is headed for catastrophe.

Vance Havner

I am a leaky vessel, and I need to keep under the tap.

D. L. Moody

It is in the closet that the battle is lost or won.

Edward Payson

He who does not first hide himself in the secret place to be alone with God is unfit to show himself in the public place to move among men.

A. T. Pierson

I frequently find that I cannot pray as a minister; I find that I cannot sometimes pray as an assured Christian, but I bless God I can pray as a sinner.

C. H. Spurgeon

The pillars on which our ministry rests are, under God, the prayers of our people.

C. H. Spurgeon

PREACHING AND PREACHERS — Qualifications

Preachers are called to be shepherds, not sheep dogs.

Anon.

If I only had three years to serve the Lord, I would spend two of them studying and preparing.

Donald Grey Barnhouse

243

To hold God in awe, to give sound biblical teaching and to live a holy life — these are the fundamental prerequisites for spiritual leadership.

John Benton

Courage ... is the indispensable requisite of any true ministry.

Phillips Brooks

The three most important ingredients in Christian work are integrity, integrity, integrity.

Charles Colson

The best sermon is preached by the minister who has a sermon to preach and not by the man who has to preach a sermon.

William Feather

Every honest minister preaches from a reservoir of guilt and grace.

Gary Gulbranson

Men who speak for God never merge into the fog around them.

Vance Havner

The man who cannot sincerely rejoice in another man's gifts has no call to the ministry.

George Johnstone Jeffrey

The man who preaches the cross must be a crucified man.

G. Campbell Morgan

No one has ever been a great preacher or a greatly-used preacher without *living* for preaching.

Iain H. Murray

The beginning and end of the pastoral vocation is this: to know Christ Jesus, and in knowing him to then strive with all our being to be like him; and in striving to be like him, to love him; and in loving him to love those whom he has entrusted to our care.

Peter Parkinson

The faithful pastor is an awful weapon in the hands of God.

C. H. Spurgeon

A ministry of growing power must be one of growing experience.

James Stalker

Unless a minister has spent the week with God and received divine communications, it would be better not to enter the pulpit or open his mouth on Sunday at all.

James Stalker

PREACHING AND PREACHERS — Results

He succeeds best who expects conversion every time he preaches.

C. H. Spurgeon

It is a poor sermon that gives no offence; that neither makes the hearer displeased with himself nor with the preacher.

George Whitefield

PREACHING AND PREACHERS — Trials

Prophets are needed but not wanted.

Vance Havner

True prophets are solitary people; eagles do not fly in flocks.

Vance Havner

The badge of New Testament ministry is suffering.

R. C. Lucas

PREACHING AND PREACHERS — Unction

Preaching that is without divine power will fall like frost on worship.

Richard Foster

Preaching has authority only when the message comes as a word from God himself.

J. I. Packer

PREDESTINATION
(See also: Election — and Conversion)

The obvious answer to those who say that they do not like the idea of predestination is that God does.

If sinners deserve the punishment inflicted on them, it cannot be unjust in the great Governor of the world to predetermine their condemnation to it.

Thomas Scott

The clamours excited against predestination, if carefully scrutinized, are generally found to be against the thing decreed, and not against the circumstance of its having been decreed from eternity.

Thomas Scott

Predestination is rooted in the character of a personal and righteous God, a God who is the sovereign Lord of history.

R. C. Sproul

I do not believe that there ever would have been a man delivered from this present evil world if it had not been according to the will, the purpose, the predestination of God.

C. H. Spurgeon

I question whether we have preached the whole counsel of God unless predestination with all its solemnity and sureness be continually declared.

C. H. Spurgeon

PREJUDICE

If we were to wake up some morning and find that everyone was the same race, creed and colour, we would find some other causes for prejudice by noon.

George Aiken

Rare is the person who can weigh the faults of others without putting his thumb on the scales.

Anon.

Weak-minded characters develop their opinions in the dark-room of prejudice.

Anon.

Man prefers to believe what he prefers to be true.

Francis Bacon

Race prejudice is as thorough a denial of the Christian God as atheism is, and it is a much more common form of apostasy.

Harry Emerson Fosdick

An unprejudiced mind is probably the rarest thing in the world.

Andre Gide

Beware lest we mistake our prejudices for our convictions.

Harry A. Ironside

The better the brain, the stronger the prejudice.

D. Martyn Lloyd-Jones

You do not take up a prejudice. It takes you up, and controls you.

D. Martyn Lloyd-Jones

Water and oil are more compatible than Christianity and prejudice.

William A. Ward

PRIDE — Characteristics

Pride is the mother of all contempt of God.

John Calvin

The whole human race is infected with the disease of pride.

John Calvin

The natural man is always play-acting, always looking at himself and admiring himself.
D. Martyn Lloyd-Jones

We are all naturally self-righteous. It is the family disease of all the children of Adam.
J. C. Ryle

Conceit of our own righteousness clings to us as the skin to the flesh.
C. H. Spurgeon

PRIDE — Effects

Most of the shadows of this life are caused by standing in one's own sunshine.
Ralph Waldo Emerson

Nearly all those evils in the world which people put down to greed or selfishness are really far more the result of pride.
C. S. Lewis

Pride was the sin that changed angels into devils.
Thomas Manton

God has nothing to say to the self-righteous.
D. L. Moody

It is easier to save us from our sins than from our righteousness.
C. H. Spurgeon

There is but a step between a proud man's glory and his disgrace.
Publilius Syrus

When we take to ourselves the place that is God's, the whole course of our lives is out of joint.
A. W. Tozer

Pride stops the current of gratitude.
Thomas Watson

PRIDE — Essence
(See also: Boasting; Conceit; Egotism; Vanity)

The root of pride is saying that we can do without God.
James Montgomery Boice

How difficult it is to awaken even Christian people to an understanding of the real nature of pride!
Frank Gabelein

A man is never so proud as when striking an attitude of humility.
C. S. Lewis

PRIDE — Folly

If you think that your best is good enough for God, you have too high an opinion of yourself and too low an opinion of God.

If you build upon yourself your edifice will be a mere ruin.
> *Augustine*

Proud people breed sad sorrows for themselves.
> *Emily Bronte*

None are so near falling as those who are most confident in their own standing.
> *William Burkitt*

A man that extols himself is a fool and an idiot.
> *John Calvin*

There is not one of us who can take to himself the least jot of glory without sacrilegious robbing of God.
> *John Calvin*

There is nothing that tends more to check a foolish eagerness for display than to reflect that we have to deal with God.
> *John Calvin*

We ought always to beware of making the smallest claim for ourselves.
> *John Calvin*

Pride shuts out grace.
> *Simon J. Kistemaker*

Vainglory is the venomous worm of all goodness.
> *Robert Leighton*

The man who feels he has arrived generally has not.
> *Tony Sargent*

Be not proud of race, face, place or grace.
> *C. H. Spurgeon*

Pride is the devil's dragnet, in which he takes more fish than in any other, except procrastination.
> *C. H. Spurgeon*

The man who clings to his own righteousness is like a man who grasps a millstone to prevent himself from sinking in the flood.
> *C. H. Spurgeon*

To glory even in the work of God the Holy Spirit in yourself is to tread dangerously near to self-adulation.
> *C. H. Spurgeon*

If pride and madness go together, so do humility and sanity.
> *John R. W. Stott*

The greatest of all disorders is to think we are whole and need no help.

Thomas Wilson

PRIDE — Opposed by God

All who exalt themselves wage war with God.

John Calvin

God ... though he abominates and resists the proud, yet knows how to bring down the stout heart, not only by the iron rod of his wrath, but by the golden sceptre of his grace.

Thomas Scott

PRINCIPLES

It is easier to fight for one's principles than to live up to them.

Alfred Adler

All too often we think we are standing on principle when in reality we may only be insisting on our opinion.

Jerry Bridges

Whenever you put your practice ahead of your principle you run into problems.

Gary Gulbranson

Some people would have higher principles if it wasn't for their interests.

Lucille Harper

There are no great principles for great duties and little ones for little duties.

Alexander MacLaren

PRIORITIES

The main thing is to make sure that the main remains the main thing.

Anon.

The last thing one knows is what to put first.

Blaise Pascal

A man's heart has only enough life in it to pursue one object fully.

C. H. Spurgeon

PROCRASTINATION

One today is worth two tomorrows.

Anon.

The lazier a man is the more he plans to do tomorrow.

Anon.

Tomorrow must be the longest day of the week — judging by the number of things we are going to do then.

Anon.

When God says 'Today' the devil says 'Tomorrow'.

Anon.

Nothing is so fatiguing as the eternal hanging on of an uncompleted task.

William James

A fool lingers on, but time hurries on.

C. H. Spurgeon

PROFANITY

God has singled out profanity for special treatment on the day of judgement.

Profanity displays more ignorance than inventiveness.

Profanity is the use of strong words by weak people.

William A. Ward

PROMISES OF GOD

(See also: Prayer — and the Promises of God)

The promises of the Bible are nothing more than God's covenant to be faithful to his people. It is his character that makes these promises valid.

Jerry Bridges

Distrust is cured by meditating upon the promises of God.

John Calvin

Men ought not to expect more than God promises.

John Calvin

Our faith should be borne up on wings by the promises of God.

John Calvin

The promises of God are ... only profitable to us when they are confirmed by the blood of Christ.

John Calvin

We are not taking any risks when we step out on the Word of God.

Vance Havner

God's promises are, virtually, obligations that he imposes upon himself.

F. W. Krummacher

It would be far easier to arrest the sun in its course than to hinder the performance of any promise that God has made to his people.

George Lawson

What greater rebellion, impiety, or insult to God can there be than not to believe his promises?

Martin Luther

God never made a promise that was too good to be true.

D. L. Moody

God's promises are made conditionally; not that the condition on our part deserves anything at God's hand, but when God hath given the condition he gives the thing promised.

Richard Sibbes

God never out-promised himself yet.

C. H. Spurgeon

God promises to keep his people, and he will keep his promise.

C. H. Spurgeon

The Lord does not play at promising.

C. H. Spurgeon

The sight of the promises themselves is good for the eye of faith: the more we study the words of grace, the more grace shall we derive from the words.

C. H. Spurgeon

There is a living God. He has spoken in the Bible. He means what he says and will do all he has promised.

J. Hudson Taylor

Let God's promises shine on your problems.

Corrie ten Boom

God's promises are sealed to us, but not dates.

Susanna Wesley

PROPHECY

God does not at this day predict hidden events; but he would have us to be satisfied with his gospel.

John Calvin

Prophecy at the present day is simply the right understanding of Scripture and the particular gift of expounding it.

John Calvin

All claims to convey some additional revelation to that which has been given by God in this body of truth are false claims and must be rejected.

George Lawlor

Since the book of Revelation was completed, no new written or verbal prophecy has ever been universally recognized by Christians as divine truth from God.

John MacArthur
251

An interest in prophecy which is merely speculative and sensational comes perilously close to being sinful.

W. Graham Scroggie

PROSPERITY

(See also: Materialism; Money; Possessions; Riches; Wealth)

It takes a strong constitution to withstand repeated attacks of prosperity.

Anon.

The cause of all prosperity is the favour of God.

John Calvin

Abundance, like want, ruins men.

Benjamin Franklin

Prosperity is a great teacher; adversity is a greater.

William Hazlitt

We can stand affliction better than we can stand prosperity, for in prosperity we forget God.

D. L. Moody

If we fail to give in prosperity, God will curse what we hold back.

Stephen Olford

PROVIDENCE

(See also: Will of God)

There is nothing of which it is more difficult to convince men than that the providence of God governs this world.

John Calvin

We declare that by God's providence, not only heaven and earth and inanimate creatures, but also the counsels and wills of men, are governed so as to move precisely to that end destined by him.

John Calvin

Providence has ordered that condition for you which is best for your eternal good. If you had more of the world than you have, your heads and hearts might not be able to manage it to your advantage.

John Flavel

Providence is much more about God's glory than about our happiness.

Geoffrey Grogan

Either directly or indirectly, every providence has a tendency to the spiritual good of those who love God.

Matthew Henry

The keys of providence swing at the girdle of Christ.

C. H. Spurgeon

PURITY

God requires an inward purity as well as an outward performance.

When God purifies the heart by faith, the market is sacred as well as the sanctuary.

Martin Luther

One of the most conclusive evidences that we do possess a pure heart is to be conscious of and burdened with the impurity which still indwells us.

A. W. Pink

Spiritual purity may be defined as undivided affections, sincerity and genuineness, godly simplicity.

A. W. Pink

God does not demand a beautiful vessel, but he does demand a clean one.

R. A. Torrey

A pure heart breathes after purity.

Thomas Watson

Most men pray more for full purses than for pure hearts.

Thomas Watson

The pure heart is God's paradise where he delights to walk. It is his lesser heaven.

Thomas Watson

PURPOSE

The least of things with a meaning is worth more in life than the greatest of things without it.

Carl Gustav Jung

One can live on less when he has more to live for.

S. S. McKenny

REASON
(See also: Education; Knowledge; Mind)

The light of human reason differs little from darkness.

John Calvin

What madness it is to embrace nothing but what commends itself to human reason!

John Calvin

God never contradicts reason, he transcends it.

Oswald Chambers

Scripture never sets faith and reason over against each other as incompatible. On the contrary, faith can only arise and grow within us by the use of our minds.

Will Metzger

Reason's last step is the recognition that there are an infinite number of things that are beyond it.

Blaise Pascal

Nothing in this world is without reason.

A. W. Tozer

RECREATION

We can play, as we can eat, to the glory of God.

C. S. Lewis

REDEMPTION
(See also: Atonement; Salvation)

The heart of the gospel is redemption, and the essence of redemption is the substitutionary sacrifice of Christ.

C. H. Spurgeon

If I had the wisdom of Solomon, the patience of Job, the meekness of Moses, the strength of Samson, the obedience of Abraham, the compassion of Joseph, the tears of Jeremiah, the poetic skill of David, the prophetic voice of Elijah, the courage of Daniel, the greatness of John the Baptist, the endurance and love of Paul, I would still need redemption through Christ's blood, the forgiveness of sin.

R. L. Wheeler

REFORMATION

All Christians are called to be reformers.

The only alternatives to continuing personal reformation are deadness and decay.

God brings about reformation when his people return to the Word of God as their sole source of doctrine and practice.

John H. Armstrong

Every Christian who thinks of reformation and revival must begin by thinking of how to give glory to God.

Tom Wells

REGENERATION
(See also: Conversion; Faith —
Saving)

Faith does not proceed from ourselves, but is the fruit of spiritual regeneration.
John Calvin

When God designs to forgive us he changes our hearts and turns us to obedience by his Spirit.
John Calvin

Regeneration, however it is described, is a divine activity in us, in which we are not the actors but the recipients.
Sinclair Ferguson

To expect Christian conduct from a person who is not born again is rank heresy.
D. Martyn Lloyd-Jones

The act of God in our regeneration is so momentous that no single category of thought is sufficient to describe the changes it brings about in and for us.
Maurice Roberts

The new creation is as much and entirely the work of God as the old creation.
C. H. Spurgeon

Regeneration gives our birth a value and our death a glory.
David Thomas

RELIGION

A religion without mystery must be a religion without God.
Anon.

Religion is bread for daily use, not cake for special occasions.
Anon.

One's religion is what he is most interested in.
J. M. Barrie

Justification by faith is the hinge on which all true religion turns.
John Calvin

No religion is pleasing to God unless founded on truth.
John Calvin

Religion separated from knowledge is nothing but the sport and delusion of Satan.
John Calvin

Let your religion be less of a theory and more of a love affair.
G. K. Chesterton

True religion consists in holy affections.

Jonathan Edwards

Religion that does not glow with love is unsatisfactory.

Richard Glover

A man may have as many religious changes in the year as there are changes in the moon, and be unchanged after all.

Rowland Hill

There are no non-religious activities; only religious and irreligious.

C. S. Lewis

The core of religion is religious experience.

H. D. Lewis

The heart of true religion is to glorify God by patient endurance and to praise him for his gracious deliverances.

J. I. Packer

Religion that is merely ritual and ceremonial can never satisfy. Neither can we be satisfied by a religion that is merely humanitarian or serviceable to mankind. Man's craving is for the spiritual.

Samuel Shoemaker

When people say that all religions are basically the same, they are actually saying that they know little or nothing about world religion.

R. C. Sproul

Banish religion and you destroy virtue.

C. H. Spurgeon

If your religion does not make you holy it will damn you. It is simply pageantry to go to hell in.

C. H. Spurgeon

What a mercy to have religion that will do to die by.

William Tiptaft

Any untrained, unprepared, unspiritual empty rattletrap of a person can start something religious and find plenty of followers who will listen and pay and promote it.

A. W. Tozer

For the true Christian the one supreme test for the present soundness and ultimate worth of everything religious must be the place our Lord occupies in it.

A. W. Tozer

The whole world has been booby-trapped by the devil, and the deadliest trap of all is the religious one.

A. W. Tozer

We have too much religion.

A. W. Tozer

That religion is suspicious which is full of faction and discord.

Thomas Watson

They who make religion a cloak for their sin shall have a hotter place in hell.

Thomas Watson

Religion is the reaction of human nature to its search for God.

Alfred North Whitehead

Unpractical religion is unscriptural religion.

James Wolfendale

The only religion ... which is of any use is that which brings us back into harmony with divine law and into the orbit of perfect fellowship with God.

Frederick P. Wood

REPENTANCE — Blessings

When we truly comprehend our own nature, repentance is no dry doctrine, no frightening message, no morbid form of self-flagellation. It is, as the early church fathers said, a gift God grants which leads to life.

Charles Colson

Every man feels more comfort and spiritual joy after true repentance for a sin, than he had in that innocence before he committed the sin.

John Donne

Repentance is the golden key that opens the palace of eternity.

John Milton

Sorrow for sin is a perpetual rain, a sweet, soft shower which, to a truly gracious man, lasts all his life long.

C. H. Spurgeon

Repentance unravels sin, and makes sin not to be.

Thomas Watson

REPENTANCE — Essence
(See also: Confession; Contrition; Conviction of Sin; Penitence)

Repentance is an attitude that leads to action.

Repentance is an inner change of heart and mind and an outward change of life.

According to the greatness of the sin must the repentance be.

Ambrose

True repentance never exists in conjunction with faith, while, on the other hand, wherever there is true faith, there is also real repentance.

Louis Berkhof

Repentance is ultimate honesty.

Dietrich Bonhoeffer

No one repents of his own accord.

John Calvin

Repentance is nothing else but a reformation of the whole life according to the Law of God.

John Calvin

The beginning of repentance is the confession of guilt.

John Calvin

No repentance is true repentance which does not recognize Jesus as Lord over every area of life.

John C. Chapman

Repentance is the process by which we see ourselves, day by day, as we really are: sinful, needy, dependent people.

Charles Colson

Repentance is the soul's divorce from sin.

Al Martin

All true repentance arises from a sight of a dying Saviour, one who has died for us.

Thomas V. Moore

Repentance is, fundamentally, a change of direction, a turning from sin to God.

James Philip

Repentance is a plant that never grows on nature's dunghill. The nature must be changed, and repentance must be implanted by the Holy Spirit, or it will never flourish in our hearts.

C. H. Spurgeon

There will never be a tear of acceptable repentance in your eye till you have first looked to Jesus Christ.

C. H. Spurgeon

We must not only abstain from sin but abhor sin.

Thomas Watson

Wouldest thou know when thou hast been humbled enough for sin? When thou art willing to let go thy sins.

Thomas Watson

REPENTANCE — False

Remorse may be a long way from repentance.

Unless there is the fruit of repentance in the life, there is no evidence of the root of repentance in the heart.

You can't purify the water by painting the pump.
                    Anon.

If we seek God for our own good and profit, we are not seeking God.
            Meister Eckhart

Repentance which is occupied with thoughts of peace is hypocrisy.
            Martin Luther

REPENTANCE — and Holiness

It is much easier to repent of sins that we have committed than to repent of those we intend to commit.
            Josh Billings

Amendment is repentance.
            Thomas Fuller

Repentance is an ongoing process ... True repentance affects the whole man and alters the entire lifestyle.
        Richard Owen Roberts

There is no repentance where there is no change of heart.
            Robert Wilson

REPENTANCE — Importance
(See also: Conversion; Faith — Saving; Regeneration)

To get the world right, start with yourself.
                    Anon.

Repentance is an inescapable consequence of regeneration.
            Charles Colson

The saint is a penitent until he reaches heaven.
            R. L. Dabney

All true believers are lifelong repenters.
            Jim Elliff

Spiritual repentance is the creation of the Spirit.
            Erroll Hulse

You cannot drive repentance out of the teaching of Christ without destroying his teaching utterly and entirely.
        D. Martyn Lloyd-Jones

We make no spiritual progress apart from repentance.

Maurice Roberts

Christ and we will never be one until we and our sin are two.

C. H. Spurgeon

Repentance and faith are like Siamese twins. If one is sick, the other cannot be well, for they live but one life.

C. H. Spurgeon

You are not living to God as you ought unless you repent daily.

C. H. Spurgeon

An unrepented sin is a continued sin.

Corrie ten Boom

I was born for nothing but repentance.

Tertullian

God will take nine steps towards us, but he will not take the tenth. He will incline us to repent, but he cannot do our repenting for us.

A. W. Tozer

REPENTANCE — Urgency

He that hath promised pardon on our repentance hath not promised to preserve our lives till we repent.

Francis Quarles

There's no repentance in the grave.

Isaac Watts

REPUTATION

A good name keeps its lustre in the dark.

Anon.

It is better to be despised for the right than praised for the wrong.

Anon.

Reputation is often got without merit and lost without fault.

Anon.

Until we have learned to set very little value upon our own reputation, we will never be inflamed with true zeal in contending for the preservation and advancement of the interest of Divine glory.

John Calvin

What I do is all that concerns me and not what people think.

Ralph Waldo Emerson

RESPONSIBILITY

(See also: Duty; Service)

Initiative is our own personal responsibility. We cannot lay this upon any other person.

E. F. Hallock

Good and evil both increase at compound interest. That is why the little decisions you and I make every day are of such infinite importance.

C. S. Lewis

Of all the awkward people in your house or job there is only one whom you can improve very much.

C. S. Lewis

The sovereignty of God never excuses us from responsibility.

Will Metzger

To be a responsible person is to find one's own role and then, funded by the grace of God, to fill this role and to delight in it.

Cornelius Plantinga

To be a man is, precisely, to be responsible.

Saint-Exupery

It is easy to dodge our responsibilities, but we cannot dodge the consequences of dodging our responsibilities.

Josiah Stamp

He who governed the world before I was born shall take care of it likewise when I am dead. My part is to improve the present moment.

John Wesley

RESURRECTION OF CHRIST

The resurrection of Christ is our receipted bill.

Donald Grey Barnhouse

The resurrection of Christ is the commencement of his reign.

John Calvin

The resurrection of Christ is the most important article of our faith.

John Calvin

At the resurrection, Christ's real self, including his divine nature and his immaterial human nature, were joined to a new, immortal, incorruptible body for ever.

Robert G. Gromacki

The resurrection of Christ, as the evidence of the sacrifice of his death being accepted, and of the validity of all his claims, is a much more decisive proof

261

of the security of all who trust in him than his death could be.

Charles Hodge

The resurrection is a fact better attested than any event recorded in any history, whether ancient or modern.

C. H. Spurgeon

RESURRECTION OF CHRISTIANS

This world is a great sculptor's shop. We are the statues and there is a rumour going around that some of us are some day going to come to life.

C. S. Lewis

Our Lord has written the promise of the resurrection not in books alone, but in every leaf in springtime.

Martin Luther

REVELATION

(See also: Bible — Divine Authorship; Knowledge of God)

A Christian cannot live by philosophy. Only the light of Christian revelation gives the end as well as the means of life.

John Jay Chapman

Revelation never contradicts or sets aside the teachings of natural religion.

J. L. Dagg

Unless God imparts the spiritual ability to hear his voice, one hears nothing but meaningless words.

Ronald Dunn

No one could ever have found God; he gave himself away.

Meister Eckhart

Science must always be prepared to alter course when new facts demand such action. Revelation, on the other hand, is final.

Brian H. Edwards

It is axiomatic in our understanding of Christian doctrine that it is only in the light of the full revelation of God in Christ that we can perceive the kingdom of darkness clearly enough to understand its powers.

Sinclair Ferguson

No one less than God can bring us true and reliable information about him: God must give it himself.

Sinclair Ferguson

God does not tell us all we want to know about anything, but he will tell us all we need to know.
Vance Havner

The natural man can never be educated into apprehension of divine truth.
Vance Havner

There is no Christianity apart from revelation.
D. Martyn Lloyd-Jones

Worship is in response to truth about God and the truth about God is revealed in his Word.
John MacArthur

God does not ordinarily shout to make himself heard.
Gordon MacDonald

We do not believe that God has added, or ever will, anything to his revelation in his Son.
C. B. Moss

Revelation is a divine activity: not, therefore, a human achievement. Revelation is not the same thing as discovery or the dawning of insight, or the emerging of a bright idea. Revelation does not mean man finding God, but God finding man, God sharing his secrets with us, God showing us himself.
J. I. Packer

Instead of complaining that God had hidden himself, you will give him thanks for having revealed so much of himself.
Blaise Pascal

We know nothing from God except by revelation.
Charles Simeon

Modern man has lost any sense of God's nearness, but Christianity teaches that God reveals himself through every single thing he has ever brought into being, whether a created object or historical event.
R. C. Sproul

We need every word that God speaks.
David Watson

We should all be incurably agnostic if God had not revealed himself.
David Watson

REVENGE
(See also: Anger; Hatred)

A man who studies revenge keeps his own wounds green.
Francis Bacon

Men must not turn into bees and kill themselves in stinging others.
Francis Bacon

263

Revenge is a passion unbecoming the children of God.
John Calvin

The noblest revenge is to forgive.
Thomas Fuller

It is more honour to bury an injury than to revenge it.
Thomas Watson

REVIVAL

Man can no more organize revival than he can dictate to the wind.

Revival cannot be planned. It is a divine interruption.

I believe nothing so distinctly causes the people of God in any generation to 'stand in awe' as when they hear of the great works of God in awakening his people powerfully.
John H. Armstrong

Evangelism is man working for God; revival is God working in a sovereign way on man's behalf.
F. Carlton Booth

While revivals do not last, the effects of revival always endure.
F. Carlton Booth

No true revival has ever fed the ego of man, or encouraged superficiality.
Bob Cotton

It is misguided to think that God will revive a people who find no time to commune with him from the heart.
Jim Faucett

A revival is a work of God's Spirit among his own people.
Vance Havner

Sunday-morning Christianity is the greatest hindrance to true revival.
Vance Havner

There never was a real revival that did not produce heartburn and hallelujahs.
Vance Havner

Revival is a sovereign act of God upon the church whereby he intervenes to lift the situation completely out of human hands and works in extraordinary power.
Geoffrey R. King

A revival never needs to be advertised, it always advertises itself.
D. Martyn Lloyd-Jones

You cannot stop a revival any more than you can start it. It is altogether in the hands of God.
D. Martyn Lloyd-Jones

The characteristic of a revival is that a profound consciousness of sin is produced in many persons at the same time by an awareness of God.
Iain H. Murray

Revival is not some emotion or worked-up excitement; it is an invasion from heaven that brings a conscious awareness of God.
Stephen Olford

A revival out of balance is soon a revival out of power.
Richard Owen Roberts

Revival is the extraordinary movement of the Holy Spirit producing extraordinary results.
Richard Owen Roberts

It is a revival of scriptural knowledge, of vital godliness and of practical obedience.
William B. Sprague

Christian men should never speak of 'getting up a revival'. Where are you going to get it up from?
C. H. Spurgeon

Divine omnipotence is the doctrine of a revival.
C. H. Spurgeon

To prepare our hearts for revival is to prepare for heaven, so that in a true sense we can say that preparation for revival *is* revival.
William Still

They tell me a revival is only temporary; so is a bath, but it does you good.
Billy Sunday

RICHES
(See also: Materialism; Money; Possessions; Prosperity; Wealth)

He is rich who has enough to be charitable.
Thomas Browne

Not possession, but use, is the only riches.
Thomas Fuller

No kind of riches is a passport to the kingdom of heaven.
C. S. Lewis

Riches are but sugared lies, pleasant impostures, like a gilded cover which has not one leaf of true comfort bound up in it.
Thomas Watson

I fear, wherever riches have increased, the essence of religion has decreased in the same proportion.

John Wesley

RUMOUR
(See also: Gossip; Slander; Speech)

Trying to squash a rumour is like trying to unring a bell.

Shana Alexander

There's only one thing as difficult as unscrambling an egg, and that's unspreading a rumour.

Anon.

There is no such thing as an 'idle rumour'. Rumours are always busy.

F. G. Kernan

I know nothing swifter in life than the voice of rumour.

Plautus

The tale-bearer is an incendiary.

Thomas Watson

SACRIFICE

Sacrifice is the giving up of something we genuinely value in order to express our devotion to God.

John Benton

I never made a sacrifice. We ought not to talk of sacrifice when we remember the great sacrifice that he made who left his Father's throne on high to give himself for us.

David Livingstone

God will be our compensation for every sacrifice we have made.

F. B. Meyer

Self-denial is not so much an impoverishment as a postponement: we make a sacrifice of a present good for the sake of a future and greater good.

George Muller

SALVATION
(See also: Atonement; Redemption)

There is no such thing as salvation by character; what men need is salvation from *character.*

To save a single soul is beyond the combined legislation of the world's parliaments, the combined power of the world's armies, the combined wealth of the world's banks and the combined skill of the world's orators.

They never sought in vain that sought the Lord aright.

Robert Burns

Our salvation consists in the doctrine of the cross.

John Calvin

Salvation is not a cafeteria where you take what you want and leave the rest. You cannot take Christ as Saviour and refuse him as Lord and be saved.

Vance Havner

Salvation originates not in man but in God.

Simon J. Kistemaker

Salvation has nothing whatever to do with temperament.

D. Martyn Lloyd-Jones

If salvation could be attained only by working hard, then surely horses and donkeys would be in heaven.

Martin Luther

Salvation is moving from living death to deathless life.

Jack Odell

Feelings of confidence about our salvation need to be tested before they are trusted.

J. I. Packer

If there is any greater exercise of power than that which brought all things out of nothing, it is that which brings a clean thing out of an unclean, or makes a saint out of a sinner.

William S. Plumer

Christ promises to save his people from their sins, not in their sins.

C. H. Spurgeon

If any man ascribes anything of salvation, even the very least thing, to the free will of man, he knows nothing of grace, and he has not learned Jesus Christ rightly.

C. H. Spurgeon

It is not your hold of Christ that saves, but his hold of you!

C. H. Spurgeon

Salvation *in* sin is not possible; it always must be salvation *from* sin.

C. H. Spurgeon

The greatest of all miracles is the salvation of a soul.

C. H. Spurgeon

SATAN — Activity

Self-righteousness is the devil's masterpiece.

Thomas Adams

The devil is not always at one door.

Anon.

The devil entangles youth with beauty, the miser with gold, the ambitious with power, the learned with false doctrine.

H. G. Bohn

Wherever God has his church, the devil will be sure to set up his chapel; not a chapel of ease for the saints, but a chapel of service for himself.

William Burkitt

The devil wrestles with God, and the field of battle is the human heart.

Fyodor Dostoyevski

It is one of Satan's deep devices to call off the attention of the church from its own state to the condition of the world without and around her.

H. G. Fish

Our adversary majors in three things: noise, hurry and crowds.

Richard J. Foster

Satan deals in subtleties. Our Lord deals in simplicities.

Vance Havner

Satan's most effective work is done when he deceives people into thinking all is well.

Will Metzger

The method of the evil one is to obscure himself behind some other object of worship.

G. Campbell Morgan

It is the oldest stratagem of Satan to disfigure the truth by misrepresentation.

Iain H. Murray

The fundamental deception of Satan is the lie that obedience can never bring happiness.

R. C. Sproul

Satan is adept in teaching us how to steal our Master's glory.

C. H. Spurgeon

Satan watches for those vessels that sail without a convoy.

George Swinnock

The devil tries to shake truth by pretending to defend it.

Tertullian

SATAN — Existence and Nature
(See also: Antichrist)

We are opposed by a living, intelligent, resourceful and cunning enemy who can outlive the oldest Christian, outwork the busiest, outfight the strongest and outwit the wisest.

The devil always leaves a stink behind him.

Anon.

To Satan no sight is beautiful but deformity itself, and no smell is sweet but filth and nastiness.

John Calvin

God is the Great I AM. Satan is the great 'I am not'; and he is never happier than when he has convinced people that he is non-existent.

Vance Havner

Of all created beings the wickedest is one who originally stood in the immediate presence of God.

C. S. Lewis

Just as God cannot lie, the devil cannot do anything else.

R. C. Lucas

Satan doesn't care what we worship, as long as we don't worship God.

D. L. Moody

There is something very comforting in the thought that the devil is an adversary. I would sooner have him for an adversary than a friend.

C. H. Spurgeon

It is the devil's concern to keep his existence, presence, and working, secret. He chooses to work in the dark.

William Still

The devil is by nature a deceiver, and what better occupation than deceiving men about himself!

William Still

SATAN — Limitations

Satan ... can do nothing without the command of God, to whose dominion he is subject.

John Calvin

The whole of Satan's kingdom is subject to the authority of Christ.

John Calvin

Everything the devil does, God overreaches to serve his own purpose.

Oswald Chambers

Satan cannot give the Christian anything, for he has everything; nor can he take away anything, because he has nothing.

Vance Havner

Satan can afflict us, tempt us, only with divine permission.

Frank Retief

269

Satan, the hinderer, may build a barrier about us, but he can never roof us in, so that we cannot look up.

J. Hudson Taylor

SATAN — Power

Wherever God erects a house
of prayer,
The devil's sure to have a
chapel there;
And 'twill be found upon
examination,
The latter has the largest congregation.

Daniel Defoe

The devil can cite Scripture for his purpose.

William Shakespeare

The devil hath power to assume a pleasing shape.

William Shakespeare

He can make men dance upon the brink of hell as though they were on the verge of heaven.

C. H. Spurgeon

SATAN — Resisting
(See also: Temptation — and Sin)

It is easy to bid the devil to be your guest, but difficult to get rid of him.

Anon.

Without a death to self, there is no escape from Satan's power over us.

William Law

'Resisting the devil' does not mean 'rebuking' him by shout-ing at him. It refers to a godly lifestyle of submission to God, a break with the friendship of the world and a spirit of per-sonal humility.

Frank Retief

SCEPTICISM

Scepticism may be a nice game to play, but there is no way one can live on the basis of it.

Clark H. Pinnock

The city of truth cannot be built upon the swampy ground of scepticism.

Albert Schweitzer

SCIENCE

A knowledge of all the sci-ences is mere smoke where the heavenly science of Christ is wanting.

John Calvin

It is a diabolical science ... which fixes our contem-plations on the works of nature and turns them away from God.

John Calvin

Most people say it is the intellect which makes a great scientist. They are wrong: it is the character.

Albert Einstein

One thing I have learned in a long life — that all our science, measured against reality, is primitive and childlike.

Albert Einstein

Science without religion is lame, religion without science is blind.

Albert Einstein

A true scientist is known by his confession of ignorance.

A. O. Foster

Our scientific power has outrun our spiritual power. We have guided missiles and misguided men.

Martin Luther King

'Science', if it contradicts Scripture, is not science but a species of blasphemy.

Maurice Roberts

Every time a scientist works in his laboratory, he assumes the reality of God though he denies God with his lips.

R. J. Rushdoony

The true scientist never loses the faculty of amazement. It is the essence of his being.

Hans Seyle

Science has nothing to say to the deepest levels of human experience. What can science say to a heart being chilled by loneliness? What can science say to a heart broken by grief? What relief can science give to a life being turned prematurely grey by unforgiven sin and guilt?

Alan Walker

SECOND COMING OF CHRIST

It is a bad sign when people start discussing eschatology instead of preparing for the coming of Christ.

Christ keeps the minds of believers in a state of suspense until the last day.

John Calvin

If this is not an integral part of the faith once given to the saints, I do not know what is.

C. S. Lewis

Precisely because we cannot predict the moment, we must be ready at all moments.

C. S. Lewis

The primitive church thought a great deal more about the coming of Christ than about death, and thought a great deal more about his coming than about heaven.

Alexander MacLaren

Christ is coming to the earth, in such form at least as shall fulfil his purposes of mercy to his friends and justice to his foes.

Thomas V. Moore

Millions of graves are dug every year, but it is inspiring to think that one generation of Christians will cheat the undertaker.

J. C. Pollock

If I knew that our Lord would come this evening, I should preach just as I mean to preach; and if I knew he would come during this sermon, I would go on preaching until he did.

C. H. Spurgeon

Since he may come any day, it is well to be ready every day.

J. Hudson Taylor

SELF
(See also: Boasting; Conceit; Egotism; Pride)

Self is always at home.

Anon.

The hardest victory is victory over self.

Anon.

Beware of no man more than thyself.

Thomas Fuller

The rise of self is the beginning of unfaithfulness.

R. F. Horton

Sensitivity about self — is not this one of the greatest curses in life? It is a result of the Fall. We spend the whole of our life watching ourselves.

D. Martyn Lloyd-Jones

The whole trouble in life is ultimately a concern about self.

D. Martyn Lloyd-Jones

We have been saved from sin and its consequences in order to be delivered from self and its complexes.

Arthur Neil

No man can free himself from himself.

Herman Olshausen

We can never distrust ourselves too much.

J. I. Packer

Most of the small quarrels and conflicts we have in life occur because self is being threatened, challenged or ignored.

Frank Retief

The greatest burden we have to carry in life is self.

Hannah Whitall Smith

I would rather go to heaven doubting all the way than be lost through self-confidence.

C. H. Spurgeon

Self-derogation is bad for the reason that self must be there to derogate self. Self, whether swaggering or grovelling, can never be anything but hateful to God.

A. W. Tozer

SELF-CONTROL
(See also: Discipline)

Never expect to govern others until you have learned to govern yourself.

Anon.

Conquer yourself and you have conquered the world.

Augustine

Self-Crucifixion

It is impossible to be a follower of Jesus without giving diligent attention in our lives to the grace of self-control.

Jerry Bridges

There is a form of self-control that says 'yes' to what we should do as well as that which says 'no' to what we shouldn't do.

Jerry Bridges

True spiritual self-discipline holds believers in bounds but never in bonds; its effect is to enlarge, expand and liberate.

D. G. Kehl

The man who disciplines himself stands out and has the mark of greatness upon him.

D. Martyn Lloyd-Jones

SELF-CRUCIFIXION
(See also: Humility; Meekness)

To resist one's cross is to make it heavier.

Henri Amiel

No man can meditate on the heavenly life unless he be dead to the world and to himself.

John Calvin

No man is qualified to be a

disciple of Christ until he has been divested of self.

John Calvin

The chief praise of Christians is self-renunciation.

John Calvin

The only source of our mortification is our participation in the death of Christ.

John Calvin

The greatest of all crosses is self — if we die in part every day we shall have but little to do on the last. These little daily deaths will destroy the power of the final dying.

François Fenelon

If we do not let go of ourselves we can never reach him who is above us.

Gregory

The only thing we should do with self is consent to its crucifixion and co-operate with God in the process.

Vance Havner

Without a death to self, there is no escape from Satan's power over us.

William Law

A rejection, or in Scripture's strong language, a crucifixion of the natural self is the pass-port to everlasting life. Nothing that has not died will be resurrected.

C. S. Lewis

Die before you die. There is no chance after.

C. S. Lewis

You will be dead so long as you refuse to die.

George MacDonald

The cross is real wood, the nails are real iron, the vinegar truly tastes bitter, and the cry of desolation is live, not recorded.

Malcolm Muggeridge

The choicest believers, who are assuredly freed from the condemning power of sin, ought yet to make it their business all their days to mortify the indwelling power of sin.

John Owen

Do we want 'unction'? Do we want 'power'? Do we want 'revival'? It would be a major step towards all three if we could only learn to crucify our accursed pride more ruthlessly.

Maurice Roberts

The way of self-mortification is irksome to flesh and blood but it is the only safe way.

Maurice Roberts

If you do not die to sin, you shall die for sin.

C. H. Spurgeon

The cross is rough, and it is deadly, but it is effective.

A. W. Tozer

SELF-DELUSION

If you feel you have no faults, that makes another one.

Anon.

The easiest person to deceive is one's own self.

Edward Bulwer-Lytton

The heart of man has so many recesses of vanity, and so many retreats of falsehood, and is so enveloped with fraudulent hypocrisy, that it frequently deceives even himself.

John Calvin

The greatest fault is to be conscious of none.

Thomas Carlyle

Show me a thoroughly satisfied man and I will show you a failure.

Thomas Edison

The fountains of self-deceit are four in number: the rarity of reliable self-knowledge, self's power to deceive self, self letting itself be deceived by others, and self deceived by Satan.

Frederick W. Faber

The ultimate tragedy of man's self-understanding is that he believes himself to be free, has all the feelings of a free agent, but does not realize that he is a slave to sin and serves the will of Satan.

Sinclair Ferguson

Self-deceivers will prove in the end self-destroyers.

Matthew Henry

We lie loudest when we lie to ourselves.

Eric Hoffer

We are so used to disguising ourselves to others that at last we become disguised even to ourselves.

François Rochefoucauld

Every man is a good man in a bad world — as he himself knows.

William Saroyan

A sin is two sins when it is defended.

Henry Smith

SELF-DENIAL

To deny self is to become a nonconformist. The Bible tells us not to be conformed to this world either physically or intellectually or spiritually.
Billy Graham

Until we cease to live for self, we have not begun to live at all.
J. R. Miller

Self-denial is a summons to submit to the authority of God as Father and of Jesus as Lord and to declare lifelong war on one's instinctive egoism.
J. I. Packer

We are as near to heaven as we are from self, and far from the love of a sinful world.
Samuel Rutherford

Self-denial is the best touchstone of sincerity.
Thomas Watson

Self-denial is the very foundation of spiritual comfort.
Robert Wilson

SELF-EXAMINATION

Disciplined self-examination before God, in order to learn what one's weaknesses, blind spots, and deepest needs are, is an ongoing necessity.

The more we know of ourselves, the more cause we have to be humble.

It is not only the most difficult thing to know oneself, but the most inconvenient one, too.
Josh Billings

No man is worse for knowing the worst of himself.
H. G. Bohn

Man never achieves a clear knowledge of himself unless he has first looked upon God's face, and then descends from contemplating him to scrutinize himself.
John Calvin

Search others for their virtues, yourself for your vices.
Benjamin Franklin

Be soonest angry with thyself.
Thomas Fuller

Self-reflection is the school of wisdom.
Baltasar Gracian

Whoever has a proper knowledge of himself will be convinced that naturally there is nothing good in him.
Robert Haldane

Whenever I look inside myself, I am afraid.

C. E. M. Joad

If you don't do a great deal of preaching to yourself, you are a very poor kind of Christian.

D. Martyn Lloyd-Jones

If your knowledge of doctrine does not make you a great man of prayer, you had better examine yourself again.

D. Martyn Lloyd-Jones

No man ever became a Christian without stopping to look at himself.

D. Martyn Lloyd-Jones

Self-examination is the high road to prayer.

D. Martyn Lloyd-Jones

The thing we have to watch most of all is our strength, our strong point. We all tend to fail ultimately at our strong point.

D. Martyn Lloyd-Jones

Not only do we know God through Jesus Christ, we only know ourselves through Jesus Christ.

Blaise Pascal

The true cure for self-righteousness is self-knowledge.

J. C. Ryle

Self-knowledge grows out of man's self-confrontation with God.

Dietrich von Hildebrand

SELFISHNESS

People who are self-centred always live in unpleasant surroundings.

Anon.

Glory built on selfish principles is shame and guilt.

William Cowper

Selfishness is the greatest curse of the human race.

W. E. Gladstone

If I really love God my innate and persistent selfishness will have received its death-blow.

Alexander Smellie

He who lives only for himself is truly dead to others.

Publilius Syrus

Selfishness is the enemy of all true affection.

Cornelius Tacitus

SELF-PITY

Everyone thinks his sack is the heaviest.

Anon.

Our tears so blind our eyes that we cannot see our mercies.
John Flavel

As Christians we should never feel sorry for ourselves. The moment we do so, we lose our energy, we lose the will to fight and the will to live, and are paralysed.
D. Martyn Lloyd-Jones

What poison is to food, self-pity is to life.
Oliver G. Wilson

SELF-RIGHTEOUSNESS

Self-righteousness is the devil's masterpiece.
Thomas Adams

Never are men's hearts in such a hopeless condition as when they are not sensible of their own sins.
J. C. Ryle

SEPARATION

When the world is at its worst, Christians must be at their best.
Anon.

Is the world against me? ... then I am against the world!
Athanasius

Before the church can make an impact on the culture it must break with the idolatries and misconceptions that dominate the culture.
Donald Bloesch

Our lifestyle should not be determined by this age.
Sinclair Ferguson

The glory of the gospel is that when the church is absolutely different from the world she invariably attracts it.
D. Martyn Lloyd-Jones

Learn to hold loosely all that is not eternal.
Agnes Maude Royden

A man is known by the company he shuns as well as by the company he keeps.
C. H. Spurgeon

I like to warm my hands; but if I cannot warm them without burning them, I would rather keep them cold. Many things are in a measure desirable, but if you cannot obtain them without exposing yourself to the smut of sin, you had better let them alone.
C. H. Spurgeon

SERVICE — Dignity

The dignity of serving God is second only to the dignity of belonging to his family.

The highest honour in the church is not government but service.

John Calvin

Serving God with our little is the way to make it more; and we must never think that wasted with which God is honoured or men are blessed.

Henrietta Mears

God wants not slaves but intelligent, grown-up children who show enthusiasm for the family business.

Cornelius Plantinga

SERVICE — God's Part

Without God, we cannot. Without us, God will not.

Augustine

I was but a pen in God's hand and what praise is due to a pen?

John Bunyan

Our service cannot be approved of God except it be founded on his Word.

John Calvin

Whatever is laudable in our works proceeds from the grace of God.

John Calvin

The Christian worker must be sent; he must not elect to go.

Oswald Chambers

It is not what we do that matters, but what a sovereign God chooses to do through us. God doesn't want our success, he wants us. He doesn't demand our achievements; he demands our obedience.

Charles Colson

The first thing we need to do in the church these days is to discover that God's work must be done by God's people in God's way.

Vance Havner

The man who knows the love of Christ in his heart can do more in one hour than the busy type of man can do in a century.

D. Martyn Lloyd-Jones

Small numbers make no difference to God. There is nothing small if God is in it.

D. L. Moody

You do not do God a favour by serving him. He honours you by allowing you to serve him.

Victor Nyquist

The men that have moved the world for God have done what they have done not because they were strong, but because they were weak, and their weakness was transfigured by grace into an instrument in the hands of God for blessing.

James Philip

There is nothing in man that God has put there which may not be employed in God's service.

C. H. Spurgeon

God uses men who are weak and feeble enough to lean on him.

J. Hudson Taylor

He who serves God has a good Master.

Torriano

God who needs no one has in sovereign condescension stooped to work by and in his obedient children.

A. W. Tozer

We should all be willing to work for the Lord, but it is a matter of grace on God's part.

A. W. Tozer

God buries his workmen but carries on his work.

Charles Wesley

To say we have not power to do what God requires of us is blasphemy.

Thomas Wilson

SERVICE — Responsibility
(See also: Duty; Responsibility)

God has no larger field for the man who is not faithfully doing his work where he is.

Anon.

No man has a right to lead such a life of contemplation as to forget in his own ease the service due to his neighbour; nor has any man a right to be so immersed in active life as to neglect the contemplation of God.

Augustine

Go, labour on; spend and be
  spent —
Thy joy to do the Father's will;
It is the way the Master went;
Should not the servant tread it
  still?

Horatius Bonar

A cup can't hold much, but it can overflow a lot.

Robert Cook

Make your life a mission — not an intermission.

Arnold Glasgow

Too many are willing to sit at God's table, but not to work in his field.

Vance Havner

Find out where you can render a service; then render it. The rest is up to the Lord.

S. S. Kresge

He is no Christian who does not seek to serve his God.

C. H. Spurgeon

It is an abomination to let the grass grow up to your knees and do nothing towards making it into hay. God never sent a man into the world to be idle.

C. H. Spurgeon

Now is the watchword of the wise.

C. H. Spurgeon

We should employ our passions in the service of life, not spend life in the service of our passions.

Richard Steele

The most important place in this church is the back door.

Sandy Williams

SERVICE — Rewards

A candle loses nothing by lighting another candle.

Anon.

God is not greater if you reverence him, but you are greater if you serve him.

Augustine

Before the judgement seat of Christ my service will not be judged by how much I have done but by how much of me there is in it.

A. W. Tozer

As God will put a veil over his people's sins, so he will in free grace set a crown upon their works.

Thomas Watson

SERVICE — Wholeheartedness
(See also: Zeal)

Christian service is not meant to be a formality burdening the mind, but a fire burning in the heart.

Keep us, Lord, so awake in the duties of our callings that we may sleep in thy peace and awake in thy glory.

John Donne

281

Wherever you are, be all there. Live to the hilt every situation you believe to be the will of God.

Jim Elliot

God wants no compulsory service. On the contrary he loves a free, willing heart that serves him with a joyful heart and soul and does what is right joyfully.

Claus Felbinger

I hate to see a thing done by halves; if it be right, do it boldly; if it be wrong, leave it undone.

Bernard Gilpin

The service that counts is the service that costs.

Howard Hendricks

Determine never to be idle ... It is wonderful how much may be done if we are always doing.

Thomas Jefferson

When the heart is right, the feet are swift.

Thomas Jefferson

The danger of mistaking our merely natural, though perhaps legitimate, enthusiasm for holy zeal is always great.

C. S. Lewis

We never test the resources of God until we attempt the impossible.

F. B. Meyer

No man ever yet lost anything by serving God with a whole heart, or gained anything by serving him with half a one.

Thomas V. Moore

SICKNESS
(See also: Pain; Suffering; Trials)

Be laid aside in bed for a week. You will soon know whether you are a Christian or not!

D. Martyn Lloyd-Jones

If cures were to be found for every illness ever known, it would make no essential difference. We should be sick, mad and blind as long as we allowed ourselves to be wholly preoccupied with the hopes and desires of this world.

Malcolm Muggeridge

The fact is that many of God's choicest saints are what they are today because God did *not* heal them.

James Philip

SILENCE

Better silent than stupid.

Anon.

Eloquent listening requires as much genius as eloquent talking.

Anon.

Eloquent silence often is better than eloquent speech.

Anon.

It takes two years to learn to talk and seventy years to learn to keep your mouth shut.

Anon.

More have repented speech than silence.

Anon.

Silence is the element in which great things fashion themselves.

Thomas Carlyle

Speech is of time, silence is of eternity.

Thomas Carlyle

Silence is foolish if we are wise, but wise if we are foolish.

C. C. Colton

Silence is wisdom when speaking is folly.

Thomas Fuller

Better to be silent and be thought a fool than to speak out and remove all doubt.

Abraham Lincoln

To sin by silence when they should protest makes cowards out of men.

Abraham Lincoln

Well-timed silence is more eloquent than speech.

Martin Tupper

SIMPLICITY

Knowledge leads us from the simple to the complex; wisdom leads us from the complex to the simple.

Anon.

The longer I live, the more I covet simplicity.

Ernest F. Kevan

The more Christian a person is, the simpler will that person's life be.

D. Martyn Lloyd-Jones

The true hallmark of greatness is simplicity. It is little minds that are complicated and involved.

D. Martyn Lloyd-Jones

Whatever is Christian is always essentially simple. Simplicity is not incompatible with depth.

D. Martyn Lloyd-Jones

283

A man is rich in proportion to the number of things he can afford to let alone.

Henry Thoreau

SIN — and the Christian

There is something in man — even regenerate man — which objects to God and seeks to be independent of him.

F. F. Bruce

The holiest person is ... one who is most conscious of what sin is.

Oswald Chambers

The best of saints may be tempted to the worst of sins.

Matthew Henry

The worst sins of men are spiritual.

C. S. Lewis

You cannot play with sin and overcome it at the same time.

J. C. MacAulay

God, in mercy, will never allow children of his to be comfortable in sin.

Will Metzger

The grace of God which is in a real Christian will not allow him to be at rest in sin. A believer who has sinned is like a man who is required to be his own executioner.

Maurice Roberts

As soon as I learn that a brother states that he has lived for months without sin, I wonder whether his secret vice is lewdness, or theft, or drink, but I feel sure that somewhere or other there is a leak in the ship.

C. H. Spurgeon

There is a little hell within the heart of every child of God, and only the great God of heaven can master that mischievous indwelling sin.

C. H. Spurgeon

Only the mature believer reaches the place both of self-disgust and self-despair.

John R. W. Stott

For the Christian, to do wrong is to wound his Friend.

William Temple

SIN — Deceitfulness

Sin keeps us from knowing the true nature of sin.

To understand the deceitfulness of sin, compare its promises and its payments.

The least sin is infinitely evil.
David Clarkson

If there is anything worse than our sins, it is our infinite capacity to rationalize it away.
Charles Colson

Nothing can deceive unless it bears a plausible resemblance to reality.
C. S. Lewis

No wickedness proceeds on any grounds of reason.
Livy

Sin is never less quiet than when it seems to be most quiet.
John Owen

Vice is a monster of such
   frightful mien
As to be hated needs but to be
   seen;
Yet seen too oft, familiar with
   her face,
We first endure, then pity, then
   embrace.
Alexander Pope

Let's not listen for a minute to the contemptible question, 'What harm is there in it?' There's nothing *but* harm if Christ is not in it.
Scott Richardson

All sin is folly; all sinners are fools.
C. H. Spurgeon

A man can no more extract blessedness out of sin than he can suck health out of poison.
Thomas Watson

SIN — Effects

As virtue is its own reward, so vice is its own punishment.
Anon.

Evil enters like a needle and spreads like an oak tree.
Anon.

He who swims in sin will sink in sorrow.
Anon.

Those who go against the grain of God's laws shouldn't complain when they get splinters.
Anon.

He that is good is free, though he is a slave; he that is evil is a slave, though he be a king.
Augustine

The punishment of sin is sin.
Augustine

The sinner sins against himself; the wrongdoer wrongs

285

himself, becoming the worse by his own action.

Marcus Aurelius

Vice always renders the mind blind, and the heart hard, and shrouds everything in the moral world in midnight.

Albert Barnes

One leak will sink a ship; and one sin will destroy a sinner.

John Bunyan

We cannot do evil to others without doing it to ourselves.

J. F. E. Desmahis

You cannot do wrong without suffering wrong.

Ralph Waldo Emerson

Sin is the most expensive thing in the universe. Nothing else can cost so much.

Charles G. Finney

Sin pays — but it pays in remorse, regret and failure.

Billy Graham

Sin has got people into more trouble than science can get them out of.

Vance Havner

Sin is spiritual cancer, and the man who tries to live with it dies of it.

Vance Havner

Every wilful sinner ought to be told that he is a dead man.

Matthew Henry

That which is won ill will never wear well.

Matthew Henry

The seeds of our punishment are sown at the same time we commit the sin.

Hesiod

If you do Satan's work you must be prepared for his wages.

C. S. Lewis

The life of sin is always in some sense a life of boredom.

D. Martyn Lloyd-Jones

The tragedy of sin is that it affects man in his highest faculties. Sin causes us to become fools, and behave in an irrational manner.

D. Martyn Lloyd-Jones

Sin is an ill guest, for it always sets its lodging on fire.

Thomas Manton

Sin is but hell in embryo; hell is but sin in fulfilment.

Thomas V. Moore

The most fearful punishment of sinners is simply to leave them to themselves.

Thomas V. Moore

Those who are under the rule of sin are also under the wrath of God.

J. I. Packer

Disobedience has a price.

James Philip

Sin always comes home to roost.

James Philip

Sin always leads us much further than we intended to go.

James Philip

Sin begins with our departure from God; it ends with our departure from God.

James Philip

The effect sin has on God is to awaken his anger.

James Philip

Sin would have few takers if its consequences occurred immediately.

W. T. Purkiser

All wars, disease, sickness, death and even natural disasters can be traced back to that one act of representative disobedience in Eden.

Frank Retief

Sin has made us all mad as well as bad.

Maurice Roberts

Sin is fatal in all languages.

Roy L. Smith

God must smite sin wherever he sees it.

C. H. Spurgeon

It is a glorious truth that God will keep his people, but it is an abominable falsehood that sin will do them no harm.

C. H. Spurgeon

It is not the nature of sin to remain in a fixed state. Like decaying fruit, it grows more rotten. The man who is bad today will be worse tomorrow.

C. H. Spurgeon

It were better to die a thousand times than to sin.

C. H. Spurgeon

Sin drives men mad. Against their reason, against their best interests, they follow after that which they know will destroy them.

C. H. Spurgeon

Sin is a thief. It will rob your soul of its life. It will rob God of his glory. Sin is a murderer. It stabbed our father Adam. It slew our purity. Sin is a traitor. It rebels against the king of heaven and earth.

C. H. Spurgeon

No sin is small. No grain of sand is small in the mechanism of a watch.
> *Jeremy Taylor*

The world's turned upside
  down, from bad to worse,
Quite out of frame, the cart
  before the horse.
> *John Taylor*

Whatever is wrongfully achieved must lead to ruin.
> *David Thomas*

Never underestimate the ability of human beings to get themselves tangled up.
> *A. W. Tozer*

Sin makes a man worse than a toad or a serpent.
> *Thomas Watson*

Sin not only makes us unlike God but contrary to God.
> *Thomas Watson*

Neither the wicked nor the righteous can sin with impunity.
> *James Wolfendale*

SIN — Essence

All wickedness flows from a disregard of God.
> *John Calvin*

Sin is not wrong doing; it is wrong being; deliberate and emphatic independence of God.
> *Oswald Chambers*

The essence of sin is my right to my claim to myself.
> *Oswald Chambers*

Sin is essentially rebellion against the rule of God.
> *Charles Colson*

The sin of the world is not that it does not *do* the will of God but that it does not *choose* the will of God.
> *Arthur C. Custance*

It is in relation to God that sin assumes its essential significance; sin is not a mere defect or weakness in man, or an unsociable action, but rather an offence against God.
> *Eryl Davies*

Sin is moral leprosy.
> *Vance Havner*

All sin has its source in apostasy from God.
> *Erroll Hulse*

What is sin? It is failure to glorify God.
> *D. Martyn Lloyd-Jones*

Sin always aims at the utmost ... Every unclean thought or glance would be adultery if it could ... every thought of unbelief would be atheism.

John Owen

Sin is not a social concept; it is a theological concept.

J. I. Packer

Sin is the contradiction of God and the antipodes of his nature.

Maurice Roberts

The essence of original sin is to hate God.

R. C. Sproul

Sin is an unlimited and unmitigated evil.

C. H. Spurgeon

Sin is Christicide.

C. H. Spurgeon

Sin is not a splash of mud on a man's exterior; it is filth generated within himself.

C. H. Spurgeon

The essence of sin is rebellion against divine authority.

A. W. Tozer

A sinner is a devil in man's shape.

Thomas Watson

SIN — Fact

Man cannot cover what God would reveal.

Thomas Campbell

The doctrine of sin is the foundation of the doctrine of grace.

David Jussely

Mere time does nothing either to the fact or the guilt of sin.

C. S. Lewis

SIN OF OMISSION
(See also: Negligence)

Our minds should not dwell upon the good we do, but upon that which we neglect to do.

Gregory the Great

I do not know any subject that so much distresses me, humbles me and lays me in the dust, as the thought of my omissions. It is not what I have done about which I think so much as of what I have not done.

C. H. Spurgeon

SIN — Power

Sin's misery and God's mercy are beyond measure.

Anon.

What a thing is sin, what a devil and master of devils is it, that it should, where it takes hold, so hang that nothing can unclinch its hold but the mercy of God and the heart-blood of his dear Son!

John Bunyan

Sin is arguably the greatest power in existence but for the power of God himself. It is not only an evil but an infinite evil. It is not merely against God but absolutely and entirely against God.

Maurice Roberts

Sin is never satisfied.

Maurice Roberts

The more men suppress the truth of God which they know, the more futile, even senseless, they become in their thinking.

John R. W. Stott

SINCERITY
(See also: Honesty)

We may truly be said to worship God though we lack perfection, but we cannot be said to worship God if we lack sincerity.

Stephen Charnock

Nothing is more pleasing to God than sincerity and plain-dealing.

Matthew Henry

The primary condition for sincerity is the same as for being humble: not to boast of it, and probably not even to be aware of it.

Henri Peyre

The conduct of our lives is the only proof of the sincerity of our hearts.

Robert Wilson

SINFUL NATURE
(See also: Depravity; Guilt; Man — a Sinner; Sin)

In the conversion of man, the properties of our original nature remain entire.

John Calvin

The ground of the soul is dark.

Meister Eckhart

Evil is the real problem in the hearts and minds of men.

Albert Einstein

Original sin is the malice that is ever flickering within us.

Eric Hoffer

The true Christian's nostril is to be continually attentive to the inner cesspool.

C. S. Lewis

Man today is as rotten as he was the moment he fell in the Garden of Eden.

D. Martyn Lloyd-Jones

Human nature is like a drunk peasant. Lift him into the saddle on one side, over he topples on the other side.

Martin Luther

I find not one corruption of my vile heart is dead, though some seem now and then asleep.

John Newton

I have a vile heart, capable of every evil; and I, in myself, am as prone to change as a weathercock.

John Newton

Beware of no man more than of yourself; we carry our worst enemies within us.

C. H. Spurgeon

During my first week the new life that was in me had been compelled to fight for its existence, and a conflict with the old nature had been vigorously carried on. This I knew to be a special token of the indwelling of grace in my soul.

C. H. Spurgeon

Our old man is crucified, but he is long at dying.

C. H. Spurgeon

The saints are sinners still.

C. H. Spurgeon

There is no doctrine more true to experience than this, that corruption remains even in the hearts of the regenerate, and that when we would do good evil is present with us.

C. H. Spurgeon

SLANDER
(See also: Gossip; Rumour; Speech)

Slanderers are the devil's bellows to blow up contention.

Anon.

Slander is best answered with silence.

Ben Johnson

Whispered insinuations are the rhetoric of the devil.

Johann Wolfgang

SOLITUDE

It is far better to be alone than to be in bad company.

Anon.

Solitude is often the best society.

Anon.

Observe what directions your thoughts and feelings most readily take when you are alone, and you will form a tolerably correct opinion of your real state.

J. A. Bengel

Solitude is the soul's best friend.

Charles Cotton

You are only what you are when no one is looking.

Robert C. Edwards

Conversation enriches the understanding, but solitude is the school of genius.

Edward Gibbon

People who cannot bear to be alone are the worst company.

Albert Guinon

It is what we do with our solitude that makes us fit for company.

C. S. Lewis

Have we not all known what it is to find that, somehow, we have less to say to God when we are alone than when we are in the presence of others?

D. Martyn Lloyd-Jones

What I am in secret, that I am in reality.

Arthur Neil

Not till we have lost the world do we begin to find ourselves.

Henry Thoreau

In the poverty of solitude all riches are present.

Paul Tillich

SORROW

He who does not sigh as a pilgrim will never rejoice as a citizen.

Augustine

There is nothing that so makes us acquainted with Christ himself as sorrow.

Horatius Bonar

No matter how great a sorrow may be, God has already suffered it.

Meister Eckhart

I wonder, many times, that ever a child of God should have a sad heart, considering what his Lord is preparing for him.

Samuel Rutherford

Better to have a Christian's days of sorrows than a worldling's joys.

C. H. Spurgeon

Sorrows are visitors that come without invitation.

C. H. Spurgeon

There is a sweet joy that comes to us through sorrow.

C. H. Spurgeon

SOUL
(See also: Heart)

Man does not have a soul, he is a soul.

James Barr

The soul is such a thing, so rich and valuable in its nature, that scarce one in twenty thousand counts of it as they should.

John Bunyan

The fundamental error of sinners is undervaluing their own souls.

Matthew Henry

The soul is the place where man's supreme and final battles are fought.

Abraham Neuman

The meaning of earthly existence lies, not as we have grown used to thinking, in prospering, but in the development of the soul.

Alexandr Solzhenitsyn

The moral character of the soul depends upon its central object.

David Thomas

SOUL-WINNING
(See also: Evangelism; Witnessing)

The level of our concern for the salvation of others reflects the condition of our own souls.

Owen French

The glory of God, and, as our only means to glorifying him, the salvation of souls, is the real business of life.

C. S. Lewis

The salvation of souls is a means to the glorifying of God because only saved souls can duly glorify him.

C. S. Lewis

The best soul-winners are those who go when it is convenient, and then go when it is not convenient.

John Rice

Better indeed for us to die than to live if souls be not saved.

C. H. Spurgeon

Have you no wish for others to be saved? Then you are not saved yourself. Be sure of that.

C. H. Spurgeon

I would sooner bring one sinner to Jesus Christ than un-pick all the mysteries of the divine Word.

C. H. Spurgeon

The soul-winner must first be a soul-lover.

C. H. Spurgeon

To be a soul-winner is the hap-piest thing in this world. And with every soul you bring to Jesus Christ you seem to get a new heaven here upon earth.

C. H. Spurgeon

It is a great work to make people fit for the cemetery.

William Tiptaft

No Christian has any right ever to feel comfortable as long as there are any anywhere who do not know Christ.

Max Warren

To bring souls to Christ should be our master passion.

Frederick P. Wood

SPEECH
(See also: Gossip; Rumour; Slander)

It is easier to look wise than to talk wisely.

Ambrose

A bird is known by his note, a man by his talk.

Anon.

Actions don't always speak louder than words — your tongue can undo everything you do.

Anon.

When you speak, remember God is one of your listeners.

Anon.

The tongue is the hinge on which everything in the per-sonality turns.

T. C. Baird

A word spoken is physically transient but morally perma-nent.

Francis Burkitt

When you have nothing to say, say nothing.

C. C. Colton

The worst of speaking without thinking is that you say what you think.

James Denney

Let thy speech be better than silence, or be silent.

Dionysius the Elder

Nothing is often a good thing to say.

Will Durant

The heart of a fool is in his mouth, but the mouth of a wise man is in his heart.

Benjamin Franklin

If nobody said anything unless he knew what he was talking about, what a ghastly hush would descend upon the earth!

A. P. Herbert

There is a time for saying nothing; there is occasionally a time for saying something; there is never a time for saying everything.

Hugh of St Victor

If you can hold your tongue you can hold anything.

E. Stanley Jones

Better to remain silent and be thought a fool than to speak out and remove all doubt.

Abraham Lincoln

The tongue is the ambassador of the heart.

John Lyly

Man's speech is like his life.

Plato

When I think over what I have said, I envy dumb people.

Seneca

If we cannot be believed on our word, we are surely not to be trusted on our oath.

C. H. Spurgeon

Speech is the mirror of the soul; as a man speaks, so he is.

Publilius Syrus

A man is hid under his tongue.

Ali Ibn-Ali-Talib

A ready tongue without an informed mind, a devout character and a holy life will hinder rather than advance the cause of Christ.

Curtis Vaughan

SPIRITUAL DARKNESS

There is no greater darkness than ignorance of God.

John Calvin

SPIRITUAL GIFTS

The things that count most cannot be counted.

Anon.

All know that the gift of healing was not perpetual ... The anointers of this day are no more ministers of the grace of which James speaks than the player who acted Agamemnon on the stage was a king.

John Calvin

All the gifts and power which men seem to possess are in the hands of God, so that he can, at any instant ... deprive them of the wisdom which he has given them.

John Calvin

It is dangerously easy to fix our hearts on the blessing rather than the Blesser.

Ronald Dunn

To place ourselves in range of God's choicest gifts, we have to walk with God, work with God, lean on God, cling to God, come to have the sense and feel of God, refer all things to God.

Cornelius Plantinga

SPIRITUAL HUNGER

God promises to fill those who hunger and thirst after righteousness, yet the sign that he is doing so is that they go on hungering and thirsting.

Taking in its widest latitude, to 'hunger and thirst after righteousness' means to yearn after God's favour, image and felicity.

A. W. Pink

They who do not thirst for righteousness shall be in perpetual hunger and thirst.

Thomas Watson

O for a heart to praise my God,
A heart from sin set free;
A heart that always feels thy blood
So freely shed for me.

Charles Wesley

SPIRITUAL RICHES

It's wiser to have your bank in heaven than to have your heaven in a bank.

Anon.

God, and God alone, is man's highest good.

Herman Bavinck

If we are spiritually impoverished, it is not because the hand of grace is tight-fisted; it is because the hand of faith is too weak.

Ronald Dunn

A man is just as rich as his investment in the bank of heaven.

Vance Havner

God wants no man to be more prosperous than his soul.

Vance Havner

It takes a radical break to turn
from earth's trash to heaven's
treasure.
Vance Havner

The trees of the age to come
extend their branches over the
wall on this side and we may
enjoy some of their fruits here
and now.
Vance Havner

A man with God on his side is
always in the majority.
John Knox

My Father, help me to learn
that I am heir to possessions
which exceed my present holding!
George Matheson

With the goodness of God to
desire our highest welfare, the
wisdom of God to plan it, and
the power of God to achieve it,
what do we lack?
A. W. Tozer

It is unlikely that God will en-
trust us with spiritual riches until he sees that we are genuinely
serving him, not mammon.
David Watson

All Christ's subjects are kings.
Thomas Watson

SPIRITUAL WARFARE

The hardest victory is victory
over self.
Anon.

Spiritual depression cannot be
resisted by flight, but must be
struggled with and resisted.
John Cassian

God has appointed this whole
life to be all as a race or a battle;
the state of rest, wherein we
shall be so out of danger as to
have no need of watching and
fighting, is for another world.
Jonathan Edwards

Jesus invited us not to a picnic
but to a pilgrimage; not to a
frolic but to a fight.
Billy Graham

The constant challenge in this
life we call Christian is the
translation of all we believe to
be true into our day-to-day lifestyle.
Tim Hansel

We are not here to commune
with darkness but to conquer it.
Vance Havner

We do not become saints in our
sleep.
Vance Havner

Sometimes we are praying when we should be resisting Satan.

D. Martyn Lloyd-Jones

Keeping our heads despite the pull of pleasure is as hard a task as any for the affluent believer.

J. I. Packer

Christianity is a battle — not a dream.

Wendell Phillips

There is no winning without warfare; there is no opportunity without opposition; there is no victory without vigilance.

Alan Redpath

There is only one attitude possible for us if we mean to get to heaven. We must wage a ceaseless warfare against sin within us all the days of our life.

Maurice Roberts

What greater encouragement can a man have to fight against his enemy than when he is sure of the victory before he fights — of final victory?

Richard Sibbes

I have never won an inch of the way to heaven without fighting for it.

C. H. Spurgeon

I thank God with all my heart that I have never known what it is to be out of the seventh of Romans, nor out of the eighth of Romans either: the whole passage has been solid truth to my experience.

C. H. Spurgeon

It strikes me that conflict is the principal feature of the Christian life this side of heaven.

C. H. Spurgeon

Dead fish go with the stream, living ones against it.

William Tiptaft

SPIRITUALITY

Attitudes to God, especially as we come to him in worship, are the true monitor of spirituality.

John Benton

It is very rare for the spirituality of a group of Christians to exceed that of its leaders.

John Benton

Sentiment is the main opponent of spirituality.

Art Glasser

Every Christian would agree that a man's spiritual health is exactly proportional to his love for God.

C. S. Lewis

The measure of our spirituality is the amount of praise and thanksgiving in our prayers.
D. Martyn Lloyd-Jones

The more spiritual we are, the more we shall think about heaven.
D. Martyn Lloyd-Jones

The ultimate test of our spirituality is the measure of our amazement at the grace of God.
D. Martyn Lloyd-Jones

Learn to hold loosely all that is not eternal.
Agnes Maude Royden

STUBBORNNESS

Ignorance is closely followed by obstinacy.
John Calvin

Hardness of heart makes a man's condition worse than all his other sins besides.
Thomas Watson

Hell is full of hard hearts; there is not one soft heart there.
Thomas Watson

SUBMISSION

(See also: Abandonment; Consecration; Zeal)

We should give God the same place in our hearts that he holds in the universe.
Anon.

I dare not choose my lot;
I would not if I might.
Choose thou for me, my God,
So shall I walk aright.
Horatius Bonar

Jesus will not be a Saviour to any man who refuses to bow to him as Lord.
Walter J. Chantry

There are no disappointments to those whose wills are buried in the will of God.
Frederick W. Faber

SUCCESS

No one ever climbed the ladder of success with his hands in his pockets.
Anon.

The dictionary is the only place where you can find success before work.
Anon.

To find his place and fill it is success for a man.

Phillips Brooks

It's a dangerous and misguided policy to measure God's blessing by standards of visible, tangible, material 'success'.

Charles Colson

The secret of success is constancy to purpose.

Benjamin Disraeli

Success can feather our nest so comfortably that we forget how to fly.

Vance Havner

Visible success has never been the proof of Jesus or his followers.

Vance Havner

Pray that success will not come any faster than you are able to endure it.

Elbert Hubbard

Many who are climbing the ladder of success have their ladders leaning against the wrong walls.

Erwin W. Lutzer

Nothing recedes like success.

Walter Winchell

SUFFERING
(See also: Pain; Sickness; Trials)

In suffering one learns to pray best of all.

Harold A. Bosley

Although the world is full of suffering, it is full also of the overcoming of it.

Helen Keller

Our sufferings are not always reasonable.

Frank Retief

Probably one of the hardest aspects of suffering to endure is the fact that our suffering is not explained. It would be much easier if we knew why.

Frank Retief

We must do away once and for all with the great myth that suffering is never part of God's will.

Frank Retief

All the suffering I could possibly endure could not earn me a place in heaven.

R. C. Sproul

God does not witness to the world by taking his people out of suffering, but rather by demonstrating his grace through them in the midst of pain.

C. Samuel Storms

SYMPATHY

Next to love, sympathy is the divinest passion of the human heart.

William Burke

Sympathy is a supporting atmosphere.

Ralph Waldo Emerson

TELEVISION

Television is called a medium because so little of it is rare or well done.

Fred Allen

Television is chewing gum for the eyes.

Fred Allen

The easiest way to find more time to do all the things you want to do is to turn off the television.

O. A. Battista

The primary danger of the television screen lies not so much in the behaviour it *produces* as the behaviour it *prevents* — the talks, the games, the family activities, and the arguments through which much of the child's learning takes place and his character is formed.

Urie Bronfenbrenner

Television is an invention that permits you to be entertained in your living room by people you wouldn't have in your home.

David Frost

Television is the literature of the illiterate.

Lee Loevinger

I find television very educating. Every time somebody turns on the set I go into the other room and read a book.

Groucho Marx

TEMPER

A man who can't control his temper is like a city without defences.

Anon.

The most important time to hold your temper is when the other person has lost his.

Harold Smith

TEMPTATION — Avoiding and Resisting

Following the lines of least resistance makes men and rivers crooked.

Anon.

He who avoids the temptation avoids the sin.

Anon.

No one can be caught in a place he does not visit.

Anon.

There is no merit in abstaining from what one is not tempted to do.

Anon.

We are never strong enough to risk walking into temptation.

Anon.

When you run away from temptation, don't leave a forwarding address.

Anon.

Each temptation leaves us better or worse; neutrality is impossible.

Erwin W. Lutzer

Our response to temptation is an accurate barometer of our love for God.

Erwin W. Lutzer

There is a time for holy running.

Al Martin

Temptations are never so dangerous as when they come to us in a religious garb.

D. L. Moody

God is better served in resisting a temptation to evil than in many formal prayers.

William Penn

The best defence against the temptation to stray from God is the possession by experience of his rich gifts that meet all desires.

James Philip

It is much easier to suppress a first desire than to satisfy those that follow.

François Rochefoucauld

Of two evils, choose neither.

C. H. Spurgeon

Things forbidden have a secret charm.

Tacitus

Temptation can cause us to succumb, sink, sin or stand.

William A. Ward

TEMPTATION — Blessing

Tempting times are teaching times.

William Bridge

The more you are tempted by Satan, the more you are pitied by God.

William Bridge

Temptation and adversity are the two best books in my library.

Martin Luther

TEMPTATION — Certainty

The man who has never been tempted doesn't know how dishonest he is.

Josh Billings

The greatest temptations sometimes follow the highest manifestation of God's love.

William Bridge

If you have not been through the devil's sifter, you are probably not worth sifting!

Vance Havner

Sin is seldom, if ever, original.

Maurice Roberts

There is no ripe fruit unpecked by the birds.

C. H. Spurgeon

We shall always be in danger as long as we are here.

C. H. Spurgeon

TEMPTATION — and Satan

(See also: Satan)

As Satan can tell how to suit temptations for you in the day of your want, so he has those that can entangle you in the day of your fulness.

John Bunyan

We cannot stand against the wiles of the devil by our wits.

Oswald Chambers

God never tempts any man. That is Satan's business.

Billy Graham

We must not so much as taste of the devil's broth, lest at last he brings us to eat of his beef.

Thomas Hall

An empty heart is an invitation to the devil.

Vance Havner

The devil can go no farther than God permits.

Vance Havner

Sometimes we are praying when we should be resisting Satan.

D. Martyn Lloyd-Jones

We must not blame the devil for our choices.

Frank Retief

303

The devil's temptations have no need to be original because the old, well-tried snares of the past are usually successful enough in each succeeding generation.

Maurice Roberts

He who will fight the devil with his own weapons must not wonder if he finds him an overmatch.

Robert South

Idle Christians are not tempted of the devil so much as they tempt the devil to tempt them.

C. H. Spurgeon

Temptation is the devil looking through the keyhole; yielding is opening the door and inviting him in.

Billy Sunday

It must not be expected that the devil will let those rest who are labouring to destroy his kingdom.

Thomas Wilson

TEMPTATION — and Sin

Temptation has its source not in the outer lure but in the inner lust.

D. Edmond Hiebert

THANKSGIVING
(See also: Gratitude)

To give thanks sincerely, one must give more than thanks.

Anon.

Thanksgiving is not a natural virtue; it is a fruit of the Spirit, given by him.

Jerry Bridges

How worthy it is to remember former benefits when we come to beg for new.

Stephen Charnock

Thankfulness grows best in the seed-bed of conviction, just as some plants must be placed in the soil in the winter if they are to flower in the summer.

Sinclair Ferguson

THEOLOGY
(See also: Bible; Doctrine)

Every Christian should be a theologian.

All theology, when separated from Christ, is not only vain and confused, but is also mad, deceitful and spurious.

John Calvin

Deep theology is the best fuel of devotion; it readily catches

fire and, once kindled, it burns
long.
Frederick W. Faber

The price of theological integrity, like that of liberty, is eternal vigilance.
Timothy George

Our theology must become biography.
Tim Hansel

Theology should be empress, and philosophy and the other arts merely her servants.
Martin Luther

Theology's proper goal is to equip the disciples of Jesus Christ for obedience.
J. I. Packer

Think of theologians as the church's sewage specialists. Their role is to detect and eliminate intellectual pollution, and to ensure, so far as man can, that God's life-giving truth flows pure and unpoisoned into Christian hearts.
J. I. Packer

A sound theology must be a theology where grace is central to it.
R. C. Sproul

Our errors in theology are rooted in our pride and our slothfulness.
R. C. Sproul

To commit theological error is to commit sin.
R. C. Sproul

Believe that all theology is rotten rubbish which is not the Word of the Lord.
C. H. Spurgeon

If your theology doesn't change your behaviour it will never change your destiny.
C. H. Spurgeon

My entire theology can be condensed into four words: 'Jesus died for me'.
C. H. Spurgeon

To be either true or useful, theology must be a passion.
Augustus H. Strong

Theological beliefs may get one into a church, but not into the kingdom of God.
Stanley I. Stuber

Theological truth is useless until it is obeyed.
A. W. Tozer

THOUGHTS
(See also: Mind)

The probable reason some people get lost in thought is because it is unfamiliar territory to them.

Anon.

Thinking evil is the same as doing it.

Anon.

Pure thoughts cannot produce evil deeds.

Augustine

One must live the way one thinks or end up thinking the way one has lived.

Paul Bourget

We allow in our minds what we would not allow in our actions, because other people cannot see our thoughts.

Jerry Bridges

To think is an effort; to think rightly is a great effort; and to think as a Christian ought to think is the greatest effort of a human soul.

Oswald Chambers

What is the hardest task in the world? To think.

Ralph Waldo Emerson

How we think is one of the great determining factors in how we live.

Sinclair Ferguson

It is right for us to take thought, but not for thought to take us!

D. Martyn Lloyd-Jones

Controlling and directing one's thoughts is a habit, and the more one practises it the better one becomes at it.

J. I. Packer

Thoughts have a moral character.

David Thomas

If we would think God's thoughts, we must learn to think continually of God.

A. W. Tozer

Guard well your thoughts; our thoughts are heard in heaven.

Owen D. Young

TIME — and Eternity

Time is nothing to God.

Oswald Chambers

It is difficult for me to understand how an intelligent person can spend all of his time building for this world and have no time for the future world.

Billy Graham

All that is not eternal is eternally out of date.
C. S. Lewis

God is not subject to time.
Dorothy L. Sayers

Right now counts for ever.
R. C. Sproul

Time is not God's master, but his servant.
William Still

God dwells in eternity, but time dwells in God. He has already lived all our tomorrows as he has lived all our yesterdays.
A. W. Tozer

TIME — Misuse

I would I could stand on a busy corner, hat in hand, and beg people to throw me all their wasted hours.
Bernard Berenson

Too often a man handles life as he does bad weather. He whiles away the time as he waits for it to stop.
Polger

Misspending a man's time is a sort of self-homicide.
George Savile

You cannot kill time without injury to eternity.
Henry Thoreau

A man has no time for which he is not accountable to God. If his very diversions are not governed by reason and religion he will one day suffer for the time he has spent in them.
Thomas Wilson

TIME — Urgency

It is better to lose anything than to lose time; we can recover lost money, but time is irrecoverable.
Chrysostom

The morning hour has gold in its hand.
Benjamin Franklin

He who neglects the present moment throws away all he has.
Johann von Schiller

TIME — Use

Time should not be spent, it should be invested in the kingdom of God.

Half our life is spent trying to

find something to do with the time we have rushed through life trying to save.

Will Rogers

TRIALS — Blessings
(See also: Pain; Sickness; Suffering)

Adversity introduces a man to himself.

Anon.

Affliction, like the iron-smith, shapes as it smites.

Anon.

Crosses are ladders that lead to heaven.

Anon.

Affliction is the shaking of the torch that it may blaze the brighter.

Horatius Bonar

In the darkness of our miseries the grace of God shines more brightly.

John Calvin

Our afflictions prepare us for receiving the grace of God.

John Calvin

Whatever poison Satan produces, God turns it into medicine for his elect.

John Calvin

The saint knows not why he suffers as he does, yet he comprehends with a knowledge that passes knowledge that all is well.

Oswald Chambers

Calamity is the perfect glass wherein we truly see and know ourselves.

William Davenant

Great men are made greater by their misfortunes.

Minucius Felix

It takes the grindstone to sharpen the axe.

Vance Havner

It is better to drink of deep griefs than to taste shallow pleasures.

William Hazlitt

Christian people are generally at their best when they are in the furnace of affliction and being persecuted and tried.

D. Martyn Lloyd-Jones

Trials and tribulations are very good for us in that they help us to know ourselves better than we knew ourselves before.

D. Martyn Lloyd-Jones

Afflictions are a fan in God's hand to separate between good and evil men.

Maurice Roberts

No enemy of Christ's cause ... has it in his competence to inflict so much as one naked blow on the Christian or on the church. Every blow is parried for our good. Every curse aimed at us is sweetened into a blessing. Every poisonous dart is deflected. Every wound is healed. Every accusation is silenced.

Maurice Roberts

Trials are the resistances God gives us to strengthen our spiritual muscles.

George Seevers

Misfortune is an occasion to demonstrate character.

Seneca

No one appears to me more pitiable than the man who has never known misfortune.

Seneca

We become wiser by adversity.

Seneca

A true Christian's losses are gains in another shape.

C. H. Spurgeon

I am afraid that all the grace that I have got out of my comfortable and easy times and happy hours might almost lie on a penny. But the good that I have received from my sorrows, and pains, and griefs, is altogether incalculable. What do I not owe to the crucible and the furnace, the bellows that have blown up the coals, and the hand which has thrust me into the heat?

C. H. Spurgeon

I am sure I have derived more real benefit and permanent strength and growth in grace, and every precious thing, from the furnace of affliction, than I have ever derived from prosperity.

C. H. Spurgeon

I bear my witness that the worst days I have ever had have turned out to be my best days.

C. H. Spurgeon

I can bear my personal testimony that the best piece of furniture that I ever had in the house was a cross. I do not mean a material cross; I mean the cross of affliction and trouble.

C. H. Spurgeon

I owe more than I can tell to the graver's tool, and I feel the lines of its cutting even now.

C. H. Spurgeon

None of us can come to the

highest maturity without enduring the summer heat of trials.

C. H. Spurgeon

On some few occasions I have had troubles which I could not tell to any but my God, and I thank God I have, for I learned more of my Lord then that at any other time.

C. H. Spurgeon

The Christian gains by his losses. He acquires health by his sickness. He wins friends through his bereavements, and he becomes a conqueror through his defeats.

C. H. Spurgeon

There is nothing that makes a man have a big heart like a great trial.

C. H. Spurgeon

We find no sword-blades so true in metal as those which have been forged in the furnace of soul-trouble.

C. H. Spurgeon

Christians are commonly best in affliction.

Thomas Watson

The eyes that sin shuts affliction opens.

Thomas Watson

We know not what we lose when we pray to be delivered out of afflictions, because God always increases his consolation and grace as afflictions abound.

Thomas Wilson

I am mended by my sickness, enriched by my poverty, and strengthened by my weakness.

Abraham Wright

What fools we are, then, to frown upon our afflictions! These, how crabbed soever, are our best friends. They are not intended for our pleasure, they are for our profit.

Abraham Wright

TRIALS — Certainty

God promises the Christian heaven after death, not before it.

Sin has turned the world from a paradise into a thicket; there is no getting through without being scratched.

Thomas Boston

The disciples of Christ must walk among thorns, and march to the cross amidst uninterrupted afflictions.

John Calvin

Perpetual sunshine is not usual in this world, even to God's true saints.

Jonathan Edwards

There is far more agony than ecstasy in this world of things as they are.

Vance Havner

Every true saint is heir to the cross.

Martin Luther

There is no guarantee that men faithful to God will be recognizable by their numbers, their talents or their success.

Iain H. Murray

Trouble-free living is not the lot of the children of Adam, even when they become the children of God.

Frank Retief

It is winter with the saints sometimes, when the tree has no leaves, yet the life is in it.

Daniel Rowland

You will not get leave to steal quietly to heaven without a conflict and a cross.

Samuel Rutherford

Christianity promises us no escape from the opposition of wicked men; indeed it teaches us to expect it.

David Thomas

You must not always expect the wind to be at your back all the way to heaven.

William Tiptaft

Afflictions fit for heaven.

Thomas Watson

Though Christ died to take away the curse from us, yet not to take away the cross from us.

Thomas Watson

TRIALS — God the Sender

Nothing that happens to the Christian is accidental or incidental.

God sends nothing but what can be borne.

Anon.

Men think that God is destroying them when he is tuning them.

Henry Ward Beecher

We are always in the forge or on the anvil; by trials God is shaping us for higher things.

Henry Ward Beecher

Affliction is the expression of paternal love.

Horatius Bonar

The Lord has given me both vinegar and honey, but he has given me the vinegar with a teaspoon and the honey with a ladle.

Billy Bray

Many crosses spring forth to us from the root of God's favour.

John Calvin

We are not afflicted by chance, but through the infallible providence of God.

John Calvin

When visited with affliction, it is of great importance that we should consider it as coming from God, and as expressly intended for our good.

John Calvin

By suffering God's will, we learn to do God's will.

Thomas Case

God does not do what false Christianity makes out — keep a man immune from trouble.

Oswald Chambers

If God has made your cup sweet, drink it with grace. If he has made it bitter, drink it in communion with him.

Oswald Chambers

God does not always spare us trouble, but he does succour us in trouble.

Vance Havner

The grace, the groans and the glory are all part of the eternal purpose. Where there is no groaning there is no growing now, nor glory to come.

Vance Havner

God ne'er afflicts us more than
    our desert,
Though he may seem to over-
    act his part.
Sometimes he strikes us more
    than flesh can bear,
But yet still less than grace can
    suffer here.

Robert Herrick

Good when he gives, su-
    premely good,
Nor less when he denies.
E'en crosses from his sover-
    eign hand
Are blessings in disguise.

James Hervey

It is a great consolation to know that dissensions ... are not fortuitous, but are ordered by the providence of God, and are designed, as storms, for the purpose of purification.

Charles Hodge

Troubles appear to be in God's catalogue of mercies, and we cannot do without them.

Thomas Jones

God, who foresaw your tribulation, has specially armed you to go through it, not without pain but without stain.

C. S. Lewis

The great thing, if one can, is to stop regarding all the unpleasant things as interruptions of one's own or real life. The truth is of course that what one calls the interruptions are precisely one's real life — the life God is sending one day by day.

C. S. Lewis

God often puts us in situations that are too much for us so that we will learn that no situation is too much for him.

Erwin W. Lutzer

Our heavenly Father never takes anything from his children unless he means to give them something better.

George Muller

God has lessons for us to learn in our times of trouble, and he is strong enough to resist our piteous cries for relief until the discipline of pain does its gracious work in our souls.

James Philip

Having called believers into his grand designs, which means into fellowship with his sufferings, God is not slow to share with them the fruits of his travail, in terms of blessing and glory, here and hereafter.

James Philip

God loves his own children too well to exempt them from affliction.

William S. Plumer

No matter how long our trial may be, it will never be too long for God's intention.

P. B. Power

God permits no suffering or trials without a purpose, even though that purpose may be hidden from us.

Frank Retief

Trials are no evidence of being without God, since trials come from God!

C. H. Spurgeon

We never have such close dealings with God as when we are in tribulation.

C. H. Spurgeon

God afflicts with the same love as he adopts.

Thomas Watson

Usually, when the Lord intends us some signal mercy, he fits us for it by some eminent trial.

Thomas Watson

TRIALS — Response

It is better to get to heaven battered, bruised and bleeding than to go happily to hell.

Anon.

The longer we dwell on our misfortunes, the greater is their power to harm us.

Anon.

It is more commendable to bear affliction patiently than to be busy in good works.

Bonaventura

Had we a clearer view of the other world, we should make so much of either the smiles or frowns of this.

Thomas Boston

The person who is patient under mistreatment by others is the person who has developed such a confidence in the wisdom, power and faithfulness of God that he willingly entrusts his circumstances into his hands.

Jerry Bridges

Every chastisement is a call to repentance.

John Calvin

Worship God in the difficult circumstances and, when he chooses, he will alter them in two seconds.

Oswald Chambers

God has not departed because the day is dark.

Vance Havner

We should glory in our infirmities, but not glorify them.

Vance Havner

When I consider my crosses, tribulations and temptations, I shame myself almost to death thinking of what they are in comparison to the sufferings of my blessed Saviour, Jesus Christ.

Martin Luther

To lie down in the time of grief, to be quiet under the stroke of adverse fortune, implies a great strength.

George Matheson

Bearing wrong is a glorious part of the fellowship with Christ's sufferings.

Andrew Murray

As mature or maturing Christians we should realize that God may not always want us to have an easy time — which is in effect what we ask for when we ask for affliction to be removed.

James Philip

It is never legitimate to be angry with God. To do so is an affront to God's holiness. It is an unspoken declaration that God has done an injustice.

R. C. Sproul

Cry for grace from God to see God's purpose in every trial, and then for grace to submit to it, at once; to accept it, to rejoice in it. This is usually the end of trouble.

C. H. Spurgeon

Let no excess of suffering drive us away from the throne of grace, but rather let it drive us closer to it.

C. H. Spurgeon

Let us be sure to praise God when things go ill with us!

C. H. Spurgeon

When a train goes through a tunnel and it gets dark, you don't throw away your ticket and jump off. You sit still and trust the engineer.

Corrie ten Boom

We are all good till we are tried.

William Tiptaft

TRIALS — Temporary Nature

The punishments inflicted by God on his servants are only temporary, and intended as medicine.

John Calvin

You can't get to tomorrow morning without going through tonight.

Elisabeth Elliot

All the tribulations of this life are but incidents on the road from groans to glory.

Vance Havner

The ills of this present life ... cannot harm us. For they are simply introductory, a kind of preface to the main theme; they are not what the real story is about.

James Philip

Light are the pains that nature
  brings;
How short our sorrows are,
When with eternal future
  things
The present we compare!
Isaac Watts

TRUTH
(See also: Honesty)

*God forbid that we should ever
be satisfied either with heated
ignorance or frozen truth.*

Add one small bit to the truth
and you inevitably subtract
from it.
Anon.

The man who speaks the truth
is always at ease.
Anon.

The trouble with stretching the
truth is that people are apt to see
through it.
Anon.

Truth needs no defence; it is
beyond attack.
James Bolen

Naked truth is too hard for
armed error.
Francis Burkitt

Nothing is deemed more
precious by God than truth.
John Calvin

Always tell the truth. Then you
don't have to worry about what
you said last.
Robert Cook

The truth does not vary because men forget or ignore or
traduce it.
Irwin Edman

It cannot be overemphasized
that men and women who have
accomplished anything in
God's strength have always
done so on the basis of their
grasp of truth.
Sinclair Ferguson

Speak boldly and speak truly.
Shame the devil!
John Fletcher

A lie stands on one leg, truth on
two.
Benjamin Franklin

Truth fears no trial.
Thomas Fuller

The temple of truth will not be
damaged half so much by
woodpeckers on the outside as
by termites on the inside.
Vance Havner

Whenever unbelief thinks it has buried the truth, the 'corpse' always comes to life in the midst of the funeral to outlive all the pallbearers.
Vance Havner

Write nothing, say nothing, think nothing that you cannot believe to be true before God.
Joseph Joubert

Absolute truth belongs to God alone.
Gotthold Lessing

Truth is always about something, but reality is that about which truth is.
C. S. Lewis

The business of the truth is to set us free from sin.
D. Martyn Lloyd-Jones

It is better that the heavens fall than that one crumb of truth perish.
Martin Luther

Seek not greatness, but seek truth and you will find both.
Horace Mann

The claims of truth are paramount.
John Murray

Right is right, even if everyone is against it; and wrong is wrong, even if everyone is for it.
William Penn

Truth often suffers more by the heat of its defenders than by the arguments of its opposers.
William Penn

There are none so bitter against the truth as those who have departed from it.
James Philip

Truth needs no flowers of speech.
Alexander Pope

There is no power on earth more formidable than the truth.
Margaret Lee Runbeck

Truth has no responsibility to make us comfortable.
David L. Russell

Nothing sets the heart on fire like truth.
John R. W. Stott

Our Lord Jesus Christ called himself the Truth not the Custom.
Tertullian

The devil tries to shake the truth by pretending to defend it.
Tertullian

Truth does not blush.
Tertullian

Truth in propositions is powerful; truth in example is more
powerful.
David Thomas

God is the source of all truth,
and every discovery is a means
of glorifying him.
Gene Veith

All truth is God's truth, and all
must ultimately be one.
J. Stafford Wright

UNBELIEF
(See also: Agnosticism; Atheism)

Living without faith is like
driving in a fog.
Anon.

Unbelief ... is always proud.
John Calvin

Unbelief makes us rebels and
deserters.
John Calvin

Unbelieving and irreligious
men have no ears.
John Calvin

Disobedience and unbelief are
two sides of the same coin.
Ronald Dunn

What loneliness is more lonely
than distrust?
George Eliot

God excludes none if they do
not exclude themselves.
William Guthrie

Unbelief is at the bottom of
what sinners do ignorantly.
Matthew Henry

Unbelief ... makes the world a
moral desert, where no divine
footsteps are heard, where no
angels ascend and descend,
where no living hand adorns
the fields, feeds the birds of
heaven, or regulates events.
F. W. Krummacher

The Bible itself gives us one
short prayer which is suitable
for all who are struggling with
the beliefs and doctrines. It is:
Lord I believe, help Thou my
unbelief.
C. S. Lewis

When you are arguing against
God you are arguing against
the very Power that makes you
able to argue at all.
C. S. Lewis

No difficulty in believing the
gospel is intellectual, it is
always moral.
D. Martyn Lloyd-Jones

As no one can give himself faith, neither can he take away his unbelief.

Martin Luther

Ultimately, the acceptance of the gospel is a moral problem not an intellectual problem.

Will Metzger

The natural man does not want to believe that God has spoken.

Tom Nettles

Unbelief makes God a liar and, worse still, a perjurer, for it accounts him as not only false to his word, but to his oath.

A. T. Pierson

No maniac ever reasoned more illogically than the unbeliever.

William S. Plumer

The difficulties of Christianity no doubt are great; but depend on it, they are nothing compared to the difficulties of infidelity.

J. C. Ryle

Those who deny God are bound to bestow all his attributes on flesh and blood.

Isaac Bashevis Singer

The revelation of the gospel is to a world that is already under indictment for its universal rejection of God the Father.

R. C. Sproul

Those who spurn the gospel challenge not the power of the church but the sovereignty of God.

R. C. Sproul

There are no infidels anywhere but on earth. There are none in heaven and there are none in hell.

C. H. Spurgeon

Unbelief calls itself 'honest doubt', and not without cause, for we should not have known it to be honest if it had not labelled itself so.

C. H. Spurgeon

Unbelief will destroy the best of us. Faith will save the worst of us.

C. H. Spurgeon

If the way to heaven is so narrow, and so few seek it, what will become of those who never seek it?

William Tiptaft

Every man will have to decide for himself whether or not he cannot afford the terrible luxury of unbelief.

A. W. Tozer

Faith unlocks the divine storehouse, but unbelief bars its doors.

Curtis Vaughan

Unbelief is the foul medley of all sins, the root and receptacle of sin.

Thomas Watson

Unbelief is the root of apostasy.

Thomas Watson

URGENCY

Making the most of today is the best way to be ready for tomorrow.

Anon.

The big word with God is *now*.

Vance Havner

Today is God's time. Tonight your soul may be required. Set your watch with heaven and not the faulty timepieces of earth.

Vance Havner

Now is the watchword of the wise.

C. H. Spurgeon

VANITY

(See also: Boasting; Conceit; Egotism; Pride)

Some people are so sensitive that when you pat them on the back their head swells.

Anon.

We know nothing vainer than the minds of men.

John Calvin

Guard against that vanity which courts a compliment, or is fed by it.

Thomas Chalmers

We are all imbued with the love of praise.

Cicero

VIGILANCE

True grace always produces vigilance rather than complacency; it always produces perseverance rather than indolence.

Jerry Bridges

The more anyone excels in grace, the more ought he to be afraid of falling.

John Calvin

Keep us, Lord, so awake in our callings that we may sleep in thy peace and awake in thy glory.

John Donne

VIRGIN BIRTH
(See also: Incarnation — Jesus Christ)

The New Testament presentation of Jesus is not an agglomeration, but an organism, and of that organism the virgin birth is an integral part. Remove the part and the whole becomes harder and not easier to accept.

J. Gresham Machen

For history the really strong argument in favour of the virgin birth is the difficulty of accounting for the story otherwise than on the assumption of its truth.

H. R. Mackintosh

It seems far more difficult to believe that the God of eternity would become a man by natural human procreative processes than to believe that he would be miraculously conceived and virgin-born!

Henry M. Morris

VIRTUE
(See also: Ethics; Goodness; Morality)

Virtue flourishes in misfortune.

Anon.

Virtue never needs the help of vice; she is self-sufficient.

Aristotle

WAR

In war all humanity and equity is buried.

John Calvin

War is one of God's judgements.

John Calvin

The tragedy of war is that it uses man's best to do man's worst.

Harry Emerson Fosdick

What a fine-looking thing is war! Yet ... what is it but murder in uniform?

Douglas Jerrold

The most persistent sound that reverberates through men's history is the beating of war drums.

Arthur Koestler

If active service does not persuade a man to prepare for death, what conceivable concatenation of circumstances would?

C. S. Lewis

O war! Thou son of hell!
William Shakespeare

No calamities have ever befallen nations that are so much to be deplored as the atrocities of war.

C. H. Spurgeon

In war there is no such thing as victor and vanquished ... There is only a loser, and that loser is mankind.

U. Thant

WEALTH
(See also: Luxury; Materialism; Money; Possessions; Prosperity; Riches)

A golden bit does not make a better horse.

Anon.

Chains of gold are stronger than chains of iron.

Anon.

Gold is the heaviest of all metals, but is made more heavy by covetousness.

Anon.

The greater our wealth, the greater our dangers.

Aristotle

All the wealth of this world is nothing else but a heap of clay.
John Calvin

Without the rich heart, wealth is an ugly beggar.
Ralph Waldo Emerson

Gold will be slave or master.
Horace

Few people have the spiritual resources to be both wealthy and godly.

Erwin W. Lutzer

Keeping our heads despite the pull of pleasure is as hard a task as any for the affluent believer.
J. I. Packer

Wisdom outweighs any wealth.

Sophocles

The streets of gold do not have too great an appeal for those who pile up gold here on earth.
A. W. Tozer

WILL
(See also: Free Will)

The Holy Spirit teaches us in

Scripture that our mind is smitten with so much blindness, that the affections of our heart are so depraved and perverted, that our whole nature is vitiated, that we can do nothing but sin until he forms a new will within us.

John Calvin

Man's will always acts in accordance with its disposition.

Jonathan Edwards

The essence of the virtue and vice of dispositions of the heart and acts of the will lies not in their cause but in their nature.

Jonathan Edwards

Such biblical emphasis on man's will as there is tends to emphasize its bondage rather than its freedom.

Sinclair Ferguson

WILL OF GOD
(See also: Guidance; Providence)

A man's heart is right when he wills what God wills.

Thomas Aquinas

The moral will is the only will of God of which we may be certain in our experience.

Jack Arnold

Our duty is found in the revealed will of God in the Scriptures. Our trust must be in the sovereign will of God, as he works in the ordinary circumstances of our daily lives for our good and for his glory.

Jerry Bridges

God cannot approve of anything that is not supported by his Word.

John Calvin

By suffering God's will, we learn to do God's will.

Thomas Case

The sin of the world is not that it does not *do* the will of God but that it does not *choose* the will of God.

Arthur C. Custance

There are no disappointments to those whose wills are buried in the will of God.

Frederick W. Faber

To walk out of God's will is to walk into nowhere.

C. S. Lewis

'Not as I will, but as thou wilt.' To be able to say these words and truly mean them is the highest point we can ever hope to attain.

Malcolm Muggeridge

We must do away once and for all with the great myth that suffering is never part of God's will.

Frank Retief

There is no other will but the Master's will, for all other wills subserve his, whether they will or no.

William Still

God's heavenly plan doesn't always make earthly sense.

Charles R. Swindoll

The power of God is identified with his will; what he cannot do is what he will not do.

Tertullian

WISDOM

Wisdom gives a balance to character.

Knowledge leads us from the simple to the complex; wisdom leads us from the complex to the simple.

Anon.

This is our wisdom, to be learners to the end.

John Calvin

To search for wisdom apart from Christ means not simply foolhardiness but utter insanity.

John Calvin

True wisdom consists in being wise according to the law of God.

John Calvin

Wisdom is not the growth of human genius. It must be sought from above.

John Calvin

The only way to know is to will to do God's will.

Oswald Chambers

Wisdom must be from God, because it can be found only in relation to him.

Edmund P. Clowney

True wisdom is always humble.

Richard Fuller

No man is really wise unless he lives in the will and for the glory of God.

Geoffrey Grogan

If you lack knowledge, go to school. If you lack wisdom, get on your knees! Knowledge is not wisdom. Wisdom is the proper use of knowledge.

Vance Havner

He who has a constant longing for wisdom will persistently pray for it.

D. Edmond Hiebert

The next best thing to being wise is to live in a circle of those who are.

C. S. Lewis

Wisdom is God-centred.

Michael Parsons

Wisdom is always an overmatch for strength.

Phaedrus

The desire of appearing to be wise often prevents our becoming so.

François Rochefoucauld

The wisest mind has something yet to learn.

George Santanaya

If ... our wisdom has been acquired without any of that eagerness and painful diligence with which the covetous man desires and seeks for his riches, it is a shrewd conjecture that it is not of the genuine sort.

Thomas Scott

Wisdom in ruling is justice; wisdom in speech is discretion; wisdom in conduct is prudence; wisdom in evaluation is discernment.

George Seevers

To know God, and Jesus Christ whom he has sent, is the highest principle and perfection of man. This attainment, infinitely above all others, constitutes true wisdom.

Charles Simeon

Wisdom outweighs any wealth.

Sophocles

We can be certain that God wants us to be wise, just as we are sure that he wants us not to sin.

R. C. Sproul

The wisest person in the world is the person who knows the most about God.

A. W. Tozer

The true test of wisdom is works, not words.

Curtis Vaughan

WITNESSING
(See also: Evangelism; Soul-Winning)

Every Christian occupies some kind of pulpit and preaches

some kind of sermon every day.

Anon.

If you want your neighbour to know what Christ will do for him, let your neighbour see what Christ has done for you.

Henry Ward Beecher

If you can't shine, at least twinkle!

Alistair Begg

Witnessing is not an effort, it is an overspill.

Robert Cook

Too many Christians live their Christian lives inside their heads; it never gets out through hands and feet and lips.

Vance Havner

We are the salt of the earth, not the sugar, and our ministry is truly to cleanse and not just to change the taste.

Vance Havner

You can never speak to the wrong man about Christ.

Peter McFarlane

God has no dumb children.

J. C. Ryle

Christians are in the world to be witnesses, and they must concentrate on their calling.

Paul B. Smith

Nothing shuts the mouth, seals the lips, ties the tongue, like the poverty of our own spiritual experience. We do not bear witness for the simple reason that we have no witness to bear.

John R. W. Stott

Only the sheer rapture of being lost in the worship of God is as exhilarating and intoxicating as telling someone about Jesus Christ.

Donald S. Whitney

The most powerful ongoing Christian witness has always been the speaking of God's Word by one who is living in God's Word.

Donald S. Whitney

WORK

Too many Christians worship their work, work at their play and play at their worship.

Anon.

Men were created to employ themselves in some work, and not to lie down in inactivity and idleness.

John Calvin

Man was made to work, because the God who made him was a 'working God'.

Sinclair Ferguson

If a man is called to be a streetsweeper, he should sweep streets even as Michelangelo painted, or Beethoven composed music, or Shakespeare poetry.

Martin Luther King

There can be intemperance in work just as in drink.

C. S. Lewis

One of the greatest blessings of humanity is that divine law which requires men to work for their livelihood.

David Thomas

No race can prosper until it learns that there is as much dignity in tilling a field as in writing a poem.

Booker T. Washington

WORLD
(See also: Worldliness)

The created world is but a small parenthesis in eternity.

Thomas Browne

What a charming place this world would be if it was not for the inhabitants.

Esther Burr

There is no neutral ground in the universe: every square inch, every split second, is claimed by God and counterclaimed by Satan.

C. S. Lewis

Nothing in the world can be properly understood unless it is understood in terms of God's design and plan.

R. C. Sproul

Without God the world would be a maze without a clue.

Woodrow Wilson

WORLDLINESS
(See also: World)

The mind of a Christian ought not to be filled with thoughts of earthly things, or find satisfaction in them, for we ought to be living as if we might have to leave this world at any moment.

John Calvin

Worldliness is rampant in the church. The devil is not fighting churches, he is joining them! He isn't persecuting Christianity, he is professing it.

Vance Havner

The health of our bodies, the passions of our minds, the noise and hurry and pleasures and business of the world, lead us on with eyes that see not and ears that hear not.

William Law

If I walk with the world, I can't walk with God.

D. L. Moody

Those who love the world serve and worship themselves every moment: it is their full-time job.

J. I. Packer

He that is in love with the world will be out of love with the cross.

Thomas Watson

WORRY
(See also: Anxiety; Fear)

Worry gives a small thing a big shadow.

Anon.

Worry is like a rocking chair; it will give you something to do, but it won't get you anywhere.

Anon.

You can't change the past, but you can ruin a perfectly good present by worrying about the future.

Anon.

Worry is to life and progress what sand is to the bearings of perfect engines.

Roger Babson

Worry is an indication that we think God cannot look after us.

Oswald Chambers

It is not work but worry that kills, and it is amazing how much wear the human mind and body can stand if it is free from friction and well oiled by the Spirit.

Vance Havner

Worry is the traitor in our camp that dampens our powder and weakens our aim.

William Jordan

The essence of worry ... is the absence of thought, a failure to think.

D. Martyn Lloyd-Jones

Not work, but worry makes us weary.

S. I. McMillen

Be careful for nothing, prayerful for everything, thankful for anything.

D. L. Moody

WORSHIP — Blessings

Worship renews the spirit as sleep renews the body.
Richard C. Cabot

An attitude of worship can cut down an avalanche of words.
Vance Havner

If we want to know God and to be blessed of God, we must start by worshipping him.
D. Martyn Lloyd-Jones

If worship does not change us it has not been worship.
John MacArthur

God is most glorified in us when we are most satisfied in him, and we are most satisfied in him in worship.
John Piper

Worship alone of all the activities of the believer will continue in heaven and will occupy the redeemed host for ever.
Robert G. Rayburn

WORSHIP — Essence

Worship does not have to be dull to be deep.

Devotion is not an activity; it is an attitude towards God.
Jerry Bridges

The beginning and perfection of lawful worship is readiness to obey.
John Calvin

Without the heart it is no worship. It is a stage play. It is an acting a part without being that person, really. It is playing the hypocrite.
Stephen Charnock

It is impossible to use God and worship him at the same time.
Larry Crabb

True worship is seen not in the ingredients of the service but in the inclination of the heart.
Brian H. Edwards

Our Lord approved neither idol worship nor idle worship, but ideal worship, in spirit and truth.
Vance Havner

True worship is a blend of godly fear and trembling together with joy that we are accepted in the Beloved.
Erroll Hulse

God is more real to me than any thought or thing or person.
William James

Worship begins in holy ecstasy; it ends in holy obedience — or it isn't worship.

John MacArthur

You cannot worship God in a vacuum. You cannot worship God apart from his revelation.

John MacArthur

Worship that costs us nothing is worth precisely what it costs.

Leon Morris

Worship is the adoration of a redeemed people, occupied with God himself.

A. W. Pink

Worship is the activity of the new life of a believer in which, recognizing the fulness of the Godhead as it is revealed in the person of Jesus Christ and his mighty redemptive acts, he seeks by the power of the Holy Spirit to render to the living God the glory, honour and submission which are his due.

Robert G. Rayburn

To worship God in truth is to worship him as he commands.

R. C. Sproul

No worship is wholly pleasing to God until there is nothing in me displeasing to God.

A. W. Tozer

True worship is to be so personally and hopelessly in love with God that the idea of a transfer of affection never even remotely exists.

A. W. Tozer

Worship in all its grades and kinds is the response of the creature to the Eternal.

Evelyn Underhill

In every part of our worship we must present Christ to God in the arms of faith.

Thomas Watson

Worship is a response to greatness.

Tom Wells

To worship God in spirit is to worship from the inside out.

Donald S. Whitney

WORSHIP — Importance
(See also: Awe; Fear of God)

Attitudes to God, especially as we come to him in worship, are the true monitor of spirituality.

John Benton

Does not every true man feel that he is himself made higher by doing reverence to what is really above him?

Thomas Carlyle

Worship ought to describe everything the people of God do when they come together, and above all in the preaching of the Word of God.

Graham Harrison

Devotion signifies a life given or devoted to God.

William Law

We — or at least I — shall not be able to adore God on the highest occasions if we have learned no habit of doing so on the lowest.

C. S. Lewis

Every man becomes the image of the man he adores. He whose worship is directed to a dead thing becomes a dead thing. He who loves corruption rots. He who loves a shadow becomes, himself, a shadow.

Thomas Merton

A man's worship is governed by what he believes, for worship is man's means of ascribing to God that adoration, reverence, praise, love, and obedience of which he sincerely believes God to be worthy.

Robert G. Rayburn

He who knows God reverences him.

Seneca

All places are places of worship to a Christian. Wherever he is, he ought to be in a worshipping frame of mind.

C. H. Spurgeon

I like, sometimes, to leave off praying, and to sit still, and just gaze upwards till my inmost soul has seen my Lord.

C. H. Spurgeon

Soul worship is the soul of worship, and if you take away the soul from worship you have killed the worship.

C. H. Spurgeon

Nowhere in Scripture is true worship portrayed in other than serious terms.

Geoff Thomas

I can safely say, on the authority of all that is revealed in the Word of God, that any man or woman on this earth who is bored and turned off by worship is not ready for heaven.

A. W. Tozer

I mean it when I say that I would rather worship God than do anything else.

A. W. Tozer

If there is any honesty left in us, it persuades us in our quieter moments that true spiritual worship is at a discouragingly low ebb among professing Christians.

A. W. Tozer

The whole course of the life is upset by failure to put God where he belongs.

A. W. Tozer

What comes into our mind when we think about God is the most important thing about us.

A. W. Tozer

YOUTH

The passions of the young are vices in the old.

Joseph Joubert

We cannot always build the future for our youth, but we can build our youth for the future.

Franklin D. Roosevelt

Youth is a time of life wherein we have too much pride to be governed by others, and too little wisdom to govern ourselves.

Henry Scougal

ZEAL

(See also: Abandonment; Consecration; Passion; Service — Wholeheartedness; Submission)

Not all Christians have great mental powers, or are extrovert personalities, but all should be zealous.

Timothy G. Alford

It is better the pot should boil over than not boil at all.

Anon.

Zeal without doctrine is like a sword in the hand of a lunatic.

John Calvin

Unless a man undertakes more than he can possibly do, he will never do all that he can.

Henry Drummond

Zeal without knowledge is fire without light.

Thomas Fuller

Earnestness commands the respect of mankind. A wavering, vacillating, dead-and-alive Christian does not get the respect of the church or of the world.

John Hall

As well a chariot without its steeds, a sun without its beams, a heaven without its joy, as a man of God without zeal.

C. H. Spurgeon

Nothing sets the heart on fire like truth.

John R. W. Stott

Lord, let me not live to be useless!

John Wesley

_____

Subject Index

Abandonment

Abortion

Actions

Activism

Addiction — see Habit

Adoption

Adoration — see Awe; Worship

Adversity — see Pain; Sickness;
    Suffering; Trials

Advice

Affliction — see Pain; Sickness;
    Suffering; Trials

Age — see Old Age

Agnosticism

Aim — see Purpose

Alcohol

Ambition

Angels

Angels — Fallen — see Demons

Anger

Annihilation

Antichrist

Antinomianism

Anxiety

Apathy

Apostasy

Arrogance — see Conceit; Pride

Art

Ascension — see Jesus Christ —
    Ascension

Assurance

Atheism

Atonement

Authority

Avarice — see Greed

Awe

Backsliding

Beauty

Behaviour — see Actions

Belief — see Faith

Bible — and Christ

Bible — Divine Authorship

Bible — Fulness

Bible — and the Holy Spirit

Bible — Inerrancy

Bible — Influence and Power

Bible — Preservation

Bible — Purpose

Bible — Relevance

Bible — Submission to

Bible — Supremacy

Bible — Unity

Bible Study

Bigotry

Blessings — see Spiritual Gifts

Boasting

Bravery — see Courage

Brokenness — see Humility;
    Repentance; Self-
    Crucifixion; Submission

Family Life — a Test of
Character
Fasting — see Prayer — and
Fasting
Fear
Fear of God
Feelings — see Emotions
Fellowship
Fellowship with God — see
Communion with God
Flattery
Forgiveness by God
Forgiveness of Others
Formalism
Fortitude — see Patience
Freedom — see Liberty
Free Will
Friendship
Fruitfulness
Fulness of Life
Future

Generosity
Gentleness
Gifts — Spiritual — see
Spiritual Gifts
Giving
Gloom — see Despair
Glory — see God — Glory
Gluttony
Goal — see Purpose
God — Eternity
God — Existence
God — Faithfulness
God — Forgiveness — see
Forgiveness by God
God — Glory
God — Goodness

God — Holiness
God — Independence
God — Inscrutability
God — Jealousy
God — Justice
God — Law — see Law of God
God — Love
God — Mercy — see Mercy
from God
God — Name
God — Omnipotence
God — Omnipresence
God — Omniscience
God — Patience
God — Perfection
God — Promises — see
Promises of God
God — Purposes
God — Sovereignty
God — Will — see Will of God
God — Wisdom
God — Wrath
Godhead
Godliness
Good Deeds
Good Works — see Good Deeds
Goodness
Gospel
Gossip
Grace — the Christian's
indebtedness to
Grace — Common Grace
Grace — Daily
Grace — Essence
Grace — and Heaven
Grace — and Salvation
Grace — Supremacy
Gratitude
Greatness

Jesus Christ — Intercession
Jesus Christ — Life and
    Influence
Jesus Christ — Lordship
Jesus Christ — Love
Jesus Christ — Perfection
Jesus Christ — Power
Jesus Christ — Resurrection
    — see Resurrection of Christ
Jesus Christ — Second
    Coming — see Second
    Coming of Christ
Jesus Christ — Teaching
Jesus Christ — Uniqueness
Joy
Judgement
Justice
Justification

Kindness
Kingdom of God
Knowledge
Knowledge of God

Law of God
Laziness — see Indolence
Leadership
Legalism
Liberalism
Liberality — see Generosity;
    Giving
Liberty
Life
Literature
Loneliness
Longsuffering — see Patience

Lord's Day
Love for Christ
Love for God
Love for Others — Definition
Love for Others — Importance
Love for Others — Measure
Love for Others — Practical
Lukewarmness — see Apathy;
    Complacency
Lust
Luxury
Lying

Malice
Man — Dignity
Man — a Failure
Man — God's Creation and
    Concern
Man — a Religious Being
Man — a Sinner
Marriage
Martyrdom
Materialism
Maturity — see Growth
Meaning — see Purpose
Meanness
Meditation
Meekness
Memory
Mercy from God
Mercy to Others
Mind
Ministry — see Preaching and
    Preachers
Miracles
Mistakes
Modernism — see Liberalism

Modesty
Money
Morality
Mortification — see Self-
    Crucifixion
Motivation — see Purpose
Motive
Murmuring
Mystery

Nature
Negligence
New Birth — see Regeneration

Obedience — Blessing
Obedience — Characteristics
Obedience — Importance
Obstinacy — see Stubbornness
Old Age
Opinion
Opportunities

Pain
Pardon — see Forgiveness by
    God; Forgiveness of Others
Parents — see Family Life
Passion
Patience
Peace
Penitence
Perfection
Persecution
Perseverance
Perseverance of Saints — see
    Eternal Security

Philosophy
Piety
Pleasures
Popularity
Possessions
Poverty
Power
Praise
Prayer — Answers
Prayer — Earnestness
Prayer — Essence
Prayer — and Faith
Prayer — and Fasting
Prayer — a Gift
Prayer — Hindrances
Prayer — and Holy Living
Prayer — Importance
Prayer — Length
Prayer — Power
Prayer — and the Promises
    of God
Prayer — Unanswered
Prayer — and the Will
    of God
Preaching and Preachers —
    Aim
Preaching and Preachers —
    Christ the Message
Preaching and Preachers —
    Dangers
Preaching and Preachers —
    Divine Calling
Preaching and Preachers —
    Doctrine
Preaching and Preachers —
    Earnestness
Preaching and Preachers —
    Glory of Preaching

Time — Urgency
Time — Use
Tongue — see Speech
Trials — Blessings
Trials — Certainty
Trials — God the Sender
Trials — Response
Trials — Temporary Nature
Trinity — see Godhead
Trust — see Faith
Truth

Unbelief
Unity — Church — see Church
   Unity
Urgency

Vanity
Vigilance
Virgin Birth
Virtue

War
Wealth
Wife — see Family Life
Will
Will of God
Wisdom
Witnessing
Wonder — see Awe; Worship
Work
Works — Good — see Good
   Deeds
World
Worldliness
Worry
Worship — Blessings
Worship — Essence
Worship — Importance

Youth

Zeal